River of Ink

Literature, History, Art

THOMAS CHRISTENSEN

Counterpoint C Berkeley

"River of Ink" appeared under the title "Remembering al-Mutanabbi" in *Al-Mutanabbi Street Starts Here: Poets and Writers Respond to the March 5th, 2007, Bombing of Baghdad's "Street of the Booksellers,"* edited by Beau Beausoleil and Deema Shehabi (PM Press, 2012), and in the online magazine phren-Z (phren-z. org). Earlier versions of some essays, or parts of them, were published, usually in quite different form, in *Treasures,* formerly the membership magazine of the Asian Art Museum, San Francisco (the current magazine is called *Asian*): "Staying Alive" as "Afghanistan's Hidden Treasures" (vol. X, no. 4, Fall 2008); "The Art of Tao" as "Taoism and the Arts of China" (vol. IV, no. 3, Winter 2000); "Before History" as "The Golden Age of Chinese Archaeology" (vol. III, no. 4, Spring 2000); and "The Temple across the Valley" as "From Guru Nanak to the Sikh Kingdoms" (vol. III, no. 1, Summer 1999). "The Winged Sphinx" appeared in *Shock and Awe: Responses to War,* edited by Peter Laufer (Berkeley: Creative Arts, 2003). "Nur Jahan," "Malik Ambar," "Harmony of the Spheres," and "Pocahontas in London" were reworked from material in my *1616: The World in Motion* (Berkeley: Counterpoint, 2012); "Pocahontas in London" also appeared in the fiftieth anniversary edition of the journal *Rosebud* (Spring 2011). Some of the essays appeared as introductions to a series of neglected literary classics published by Mercury House, San Francisco: "Getting Henry" in Henry Handel Richardson, *The Getting of Wisdom* (1993), "Dodgson's Dodges" in Lewis Carroll, *The Complete Sylvie and Bruno* (1991), "A Horace Reading" in Horace Walpole, *Hieroglyphic Tales* (1993). "The Nightingale and You" was a translator's preface in *Landscape with Yellow Birds: Selected Poems of José Ángel Valente* (New York: Archipelago, 2013) and "Dance Macabre" was a translator's preface to Louis-Ferdinand Céline, *Ballets without Music, without Dancers, without Anything* (Los Angeles: Green Integer, 1999). "New World / New Words" was published in my *New World / New Words: Recent Writing from the Americas* (San Francisco: Two Lines, 2007). "Eva Perón in Life and Myth" draws on material from a Nov. 3, 1996, book review in the *San Francisco Chronicle Book Review.* "This World Makes Trickster" appeared in *Terrain: A Journal of the Built and Natural Environments* no. 8 (Autumn 2000). "Natural Man" appeared as "Beyond Taxonomy" in *Terra Nova* vol. 2 no. 1 (Winter 1997). "#OccupyXmas" appeared online at Salon.com, Dec. 24, 2011.

Library of Congress Cataloging-in-Publication Data
Christensen, Thomas, 1948–
  River of ink : literature, history and art / Thomas Christensen.
    pages cm
  ISBN 978-1-61902-426-7 (hardback)
1. Literature and history. 2. Arts and history. 3. Literacy—History. 4. Printing—History. 5. Books and reading—History. 6. Intellectual life—History. 7. Literature and society—History. 8. Arts and society—History. 9. World history. I. Title.
PN50.C525 2014
909—dc23
    2014014418

COUNTERPOINT
2560 Ninth Street, Suite 318
Berkeley, CA 94710
www.counterpointpress.com

 Book design by the author
www.rightreading.com

With respect to images, profound thanks are owed to friends, colleagues, and fellow travelers at Arthur M. Sackler Gallery, Smithsonian Institution; Asian Art Museum; Bibliothèque Nationale de France; British Library; British Museum; Chester Beatty Library, Dublin; Collection of Dorothea Gilliland; Collection of Gursharan and Elvira Sidhu; French National Archives; the Kapany Collection; *Koreana*; Kupferstichkabinett, Dresden; Los Angeles County Museum of Art; Louvre Museum; Metropolitan Museum of Art; Morgan Library and Museum; Musée des Arts Asiatiques Guimet, Paris; Musée du Quai Branly; Museum of Modern Art, New York; Museum of the Argentine Bicentennial, Buenos Aires; Museum fur Volkerkunde, Berlin; National Library of Australia; National Palace Museum, Taiwan; Palace Museum, Beijing; Radio Nederland Wereldomroep; Richard Rosenblum Family Collection, Newton Center, Massachusetts; Staatsbibliothek zu Berlin; University of Arizona Press; University of Chicago Library, East Asian Collection; Victoria and Albert Museum; and the Yanaguana Society, Daughters of the Republic of Texas Library, as well as to photographers Marshall Astor; Zaida Ben-Yusuf; Adrienne Barti; Ellen Christensen; Charles W. Clark; Coro; Howard and Joan Coster; cotaro70; Daderot; B. J. Falk; Editions Gallimard; ellenm1; Mark Fenn; Jonathan Harrell; Indi Samarajiva; kudumomo; Christopher, Tania, and Isabelle Luna; Lupin; Luis Matilla; Carl Montgomery; William Navarrete; rajkumar1220; Patrick A. Rogers; Holger Uwe Schmitt; Tervlugt; Kaz Tsuruta; Jun Wang; Wmpearl; Zaccarias; and Arian Zwegers. Copyright on all of the images in this book remains lodged with their respective copyright holders, irrespective of the appearance of those images in these pages.

Printed by RR Donnelley in China

Distributed by Publishers Group West

10 9 8 7 6 5 4 3 2 1

For Carol

Contents

⁓⁓⁓⁓

Preface

Our lives, it is often remarked, are but the blink of an eye in the grand sweep of time. But lately I've been struck by the feeling not of how distant events in human history and prehistory are, but of how recent they seem. Not of how archaic ancient things look, but of how close they appear. Not of how fusty ancient verses — Homer, Vedas, Book of Songs — feel, but of how alive they are.

I'm not talking about what Rose Macaulay called "ruin lust" or Peter Aspden "archaeolatreia" — romantic nostalgia for the crumbling debris of the ancients.[1] I'm talking about the past as vitally present. A thousand years ago Song-dynasty artists painted landscapes that still seem fresh today, and continue to influence contemporary artworks, such as the monumental fine-brush landscapes of Li Huayi. Two thousand years ago the prophets of many of today's major religions had already preached their messages (with some notable exceptions like Muhammad and Guru Nanak, along with a few Johnny-come-latelies such as Joseph Smith and L. Ron Hubbard); some people are still fighting over them. Three thousand years ago Greek epic poets were working up early drafts of what have turned into modern Hollywood screenplays.

A millennium is nothing. Yet the Lascaux cave paintings, which are among the earliest expressions of human culture, were made a mere seventeen millennia ago — just seventeen![2] Visiting the caves,

---

1   Peter Aspden, "The Joy of Archaeolatreia," *Financial Times,* 8–9 March, 2014. Aspden discusses Macaulay.

2   Some considerably earlier objects exist, but the cave paintings are conventionally taken to represent the dawn of human artistic activity. Women may have led the way: recent analysis by Dean Snow of Pennsylvania State University of handprints at cave painting sites suggests that most of the early artists, despite the images' hunting themes, were women.

◁ This ivory lion-man was discovered in 1939 in the Swabian Alps of southwestern Germany. Made forty millennia ago from Mammoth ivory, it is the oldest-known figural sculpture. Yet it would not look out of place on a contemporary coffee table. It is now in the Ulm museum, Germany. *Photo by Holger Uwe Schmitt, http://bit.ly/14VoLuz.*

Pablo Picasso remarked, "We have learned nothing." Well, we haven't had time. Homo sapiens has barely been around a couple of hundred millennia altogether.

Time whizzes by, like the strobe of images in some MTV video montage (a genre that is itself passing, or has passed, into the realm of history). Wasn't it just yesterday that I was still a young man?[3] Yet the past clings to us.[4] (Actually, according to the philosopher Martin Heidegger, we are ourselves the stuff of time.) It can weigh us down or it can enrich us.

To explore other times and other cultures is really to explore our own time and our own culture (and the corollary is that to view oneself is necessarily to view an Other).[5] It is to polish up a mirror

---

3 Simone de Beauvoir was famously troubled by this sort of question. "How is it," she asked in *Force of Circumstance* (*La Force des Choses,* 1963, published when she was fifty-five), "that time, which has no form nor substance, can crush me with so huge a weight that I can no longer breathe?" At that age she would dream that she was a thirty-year-old woman who was dreaming that she was in her fifties. In her dream, "I awake and find I'm only thirty. 'What a terrible nightmare I had,' says the woman who thinks she's awake" — then she would awake to find that she was indeed in her fifties. Eventually she concluded that old age is an internalized Other who inhabits our selves throughout our lives.

   Speaking of aging, you know those "senior moments," when people of a certain age struggle to retrieve names from their cranial memory banks? According to a study led by Michael Ramscar of the University of Tübingen, Germany, that is not a sign of cognitive decline. Rather, it is a side effect of increased knowledge, as the limited free space in the storage capacity of older brains filled with years of information results in sluggish data retrieval. Sherlock Holmes was right! (In the first Holmes story, Watson informs Holmes that the earth revolves around the sun and Holmes says he will endeavor to forget that, so that his brain will not fill up with facts that aren't pertinent to solving crimes. Or so I recall.)

4 We live our lives in the past. Our consciousness lags eighty milliseconds behind actual events. "When you think an event occurs," says David Eagleman of the Baylor College of Medicine, whose research recently established this, "it has already happened."

5 Other places, other times — equally distant from the here and now. Since Einstein, many theoretical physicists have speculated that space and time may be modes of the same thing — which might

that reveals the form and pressure of the very age and body of time. Without such a mirror, how can we see ourselves? Michel de Montaigne, more or less the inventor of the modern essay, recognized this when he wrote, "I am myself the subject of my book."

To essay is to make an attempt (the French verb is *essayer*, "to try"). Etymologically, the word connotes weighing or measuring—I imagine that is why Kenneth Rexroth entitled his selected essays *Assays*. For Montaigne each prose piece was a new *essai*, a new take on the world. Analogy could be made to the jazz "take," which is a discreet and unique performance, as distinguished from practice, the same piece repeated over and over again. Argentine writer Julio Cortázar wrote in *Around the Day in Eighty Worlds* (*La Vuelta al Día en Ochenta Mundos*):

> The best literature is always a take: there is an implicit risk in
> its execution, a margin of danger that is the pleasure of the
> flight, or the love, carrying with it a tangible loss but also a
> total engagement that, on another level, lends the theater its
> unparalleled imperfection faced with the perfection of film.
>   I don't want to write anything but takes.

Which reminds me of Julio's novel *Hopscotch* (*Rayuela*), in which he offers the reader the choice of proceeding linearly in the traditional manner or hopping around from chapter to chapter in a prescribed but discontinuous route — something like the route taken in playing the game that gives the book its name. The object of that game is to skip from space to space to pick up a token and return home safely with it. The idea is to complete a journey around the world, or around the universe, or any number of other metaphorical journeys. (The French version, incidentally, is called "Escargot" and is played on a spiral course.)

---

well be imaginary. Certainly there is a strange parallel between past and future. Amnesiacs do not simply lose their past, they also lose the ability to imagine the future. And brain scans of subjects recalling past events are remarkably similar to those of people imagining future ones. Forgetting the past imperils the future.

LEFT | RIGHT
HEAVEN

SEVEN
FOR A SECRET
NEVER TO BE TOLD

SIX
FOR POOR

FIVE
FOR RICH

FOUR
FOR A BIRTH

THREE
FOR A
WEDDING

TWO
FOR MIRTH

ONE
FOR SORROW

EARTH

The great thing about being a nonspecialist — I'm only a specialist in making books[6] — is that you are free to write about whatever you want — to skip from one station to another like a child on a playground. Academic scholars don't do takes. The synopses at the heads of their articles in learned journals often begin "I argue...." Indeed.

So each of these essays (most written for particular occasions but some specifically for this book, and others so changed as if to be) is, to a greater or lesser degree, a take, each one a try at making sense of a little corner of things, each one starting from a different thread of the fabric of everything. Looking back at them, I realized that put together they composed a sort of hopscotch journey around the world — around the day, I suppose Julio might have said, in thirty worlds — so I have arranged them by continent. There is a point to that. In the twenty-first century we can no longer responsibly exclude or ignore any part of our shrinking world. For better or worse, we are globalized beings. From my home in the San Francisco Bay Area, a trip to China and back would have meant committing about a year of my life during the early modern period that I wrote about in *1616: The World in Motion*. Today it could easily be done in a weekend.

Julio invited his readers to hop around from text to text "with a clear conscience," and I suppose I would do the same. But for those of a linear bent (is that an oxymoron?), the journey begins in the "cradle of civilization," which is to say West Asia (what people who define things in terms of their relation to Europe call the "Near East" or "Middle East"). It ends in North America, in the person of Sadakichi Hartmann, who embodied the wider world and brought it to America. Hartmann hopped around a lot. His personal odyssey led him from east to west — from Japan to Europe to the East Coast of the U.S., and finally to California, where I have lived since the 1970s. Odysseus returned to Penelope, Bloom to Molly. For any player of hopscotch, the odyssey always leads back home.

---

6   "Of making many books," Ecclesiastes warns us, "there is no end." I am not among those doomsayers who say that digital media are a dying technology that will soon be pushed aside by the clear superiority of print. I feel sure there is room for both media.

◀ Hopscotch court, Stone Jetty, Morecambe, England. *Photo by Lupin, http://bit.ly/18m7OCo.*

River of Ink

WEST ASIA

River of Ink

❧

Some day we'll stop making the goddam funeral pyres and jumping into the middle of them. We pick up a few more people that remember, every generation.
— *Fahrenheit 451*

As the fifteenth century was drawing to a close, William Caxton, England's first printer, traveled to the Flemish city of Bruges. Today the city, with its late medieval architecture and meandering cobbled streets, seems a museum piece, but then it was a lively trading center where Italians, Germans, Spaniards, and others met and exchanged goods — and ideas. Arts and culture flourished, and new technology was everywhere. Visitors were assured of eating well thanks to the invention of drift nets, which resulted in an abundance of seafood. Followers of Jan van Eyck and Hans Memling were filling the city with paintings in a medium new to northern Europe, oils. And the printing press with movable type — the machine on which Johannes Gutenberg had printed his forty-two-line Bible a couple of decades before — was changing the intellectual life of the city. (Printing on movable metal type was well established in Korea, and information about it could have traveled through the vast Mongol empire to West Asia, and from there to Europe.)

There in Bruges, at a table overlooking a foggy canal, over a meal of mussels and ale, Caxton would discuss the new printed texts with scholars and artists who were arriving from all across Europe. Among those joining him would have been Colard Mansion, a Flemish scribe who printed the first book using copper engravings, as well as the first books in English and French. Also at the table would have been Anthony Woodville, the second Earl Rivers, an English Francophile and translator. Woodville had recently completed a translation of a French text called *Les Dits*

◀ Mongols besiege a city, 14th c. Persia. Painting. *Heinrich von Diez Albums, Staatsbibliothek zu Berlin.*

Moraulx des Philosophes. The book was a compendium of the wisdom of ancient philosophers. Would Caxton have a look at it?

The Englishman set about editing and proofreading the translation. In Bruges, working with Mansion, he mastered the art of printing, and when he returned to England he established a press there and made *Dictes and Sayings of the Philosophers* the first dated book printed in England.

So it is that the seed of free speech that was planted by followers of Muhammad found fruit at the very inception of bookmaking in England — for, while the French version of *Dictes and Sayings of the Philosophers* was itself a translation from Latin, the English text was in fact a translation of a translation of a translation. The Latin text was a translation of an Arabic text, called *Muhtar al hikamwa-mahasin al kalim* (Choice maxims and finest sayings), which was written in the eleventh century by Abul Wafa Mubasshir ibn Fatik, an Egyptian emir.

The Islamic world was at that time one of the great centers of book production. Arabic calligraphy lends itself to textual decoration, and demand for glorious Qur'ans spurred book arts to unprecedented heights. But another factor was equally important in the flourishing of Islamic bookmaking — its tradition of freedom of speech.

Umar, the second caliph, whose caliphate began just two years after the death of Muhammad in the seventh century, declared that the weak must be allowed to "express themselves freely and without fear." Subsequent caliphs expanded on Umar's notion and established a system of *madrasahs*, or educational centers, in part to encourage such expression. This system became the explicit model for the concept of academic freedom in European universities.

But freedom of expression is never an easy sell — shifting shape like a djinn, it all too readily assumes the form "You are free to express your agreement with my beliefs." In the mid-seventh century, Umar's successor, the third caliph, Uthman, established an authoritative Qur'an through the simple expedient of burning competing editions. In the eleventh century, as Abul Wafa Mubasshir ibn Fatik was writing the text that would journey through Latin and French to become the first dated book printed in England, Turkish forces were busy demolishing the Royal Library of the Samanid dynasty in Persia (which contained one of the earliest Qur'ans and other rare books).

Two centuries later, in 1258, the Abbasid caliphate's great flowering of Islamic scholarship was dealt a harsh blow when Mongol forces under Hulagu Khan besieged Baghdad. The city was then a place of parks, libraries, and book stalls. Its gardens produced fruits and spices. It boasted palaces of marble, jade, and alabaster. A European visitor said that the Tigris ran between the eastern and western parts of the city "like a string of pearls between two breasts." But, with the help of Nestorian Christian and Shiite Muslim allies, the Mongols breached the city walls. It is estimated that over the following week of rampage they killed hundreds of thousands of the city's residents, and they laid waste to many of its buildings and monuments. Among their targets was the Grand Library — known as the House of Wisdom — which was perhaps the greatest repository of historic, scientific, and literary documents of its age. So many of its books were flung into the Tigris that it was said a man could cross the river on horseback over the pile. For six months, it was reported, the waters of the Tigris flowed black from the ink of the books (along with red from the blood of scholars). It was a river of ink.

In an echo of that event Iraq's national library was burned following the U. S. invasion in 2003.

Even as Caxton was publishing *Dictes and Sayings of the Philosophers*, Jewish and Islamic literatures were being destroyed in Spain. Of the Spanish auto-da-fé the nineteenth-century German poet Heinrich Heine would say, "Where they burn books, they will also, in the end, burn humans." His observation is recorded on a memorial at the concentration camp at Dachau, so that we will not forget the Nazi book burnings that began in 1933, when twenty thousand books were burned in a single public spectacle, nor the larger and more terrible holocaust that followed. Such memorials are important, for tyranny hates memory.

And so Mutanabbi Street starts here — it starts wherever books are made, exchanged, and shared. It starts when we remember the bomb that destroyed part of Baghdad's historic booksellers row, on March 5, 2007, killing more than thirty people and injuring many more. The intent of the bomber was to prevent the free discussion that books attract. And, to a degree, he was successful. But so long as we do not forget to remember, he will not, in the end, prevail.

Mutanabbi Street is named for Abou-t-Tayyib Ahmad ibn al-Husayn al-Mutanabbi (915–965), one of the great poets of the Arabic language. Mutanabbi is also renowned for an extraordinary feat of memory: he is said to have memorized the contents of a thirty-folio book in a single reading. Tyrants and bigots — like First Emperor Qin Shihuang of China's Qin dynasty, who was said by the historian Sima Qian to have burned most of the country's ancient literature (and buried many of its scholars alive) or the priest Diego de Landa, who destroyed the entire written literature of the Maya people with the exception of four codices — seek to erase cultural memory in order to bask in the eternal sunshine of the cleansed cultural mind. For them, books are a target, because they represent and enable remembering.

Consider the case of Afghanistan's Taliban, who tried hard to enforce forgetting throughout that unfortunate country. As described in the following essay, in an effort to erase all trace of the region's pre-Muslim past they blasted into bits the monumental Buddhas of Bamiyan, and they smashed artworks and destroyed books wherever they could find them. They destroyed the National Museum in Kabul and shattered most of its contents.

But even as they did their worst, the museum's staff found a way to hide many prize items, and over the years of Taliban rule they refused to divulge their locations despite intense persecution. Years after the museum had been destroyed, when the Taliban had been driven from power, those artworks were brought forth from their hiding places. The museum itself was rebuilt. The art objects went on a world tour to demonstrate that Afghanistan's cultural heritage had survived.

Today, in bold Arabic script on a banner above the museum's entrance, a new motto is written: "A nation stays alive when its culture stays alive." Through his act of remembering, Mutanabbi helped to keep his culture alive. By remembering the poet, Mutanabbi Street did the same. And by remembering Mutanabbi Street, we keep alive the seeds of freedom.

The Grand Library ("House of Wisdom," detail), 13th c. Painting. Baghdad. *Bibliothèque Nationale de France.*

Staying Alive

AFGHANISTAN'S HIDDEN TREASURES

～∾～

Ovid said that "all that's noblest will survive." If only it were that easy. The story of Afghanistan's artistic legacy is one of survival against great odds.

Afghanistan occupies a place along the ancient Silk Road — not really a road but rather a network of local connections that collectively stretched thousands of miles — where trade routes to East Asia, South Asia, and the West converged. As a result, many luxury goods moved through the region, and its inhabitants were exposed to the products of diverse cultures.

But Afghanistan was not just a trader of goods produced elsewhere. It was also a producer of objects for local consumption as well as for trade. Recent archaeological discoveries suggest that more objects were created in Afghanistan than was once supposed.

Unfortunately, the same crossroads location that made the region a hub of trade also made it a target, as did its own deposits of gold, copper, tin, lapis lazuli, garnet, and carnelian. Over the centuries, Afghanistan's treasures have been a lure for countless invaders and looters. More recently, the problem has been compounded by local iconoclasts who have sought to destroy works of art they find objectionable. The wonder is that so many have somehow survived. That survival is in part a testament to acts of extraordinary courage.

THE OXUS, A BRONZE-AGE CIVILIZATION

The beginnings of the story are located four thousand years ago, in the Bronze Age, when, "between the Indus Civilization and Mesopotamia, a 'new' civilization emerged," as Paris's Guimet Museum's website has it, "with its bronze seals, its composite statues of

◀ Gargoyle-head waterspout, 2nd c. BCE, from the archaeological site of Ai Khanum. The fountain of which this was a part may have served as a bath — a gymnasium was adjacent. *Photo by Adrienne Barti, http://bit.ly/1jr3qpK.*

This ceremonial plate (detail), one of the oldest objects found at Al Khanum, demonstrates the ancient world's interconnectivity. The deities are Cybele, goddess of nature, and Nike, god of victory. These gods, adopted by the Greeks, arose in Anatolia. But the priests and chariot are drawn from ancient Syrian or Persian cultural sources. *Photo by Adrienne Barti, http://bit.ly/1jr4bXA.*

'goddesses' in abstract silhouette, its gold and silver cups decorated with animals set in landscapes, with its troupe of strange creatures and bearded bulls, or geometric motifs." This culture has been named the Oxus civilization, after the Oxus (current Amu Darya) River, which flows out of Afghanistan and into the Aral Sea.

In this location, in 1960, a group of farmers found a hoard of gold and silver bowls. In order to apportion the loot, they hacked the objects into pieces with an axe, before local authorities intervened.

Objects from the site showed similarities to works from cultures ranging from Mesopotamia to the Indus Valley in modern-day Pakistan. Nobody is exactly sure how it all worked, but the implication that the region was already active in cultural exchange at this very early date (roughly the time of Egypt's Middle Kingdom and China's semi-legendary Xia dynasty) is inescapable. As a general rule, we tend to imagine that where we are unaware of connections between cultures they must not have existed, but time and again new knowledge proves interconnectivity surpassing our expectations.

AI KHANUM, A ROYAL GREEK BACTRIAN CITY

Flash forward a couple of millennia and we find a new intruder in the area — Alexander the Great, who conquered Bactria, as the region was known in antiquity, around 328 BCE. Alexander's forces made Greek the language of government and introduced Greek art and religion.

One of Alexander's successors founded a city called Ai Khanum ("Lady Moon") at a strategic location along the Oxus River, at the frontier with nomadic tribes to the north. The city was built on a Greek plan. Excavations have revealed a theater, a gymnasium, a fountain, tombs, a temple, and a residential district. It also contained a building that archaeologists identify as a palace, suggesting that it was a royal city. The city flourished until about 145 BCE, when it was destroyed by another wave of invaders, this time from the northern steppes of Eurasia.

BEGRAM, A TRADING SETTLEMENT

In the first century BCE, the Kushans, a people originating in Central Asia, consolidated power in Bactria and established the Kushan dynasty, which would be a center of exchange for centuries. The Kushans borrowed much from their Greek predecessors, such as

This gold crown from Tillya Tepe features five trees attached by rods inserted into gold tubes on the inside of a diadem. The trees might represent the Tree of Life. *Photo by Adrienne Barti, http://bit.ly/1kzQA6R.*

the use of the Greek alphabet to write their own language and the application of Greek models of coinage.

Under the Kushans, Afghanistan continued to serve as an entrepot for trade, as evidenced by two sealed storerooms that were excavated at Begram in the 1930s and 1940s. The rooms were filled with art objects from distant lands, including bronzes from Greece, glassware from Egypt, and lacquered bowls from China. The rooms also contained large amounts of ivory, some of which probably came from India. Filled with objects from the first and second centuries, the storerooms seem somehow to have survived intact since around that time. Were these treasures a secret hoard of the Kushan kings? Were they a forgotten warehouse of goods intended for trade? The answer is uncertain, but either way this large cache of diverse objects makes it clear that Begram was active in exchange, either directly or indirectly, with a variety of distant cultures.

TILLYA TEPE, THE TOMB OF A NOMADIC CHIEFTAIN

The first extensive archaeological evidence of the nomadic invaders who overran Bactria around 145 BCE was found at Tillya Tepe, a name meaning "Hill of Gold." The site consists of a series of graves (identified by numbers corresponding to the order in which they were discovered). Here the bodies of a man and five women were found, adorned with all manner of precious objects, including jewelry, belts, coins, hair ornaments, and a crown — more than twenty thousand objects were found in the tombs. The man's head was resting in a golden bowl, and one of the women wore footwear with golden soles. This funerary gold is known today as the "Bactrian Hoard."

Probably imported from Egypt or the eastern Mediterranean, this glass goblet from Begram depicts women and men gathering dates. It is a striking testament to the stubborn will for survival of human culture. *Photo by Adrienne Barti, http://bit.ly/RfId7v.*

The Bactrian gold from Tillya Tepe is rather uniform in style and materials, and stones such as turquoise that were used for inlays appear to have come from nearby sources. While this suggests that the objects were made locally, perhaps from a single workshop, rather

than imported through trade, it is clear that the artists were influenced by objects that had traveled along the Silk Road and other trade routes — a small "goddess of love," for example, combines aspects of the Greek goddess Aphrodite along with qualities reminiscent of South Asian figures.

One might have expected this nomadic people to have amassed a collection of objects from the many cultures that passed along the Silk Road. Instead, it appears that they observed those objects

Taller Buddha of Bamiyan before and after destruction by the Taliban. Figures in the foreground give a sense of scale. Approaches to reconstruction are currently being discussed. *Photos by Zaccarias and Carl Montgomery, http://bit.ly/1p7wMsi.*

and adapted aspects of them to fashion a style to their own taste, producing large numbers of objects apparently intended for their own use.

PRESERVING AFGHANISTAN'S ARTISTIC HERITAGE

As we know all too well, Alexander and the northern nomads who left the graves at Tillya Tepe were hardly the last invaders of northern Afghanistan. Among subsequent attacks were those of Chinggis Khan, who overran the region in the early thirteenth century. His Mongol forces killed all of the inhabitants of Bamiyan, a city at the southern edge of Bactria, where there was a strong South Asian influence, including the presence of Buddhism.

The Mongols spared the stone Buddhas that were carved into

a cliff near Bamiyan. Despite some damage, the enormous statues (more than 120 feet tall) continued to stand where they had been constructed in the early to mid-500s. Until 2001, when the Taliban dynamited them on the grounds that they were idols.

That same year, the Taliban also destroyed the National Museum of Afghanistan, which had been built in 1922. Omara Khan Massoudi, director of the museum, has written:

> At the beginning of 2001 ... the Taliban decided that all images must be destroyed. A special group was charged with this task. They destroyed about 2,500 works of art.... These barbaric acts, which filled the heart of every decent Afghan with anger, represented an irreplaceable loss. Terrible damage was caused at every archaeological site in the country. Neither the coming generations of Afghans nor human history will forget this era of tyranny and destruction.

Facing political turmoil, warfare, and social chaos, in 1988 the museum placed its prized artworks in the vaults of the Central Bank of Afghanistan. Only its staff knew their exact location. Despite extreme pressures during the ensuing years of turmoil, during which its employees were arrested, mistreated, and even killed, no member of the museum staff revealed the secret of the objects' location.

Finally, in 2003, with the Taliban out of power, the storerooms were opened. A count revealed that 22,607 objects (less than a third of the museum's original holdings) had been spared, thanks to the courage of the museum's staff. In 2004, the museum was reopened to the public, making this legacy of the country's rich artistic and cultural heritage once again available to the public and to scholars, in Afghanistan and throughout the world. Reviewing an exhibition of some of the treasures at the Metropolitan Museum in New York, Roberta Smith called the display "at once revelatory and heart-rending."

The Unfinished Bridge

DECONSTRUCTING TURKEY

~~~~~

On May 29, 2013, construction workers laid the first foundation stone for a new bridge across the Bosphorus. More than a mile in length, the bridge will be the third over the divide that is traditionally considered to mark the boundary between Europe and Asia. It will be the world's longest bridge accommodating both vehicular and rail travel, and the world's ninth-longest suspension span.

The May 29 date was carefully chosen. On that day, 560 years before, Ottoman forces under Sultan Mehmed II, "The Conqueror," defeated Byzantine defenders and took Constantinople, which would thereafter be known as Istanbul ("The City"). But one of Istanbul's existing bridges is already named for Mehmed, so the new bridge is to be named for Sultan Selim I, known as "The Grim." Selim is best known for tripling the size of the Ottoman empire, primarily through expansion into Egypt and North Africa. Because he was also known for the slaughter of minority populations (Alevis, Kurds, Turkmens, and others), the choice of name was seen as a slap in the face to Turkish minorities.

Turkey is a country rich in symbolism, and the symbols associated with the new bridge underscored prime minister Recep Tayyip Erdogan's nostalgia for the vanished Ottoman empire, which was overthrown in 1922 by the founder of the modern Turkish state, Mustafa Kemal Ataturk.[1] (Ataturk means, roughly, "Father of the Turks.") The movement that claims the most direct lineage from Ataturk, called Kemalism, dominated Turkey's politics through most of the twentieth century, before being supplanted by the Islamist government headed by Erdogan.

Erdogan's "Ottomanalgia" echoed throughout Turkey. A popular

---

1   Erdoğan. Atatürk. This essay omits diacritics in transliterating Turkish.

◄ Satellite image of Istanbul (taken by the crew of the International Space Station on April 16, 2004) divided by the Bosphorus, the traditional divide between Europe and Asia.

television soap opera called *Muhtesem Yuzil* (Magnificent century) was set in the court of Sultan Suleiman, "The Magnificent" or "The Lawgiver." *Fetih 1453* (Conquest 1453), a big-budget epic film released in 2012, centered on the Ottomans' capture of Constantinople. The film, which employed thousands of actors (real or digitized) in massive battle scenes, depicted the fall of the city as the fulfillment of a prophesy supposedly made by Muhammad, eight hundred years before.

Protests that erupted in Istanbul's Gezi Park in Taksim Square in the spring of 2013 were set against this backdrop. Erdogan's government has been engaged in a project of "Ottomanization" of the city's public spaces, a project that flies in the face of Ataturk's secularization of government. Some have seen the plans — which call for demolishing the Ataturk cultural center and rebuilding the Ottoman barracks that were the site of an early twentieth-century attempt to stave off the liberal reforms that led to Ataturk's revolt — as a further assault on Ataturk and his legacy. Erdogan, who also banned the sale of alcohol after 10:00 PM (which did not sit well with some Turks who depend on tourism for their livelihood) has even gone so far as to suggest that Ataturk was a drunkard, undercutting nearly a century of almost religious respect given him.

It's all part of the complex of contradictions that make up modern Turkey, a country that straddles Europe and Asia, where authoritarianism competes with democratization, where there is a constant strain between the religious and the secular, where rural farmworkers are often at odds with the urban elite, where military and religious leaders have traditionally been in opposition, and where a reputation for tolerance dating from the days of empire is undercut by repression of Kurds and other ethnic minorities — all of this wrapped up in a nostalgia for the past that plays out amid the razing of historical structures and their replacement with gleaming new high-rises, as old-timers lament the loss of the past and the young embrace social media and the international Internet culture.

▶ Poster for the Turkish movie *Fetih 1453* (Conquest 1453).

YA BEN İSTANBUL'U ALACAĞIM, YA İSTANBUL BENİ!

FARUK AKSOY
SUNAR

FETİH
1453

BIR AKSOY FILM YAPIMI "FETİH 1453" MED YAPIM ORTAKLIĞIYLA

DEVRİM EVİN İBRAHİM ÇELİKKOL DİLEK SERBEST CENGİZ COŞKUN RECEP AKTUĞ ŞAHİKA KOLDEMİR ERDEN ALKAN NACİ ADIGÜZEL ERDOĞAN AYDEMİR
GÖRÜNTÜ YÖNETMENİ SRDJAN KURPJEL KOSTÜM TASARIMI CANAN GÖKNİL GÖRSEL EFEKT SÜPERVİZÖRÜ SERKAN ZELZELE YÖNETMEN YARDIMCISI GÜLÇİN ÖNEL YAPIM YÖNETMENİ FARUK METİN SANAT YÖNETMENİ SERVET AKSOY KURGU ERKAN ÖZEKAN
MÜZİK BENJAMIN WALLFISCH SEVGİ VE SESİN YÖNETMENİ MIRSAD HEROVIC HASAN GERGİN CO-SENARIST İRFAN SARUHAN FARUK AKSOY SENARİST ATİLLA ENGİN
ORTAK YAPIMCI HAMİT KELEŞ YAPIMCI FARUK AKSOY SERVET AKSOY AYŞE GERMEN YÖNETMEN FARUK AKSOY

www.fetih1453movie.com

Flash back about four hundred years, to a hot summer day in 1605, when an aging Spanish hidalgo, accompanied by a single manservant, saddled up his nag and set out to see the world. That day, according to Mexican writer Carlos Fuentes, the modern world began.

The history of that gentleman's journey — in the course of which he discovered that the world did not resemble what he had read about it — has been passed down to us by Miguel de Cervantes. But his text, Cervantes assures us, is not original: it is a translation from the Arabic of the work of a Muslim writer, *The History of Don Quixote of La Mancha,* written by Cide Hamete Benengeli.

Cervantes had fought and lost the use of an arm in the epic naval battle of Lepanto in 1571, when the Ottomans' ambitions of steamrolling through Europe were stalled by a coalition of Western forces. A few years later, on his way back to Spain, he was captured by North African corsairs and sent to Algiers, where he would endure five years as a slave. If, as Fuentes asserts, the modern world began with Cervantes, then it was a world colored by Islam and by Ottoman might. The view of Spanish society that Cervantes elaborated was conceived at a fundamental level, according to the great Spanish writer Juan Goytisolo, "from the other shore."

Cervantes in effect provided a bridge between the Christian West and the Islamic East at the beginnings of the modern age. At the time of his birth, the West lagged behind the East in most important measures: Muslim military might was greater, its economy stronger, its scientific and scholarly achievements more distinguished. At that time it was more tolerant of diversity than were Christian nations — the Jews expelled from Cervantes's Spain were accepted into the empire. The modern world, it appeared then, would be dominated by Islam, with the Ottoman empire as its vehicle.

According to a contemporary of Cervantes, the Flemish diplomat Ogier Ghiselin de Busbecq, the Ottomans would have overrun Europe had it not been for the threat from Persia on their east. Instead, this turned out to be near the high-water mark of the Ottoman empire. Within Cervantes's lifetime the balance began to shift.

By the end of the seventeenth century a second Ottoman siege of Vienna would fail, and it would be followed by a succession of further crushing defeats. After a series of losses in battles in Serbia, the Ottomans would be forced to concede defeat in the Treaty of Karlowitz, their first major formal concession to Western military force.

THE LONG DECLINE

We might think of the long conflict between the Islamic East and the Christian West as an epic battle between near equals, carried out over centuries and focused on the Holy Land, which time and again would be won and lost, with neither side able to claim the upper hand for long. If so, we would be wrong. For the first millennium of Islam the real story was mostly one of steady conquest and glory. At the time of the birth of the prophet Muhammad in Mecca around 570, the entire Mediterranean region, including North Africa and the so-called Middle East, extending at least into Persia, was predominantly Christian. Pretty quickly Islam largely supplanted that well-established religion. Already in the prophet's lifetime his message had spread through much of the Arabian Peninsula. Within thirty years of his death — under the first four caliphs — Islam had reached as far as Egypt and had won territory from the greatest established powers of the time, Byzantium and Sassanid Persia. Within another century it had extended its domain all the way to the Iberian Peninsula in the west and had made contact with South Asia in the east.

But, not long after the age of Cervantes, the Ottomans shifted from a mode of expansion of the empire to one of preservation. Leadership in science and technology passed to the West, and in the Muslim world these fields began a long decline, which has never fully been reversed. It had been the Muslim world that had preserved ancient Greek science, and Muslim scientists who had influenced Europe's technical and scientific revolution. Why did this regression occur just as the empire appeared poised to advance into Europe? Many reasons have been adduced, but I think the major factor was the opening of international maritime trade routes in the sixteenth and seventeenth centuries (the time of Europe's scientific revolution). Maritime discoveries introduced the Europeans to new peoples and ideas, and caused them to reexamine accepted beliefs. By contrast, in failing to continue their advance, and with a reduction in trade, the Ottomans were increasingly closed off to new encounters and new ideas. And it was now possible for Europeans to circumvent the Ottoman empire in obtaining spices, textiles, and other luxury goods from the East. As the empire lost the wealth that had resulted from its strategic position along the old land routes, it became less capable of supporting education, scholarship, and innovation. On the military side, it compensated for its technological disadvantage by putting large resources into manpower (as late as World War I the military resilience of the Ottomans remained notable).

In this way, the empire was sustained into the early twentieth century without recapturing the vigor that had marked it at its height. At the turn of the century a group of "Young Turks" seized administrative control (officially they were heads of a political group called the Committee of Union and Progress, or CUP), though they remained within the Ottoman structure, and sought to modernize the country. Unfortunately, they ended up making a fair mess of things. Genocide of Armenians and Kurds accelerated the diminishment of diversity within the empire. It is estimated that as many as two million Armenians may have been killed by the Turks. Alliance with Germany and the Central Powers brought the country into conflict with Russia and with England, who helped drive a wedge in Turkish-Arab relations, leading to the secession of Arab lands from the empire. After defeat in the war the ruling CUP triumvirate — the "Three Pashas" — fled to Germany, but by 1922 all three had been killed.

A NEW NATION

The massacre of the Armenians was a great self-inflicted wound to the body of Turkey. Mounting internal tensions combined with external defeats brought about the collapse of the empire, which was forced to give up large portions of its territory and endure the occupation of parts of the country by European powers. But Mustafa Kemal successfully led a Turkish independence movement. Kemal was a capable military leader, and the world was weary of war. In 1922 a newly formed parliament officially abolished the Ottoman sultanate. The empire had endured 623 years, one of the longest spans in history.

Not much remained to admire in it. The modern Turkish state Kemal founded amounted to a sharp repudiation of its Ottoman past. The new state was to be politically secular, the fez and the veil were outlawed, polygamy was abolished, and new rights were given to women. Turkey would no longer be "The Sick Man of Europe." It was to be a fully modern nation.

Which meant a European one. Turks were now to have Western-style surnames. They were to write in Roman rather than Arabic script. They were to adopt the Western calendar. From its perch on the Bosphorus, Turkey was to look west as much as east. Perhaps Turkey could be the bridge between East and West. Kipling notwithstanding, could the twain meet after all?

Ironically, the postwar peace settlement had transformed Turkey geographically into a mostly Asian nation, even as Ataturk was seeking to bring Turkey into Europe (an effort that continues today — Turkey officially applied to join the European Union in 1987, and it is currently projected that Turkey will join the union in 2023, a century after the founding of the Turkish state). Where once the empire had embraced three continents — Europe, Asia, and Africa — it was now contracted to its Anatolian base, apart from the toehold of the portion of Istanbul that lay on the European side of the Bosphorus. The results of this would be slow to manifest themselves, but I believe we are seeing them today.

BRIDGE TO NOWHERE?

Erdogan was elected prime minister in 2002 with strong support from the country's Anatolian heartland. Though pro-business, he is a cultural conservative, much like some highly vocal politicans in my own country. His nostalgia for the Ottoman empire reflects the common tendency to blame problems on the abandonment of traditional values and to seek solutions in a return to the old ways. It also represents a reassertion of Turkish ambition in the interna-

Istanbul's Fatih Mosque complex (left) was first constructed in 1470 under Sultan Mehmet II, "The Conqueror," over the ruins of a Byzantine church. It included a hospital, university, and soup kitchen, as well as a caravansary offering free lodging for travelers and the homeless. On the right is a design for a new shopping complex in Taksim Gezi Park, which will also feature a mosque. The proposed project, part of Prime Minister Erdogan's "Ottomization" program, led to protests, which were sharply repressed.

tional arena. The urban development plan for Taksim Gezi Park could be viewed in this light, as it expresses the desire to return to a more Islamicized state.

One of the pillars of Islam is daily prayer. While prayer can be done anywhere, it is preferable to pray in a mosque. The earliest mosques were simple buildings but, over time, a complex of such structures as hospitals, schools, libraries, and inns grew up around many of the mosques. Fountains were provided for ritual cleaning, and minarets served to call the faithful to prayer. In Cervante's time, the impressive mosques of Istanbul represented the marvel and might of the Muslim world, and the highest achievement of Ottoman art and architecture. In Erdogan's Turkey, the contemporary equivalent of these complexes is the shopping mall.

Although he admonished former Egyptian dictator Hosni Mubarak that "no government can survive against the will of its people," Erdogan does not freely entertain alternative views. He brooks no dissent to his policies and dismisses protestors as looters, bums, and subversives. Protestors have been attacked with water cannons and tear gas.

Erdogan denies the Armenian holocaust. "It's not possible for a Muslim," he has said, "to commit genocide." In 2005 Turkish Nobel-winning novelist Orhan Pamuk was quoted in *Swiss* publications as having told an interviewer, "Thirty thousand Kurds have been killed here, and a million Armenians. And almost nobody dares to mention that. So I do." Several months later, Turkey instituted a new law dictating that "a person who, being a Turk, explicitly insults the Republic or Turkish Grand National Assembly, shall be punishable by imprisonment of between six months to three years." Pamuk was put on trial in Turkey for having violated the law (retroactively) — for "insulting Turkishness." Authors José Saramago, Gabriel García Márquez, Günter Grass, Umberto Eco, Carlos Fuentes, Juan Goytisolo, John Updike, and Mario Vargas Llosa, who issued a joint statement in his support, were among Pamuk's international advocates; nonetheless, in 2011 he was found guilty and ordered to pay a fine for insulting Turkish honor.

In 2013, prime minister Erdogan threatened to sue the *Times* of London for publishing an open letter criticizing his handling of anti-government protests. At the same time, the publisher and translator of a Turkish edition of Guillaume Apollinaire's *The Exploits of a Young Don Juan* were facing potential ten-year prison sentences for "exploiting and arousing the sexual desires and harming the modesty of society." (One of those corrupted by the original book must have been Pablo Picasso, to whom the author gave the original manuscript, and who considered it one of his most prized possessions.) Clearly freedom of speech has its limits in twenty-first-century Turkey.

So the bridge between Europe and Asia remains unfinished, as Turkey wavers between authoritarianism and democratization, between the religious and the secular, between tolerance and repression, and between the past and the future. Will this bridge ever be complete?

The Winged Sphinx

Every writer worth his salt should do an antiwar essay.
This was my effort in the genre.

What we gotta do is grab these Arabs, and get a big stick,
and hit them over the head but good — hit 'em and hit 'em
until they stop hating us.
> — Cab driver quoted in Shulamith Hareven,
> *The Vocabulary of Peace*

To raise one's voice against the war in Iraq — what is the point? As I write this it is early in April 2003. U. S. tanks have entered Baghdad, and by the time this sees print Saddam Hussein's Baathite party will have been driven from power. Iraqis will cheer the fall of that repressive government, and I will share the world's cheer at seeing Saddam removed after so many brutal years.

Often it seems there is too much chatter in our lives, too little silence, too little reflection — why add to that noise now, when victory is at hand?

My happiness at the removal of Saddam is balanced by my sorrow at the consequences of our embracing the rule of force and ignoring the rule of law. The immediate consequences are death and mutilation, mostly of Iraqi civilians but also of American, British, and Iraqi soldiers, along with some reporters, aid workers, and observers. *San Francisco Chronicle* columnist Jon Carroll has observed that the Bush administration likes to call the dead Iraqis enemy casualties. "It is not clear," he says, "how the dead people, previously victims of known tyrant Saddam Hussein, became the enemy. Maybe their deaths proved that their intentions were hostile after all." One thing is certain: the war has brought a great deal of death and destruction.

◀ Cheekpiece of a horse bridle in the form of a mythical creature, ca. 800–700 BCE. Luristan region, Iran. Bronze. *Asian Art Museum, The Avery Brundage Collection*, B60B17+.

The long-term consequences are less certain. We have gained a foothold in West Asia, which seems to be what the Bush administration has been seeking. But why should we not suffer the drawn-out agonies of other colonial powers that have stubbornly sought to impose their will on an alien population, whose culture and values they disregard or imperfectly understand? British troops at present are struggling to control an anarchic situation in Basra — perhaps the grandparents of these soldiers experienced something similar. In 1941, Britain, angry at Iraq's noncompliance with a twenty-five-year treaty it had been forced to sign at the end of the colonial period, moved into Basra. Initially there was stiff resistance, but it faded away within weeks in the face of overwhelming superior force. Britain sentenced most of the opposition leaders to death; others it imprisoned. One of these was the uncle of Saddam Hussein, a man named Khairallah Talfah, with whom Saddam lived during his secondary school years, when he formed a bitter hatred of foreign influence. Now the Brits are back in Basra, and nothing seems to have been gained in the intervening seventy-two years. Are a new teenage tyrant-to-be's attitudes being shaped by the present invasion?

The word *victory* comes from a Latin root meaning "to conquer." A victor is someone who suppresses an opponent by force. But "victors," John Dryden said, "are by victory undone." Recall arrogant Goliath, felled by young David, and David as king in turn brought down by his own arrogance. I hope that we will not end up being undone by our victory in Iraq. The sage Laozi understood the danger two and a half millennia ago, when he wrote in the *Daode jing*:

> Trying to govern the world with force
> I see this not succeeding
> the world is a spiritual thing
> it can't be forced
> to force it is to harm it
> to control it is to lose it
>   (tr. Red Pine)

So why speak up? Better ask, why be silent? One of the lessons of the twentieth century was that silence can become complicity. Again and again in that troubled century the interests of power sought to control the very language we speak. So now "attack" is recast as "liberation," "assassination" is called "regime change," and uncritical compliance is equated with patriotism, as a silent majority is posited and pointed to for validation. But "amnesia," Edward R. Murrow observed, "is not a requirement for patriotism.... We must not confuse dissent with disloyalty. When the loyal opposition dies, I think the soul of America dies with it." Only by calling things by their true names can we overcome the humpty-dumpty logomachy of power and allow language to spread its magic circle around the world and reveal it as it really is. To speak is our patriotic duty.

COLLATERAL DAMAGE

> That use which is collateral and intervenient is no less
> worthy than that which is principal and intended.
> — Roger Bacon, *A History of Mathematics*

Something that is collateral is something that is secondary, something that is extrinsic to a main consideration. Indeed, one of its meanings is "odds and ends of trash" or "rubbish" ("a woodshed full of collateral"). The people who live in the region we have invaded seem to be regarded by some as collateral — they are secondary to the main interests of the war makers. Their deaths are deplored but shrugged off as inevitable — President Bush, my newspaper tells me, is untroubled by his decision to go to war and "sleeps like a baby."

There is another definition of collateral, one in which what is secondary comes to the forefront. A person applying for a loan is asked for "collateral security." The collateral is secondary to the loan, but it is a primary asset, without which the loan could not be obtained. I suggest that a nation's people are collateral in this sense: they are the raw material of the future. They are, indeed, the nation. Without drawing on this collateral one cannot build anything lasting. A wise leader considers the effect his action has on the people, for resentment can linger for decades, centuries, or even millennia, as we have seen in Palestine. I fear that our obstinate display of military might has damaged our Gulf collateral for many years into the future.

Bakhat Hassan is collateral. He was a "dirt farmer," according to a Knight Ridder report filed by Meg Laughlin (which is my source for the following). On the last day of March, he grabbed a leaflet dropped from an American helicopter. The leaflet advised him to "be safe" and flee his village of Karbala.

Hassan and his family dressed in their best clothes — "to look American," he explained. His father put on a pinstriped suit. Hassan piled more than a dozen family members into a vehicle. When the family approached a first U.S. checkpoint, they waved to the soldiers, and in turn were waved through. "We were thinking these Americans want us to be safe," Hassan said. Then they approached a second checkpoint. Again they waved, but this time the soldiers responded by firing on them. Hassan lost his daughters, age two and five, and his son, age three. He lost both his parents. He lost two older brothers, their wives, and two nieces, age twelve and fifteen.

"I saw the heads of my two little girls come off," cried Hassan's wife, who is nine months pregnant. "It would be better not to have the baby," she added. "Our lives are over."

An army report termed the incident "miscommunication."

Another article in my local paper explains that fatigue is the soldiers' worst enemy, so they are kept jazzed up on dexadrine. Truckers, hipsters, and children of the sixties (and probably military leaders as well) know that a diet of dex will turn a person edgy, jumpy, paranoid, and aggressive.

But it's all collateral damage, and it surprises no one, least of all the masterminds of this war, who are constantly reminding us that war is a dirty business. The war may be illegal, unnecessary, and unjust, but these planners' global vision does not give much weight to "collateral damage."

PREEMPTIVE ACTION

> *Cuando la fuerza ríe, la razón llora.* (When force laughs, reason cries.)
> — Latino dicho

Long before the 9/11 terrorist attack on the World Trade Center, plans to invade Iraq were hatched by a group of neoconservatives including President Bush and his brother Florida governor Jeb Bush, Vice President Richard Cheney, Cheney's chief-of-staff I. Lewis Libby, Defense Secretary Donald Rumsfeld, Deputy Secretary of Defense Paul Wolfowitz, and other like-minded political players and theorists. In 1992, while at the Pentagon, Wolfowitz and Libby, under the general direction of Cheney, produced a document called *Defense Policy Guidance,* which called for preemptive attack on any states suspected of developing weapons of mass destruction. The document urged military intervention in Iraq to ensure "access to vital raw material, primarily Persian Gulf oil." Indeed, it envisioned U.S. military intervention abroad as "a constant feature" of the new world order.

In 1997, the neoconservative Project for the New American Century issued a Statement of Principles (signed by Wolfowitz, Libby, Cheney, and Rumsfeld, among others), which argued that "it is important to shape circumstances before crises emerge, and to meet threats before they become dire." The same group issued a strategy document in 2000 entitled *Rebuilding America's Defenses: Strategies, Forces, and Resources for a New Century,* which called for "a global first-strike force." The document identified North Korea, Iran, and Iraq — later designated the "axis of evil" — as candidates for regime change (together with Syria and China).

A passage in this document is worth quoting: "The United States," it argues, "has for decades sought to play a more permanent role in Gulf regional security. While the unresolved conflict with Iraq provides the immediate justification, the need for a substantial American force presence in the Gulf transcends the issue of the regime of Saddam Hussein." In other words, the war makers were determined to take over Iraq, regardless of whether Saddam Hussein was in power or not. The document projects a "cavalry of the new American frontier" in which there is a permanent U.S. presence in the Gulf, including Saudi Arabia, Kuwait, Iraq, and elsewhere. The plan calls on the U.S. to consider developing biological weapons of mass destruction.

Also in 2000, PNAC directors Robert Kagan and William Kristol edited a book called *Present Dangers: Crisis and Opportunities in American Foreign and Defense Policy,* which repeated the call for regime change not just in Iraq, Iran, and North Korea, but also in mainland China. The neoconservative American Enterprise Institute, which included Richard Perle, chair of Rumsfeld's Defense Planning Board until he was forced to resign because of conflict of interest issues, promoted the notion that conflict with China is inevitable.

In June 2001, President Bush told the graduating class at West Point that "we must take the battle to the enemy, disrupt his plans, and confront the worst threats before they emerge." In 2002 he sent an official "National Security Strategy" to Capitol Hill in which he repeated that "America will act against such emerging threats before they are fully formed."

The point is that 9/11 provided this group a convenient smokescreen to put into action plans that had been formulated for at least a decade (it ought by now to go without saying that the purported links between Iraq and Al-Qaeda are, to be charitable, tenuous). With the fall of the Soviets as a formidable counterbalance, these visionaries sought to seize the "unipolar moment" and achieve "full spectrum dominance" — a phrase that figures prominently in an official U.S. Department of Defense document: "The United States," it says, "must maintain ... the ability to rapidly project power worldwide in order to achieve full spectrum dominance." This will enable the country to "control any situation," the document explains, by the application of military force.

And that is what all this theorizing comes down to — the application of superior force, pure and simple. We invade Iraq because we can. Perhaps Syria will be next. For now, we are powerful, and we can do as we wish.

But power has a funny way of fading away. In the collections of the Asian Art Museum in San Francisco is a small, ancient, mysterious cheekpiece of a horse bridle in the form of a winged creature. It comes from the mountains that separate Iran from Iraq, a region hit hard in the first Gulf War. People from this region conquered Babylon and briefly won full-spectrum dominance over the cradle of civilization. But when the wind blows the cradle will rock. The one-time conquerors vanished, leaving only a few intriguing bronzes like this one to mark their moment of glory. We can only speculate at the meaning of the creature I am calling a winged sphinx. Who knows what significance it had for its makers? It bears horns on its head, and some sort of predator emerges from its wings. It tramples a creature the museum's curators describe as an antelope. What are the meanings of these features? And how did the sphinx's mirror image, from the other side of the bridle, end up in the Louvre, nearly six thousand miles distant? The answer, I suppose, is blowing in the wind.

So empires rise and decline. What will be the legacy of our moment in the sun? A legacy of force or a legacy of reason? For all their flaws (such as tolerance of slavery), our forefathers forged a constitution that was constructed on principles of fairness and justice. I wish that we would honor those principles now. "Legal war" may seem an odd concept, but wars of self-defense can be justified in the community of nations. This, however, is not such a war. Saddam Hussein's aggression against his neighbors Iran (we generally supported Iraq in that conflict) and Kuwait came to a halt after the first Gulf War. He is (by the time this sees print the verb will probably be *was*) a despot and a villain, a cruel man who deserved to be overthrown, but he posed no immediate threat to the U.S. By invading Iraq and causing large numbers of civilian casualties, we cannot help but turn many of its people against us, just as young Saddam turned against an earlier wave of British invaders. By invading we damage our collateral. If we had offered more substantial support to the Iraqi opposition (recall the lingering resentment from our failure to deliver promised support to Kurdish opposition factions) we could likely have worked to oust Saddam in a way that would have won us more good will and less ill will.

MOOD OF THE NATION

> Why am I so soft in the middle
> When the rest of my life is so hard?
> — Paul Simon, "You Can Call Me Al"

According to polls, support for the war has stayed steady at about 70 percent. (In the U.S., that is; hardly anywhere else in the world can substantial popular support be found.) The numbers further break down as 40 percent strongly for the war and 20 percent strongly against. Of the remaining 40 percent, three out of four "softly" favor the war. Which means that if the last statistic could be turned around, if three out of four of the soft group could be turned against the war — or if it is too late for this war, against the next "preemptive" war — then the opposition would include half of all Americans.

In his novel *Brighton Rock,* Graham Greene explores the mind of a serial killer. Essentially he contrasts a bad person, a good person, and an indifferent one, and he suggests that in some ways the indifferent person is the worst — for Greene it is better to acknowledge goodness by turning against it than to pay it no mind, for rejection is but one step from redemption. It's hard to subscribe to that point of view without reservation, but sometimes I do wonder which is worse, the muddle in the middle or the pro-war camp, some of whom seem to be acting from a sincere and coherent system of beliefs (though many seem suspiciously often to personally profit from actions taken). How can a person be indifferent or unsure in a case such as this?

Well, they have their own lives to be concerned with, and it would be condescending to pass judgment without knowing their circumstances. All we can do is speak up. An informed and educated public, we must presume, will make better decisions than an ignorant one. Perhaps in time the muddled middle will come to be appalled by endless atrocities, and it will turn against unnecessary wars.[1]

Having written these words, I turn on the television, and I see a report on "the mood of the nation." The visual shows people watching the very program that is broadcasting the report — the nation is in the mood to watch this same channel. We are, it seems, all embedded together. At the bottom of the screen stock prices parade by in a row.

---

[1] Rereading this a decade later, I find that day has, to some extent, arrived, as America is greeting President Obama's proposal to bomb Syria with appropriate and reasonable skepticism.

EAST ASIA

Gutenberg and the Koreans

Left: Jost Amman, "The Printer's Workshop," from *The Book of Trades,* woodcut, Germany, 1568. Right: Illustration from *Imperial Printing Office Manual for Moving Type,* China, 1733.

Johannes Gutenberg's development, in mid-fifteenth-century Mainz, of printing with movable metal type was enormously consequential — it made texts available to an increasing percentage of the population and helped to spark the European Renaissance.[1] So

---

1   Although Gutenberg is widely acknowledged as the first European to print with movable metal type, that honor is sometimes claimed for a handful of other printers. This dispute has little bearing on the present argument.

◄ Replica of type used for the earliest extant book printed with movable metal type, 1377. Korean Culture Museum, Incheon Airport, Seoul, South Korea. *Photo by Daderot, http://bit.ly/1nkotxA.*

it is surprising how much remains unknown about Gutenberg and his invention, such as its year of creation, what the press looked like, what tools were used to prepare the type, or what financial structure supported the print operation.

Another question also remains unanswered: was Gutenberg aware that he was far from the first to print with movable metal type, and that printing in this manner had been done in Asia since the early thirteenth century? "The question if there was a direct influence from the orient on the invention of printing with movable type in Germany around 1440," says Eva-Maria Hanebutt-Benz of the Gutenberg Museum in Mainz, "cannot be solved so far in the context of the scholarly research."[2] What is certain, however, is that printing with movable wooden type is documented from the eleventh century; that printing with movable metal type had been an active enterprise in Korea since 1234; that other printing technologies had Asian origins and were subsequently transmitted to the West; that a single empire (the Mongol khanates) stretched from Korea to Europe through much of the thirteenth and fourteenth centuries, facilitating cross-cultural exchange across a vast region; that there

Passport (*paiza*), 13th c., enabling travel through the Mongol empire. Iron with silver inlay. *Metropolitan Museum of Art. Purchase, Bequest of Dorothy Graham Bennett, 1993 (1993.256).*

---

2   Hanebutt-Benz, 41. For bibliographical information on citations see the list of selected readings at the end of this essay.

was considerable East–West travel, contact, and exchange during this period; that the written record of such contacts records only a fraction of what actually occurred; and that there was awareness of Asian printing in Europe in the centuries before Gutenberg.

For all these reasons it is likely that Europe's print revolution did not occur independently but was influenced or inspired by similar printing in Asia.

PRINT TECHNOLOGY AND SOCIETY

Gutenberg is rightly lauded for his resourcefulness, inventiveness, and skill, but the impact of printing was more a manifestation of social change than of a single technological innovation. Print technology fueled or accelerated social developments, but at the same time it was a response to them. Moreover, print technology is a complex system of interactions rather than just a single machine — it involves technologies of papermaking, ink production, metal-casting, distribution, and so on. These technologies differed between East and West, in part because of the materials available, so movable-type printing differed as well.[3]

What is printing for? Printing is above all a duplicating process, and Gutenberg was the Xerox of his time.[4] Printing does not directly produce knowledge; it facilitates the spread of existing knowledge. Therefore, the first requirement for the development of printing is a demand for texts and for duplication of documents. In Gutenberg's Europe such demand was exploding, and printing responded to this existing market — demand for books was so great

---

3   See Hanebutt-Benz for a discussion of some of the technical differences.

4   Photocopying is a type of printing. The Internet, on the other hand, inverts printing's solution to the replication of documents. While printing creates many copies, each providing one view at a time, the Internet enables one document to have multiple simultaneous views. Therefore it can be regarded as a profound technological development, comparable in magnitude to printing.

Pages from the *Pulcho Chikchi Simch'e Yoyol* (Selected teachings of Buddhist sages and Son masters), the earliest extant book printed with movable metal type, dated 1377, Hungdok-sa Temple, Korea. *Bibliothèque Nationale de France. Photo by Jonathan Harrell, http://bit.ly/1st4Eow.*

in the mid-fifteenth century that a single bookseller might employ five hundred scribes; by the end of the century there were 150 printing presses in Venice alone, and nearly 15 million books had been printed. The happy result for many publishers was a dynamic in which increasing supply fed increasing demand.

But there is another, perhaps less evident, function of printing. This is standardization. To generalize, the duplicative function was given more weight in the West and the standardizing function more weight in East Asia. The reason for this lies in the different social contexts of printing in the two areas. In the West, early Renaissance printing had a subversive tinge — in the Italianate states where it first caught hold in a major way it was associated with capitalist enterprise that tended to undercut the authority of church and

Scholars waiting for the results of the civil service exam to be posted (detail). Hand-scroll attributed to Qiu Ying (active 1530–1552). *National Palace Museum, Taipei.*

nobility by creating new sources of wealth and by extending publications beyond the inner circles of the traditional literate elite.[5]

In East Asia, and especially in Korea, where printing with movable metal type was perfected, the situation was different. During the period when this process was regularly used, Korea was governed by the Goryeo dynasty, which had made Buddhism the state religion. In the face of a looming Mongol threat, Goryeo scriptoria were charged with making copies of the Buddhist canon (called the Tripitaka) in order to preserve the Buddhist dharma. (This was a large project — the first Korean woodblock printing of the Tripitaka, from about 1014, consisted of 5,058 chapters, and later editions substantially enlarged the total. This required more than 130,000 blocks, for which a special storehouse had to be built.) But copyists sometimes imposed, whether intentionally or accidentally, differences in rendering the texts. Since the documents represented Buddhist scriptural orthodoxy, it was important for doctrinal reasons that they be standardized. Movable type may have been seen as contributing to such standardization by codifying the character set and enabling multiple documents to be produced from the same set of materials rather than being assigned to different carvers.

The Chinese-style civil service examination system, which was exported to Korea at least by the time of the unification of its states in the seventh century, also contributed to a demand for standardization. A national institute for higher education was established, and private schools existed in various parts of the country to prepare students for the state-run exams. When a provincial school complained about the unreliability of texts, the government ordered

---

5   According to Marshall McLuhan, "Print created national uniformity and government centralism, but also individualism and opposition to government as such" (255). The democratizing element of printing may seem inevitable from the perspective of the European tradition — to Hellmut Lehmann-Haupt, for example, "it seems quite understandable that printing ... should have become associated with popular and democratic rather than aristocratic levels of cultural expression" (75). But this is not as strongly the case from the Asian perspective.

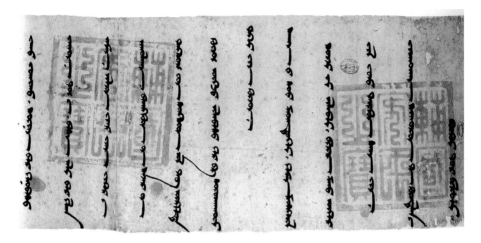

From a letter from the Il-khan Arghun to Philip IV "The Fair" of France, in Uighur script, dated 1289. *French National Archives.*

copies of books made and delivered to the provincial capital.[6] So in East Asia, both for reasons of state and reasons of religion, printing was not subversive but state-mandated, and its primary motivation was as much standardization as duplication.

The Mongol empire spread knowledge of printing. Chinese book production was described in detail by one of the most important chroniclers of the Mongol period, the Persian official Rashid al-Din, in his early fourteenth-century history. According to Rashid, "when any book was desired, a copy was made by a skillful calligrapher on tablets and carefully corrected by proofreaders whose names were inscribed on the back of the tablets. The letters were then cut out by expert engravers, and all pages of the books consecutively numbered. When completed, the tablets were placed in sealed bags to be kept by reliable persons, and if anyone wanted a copy of the book, he paid the charges fixed by the government. The tablets were then taken out of the bags and imposed on leaves of paper to obtain the printed sheets as desired. In this way, alterations could not be made and documents

---

6   Sohn (1959), 96–97.

could be faithfully transmitted."[7] Rashid's report confirms that control of texts was a primary motivation for Chinese printing. It also establishes beyond any doubt that detailed knowledge of woodblock printing was transmitted across the Mongol empire from East Asia to West Asia. It is likely that information about cast-type printing would have been similarly conveyed.

The Persian Ilkhanate (one of the four states of the Mongol empire) was at this time in regular contact not just with East Asia but also with Europe (in part because the Persian and the European states shared a common enemy in the Mamluk sultanate), frequently exchanging emissaries and documents. Indeed, Rashid himself gives a full account of the arrival of the embassy with which Marco Polo reported returning from China.[8] Rashid also demonstrated the Ilkhanate's interest in Europe by writing a History of the Franks, which reveals a fair understanding of Western Europe, considering that "the Muslims regarded Europe as a remote and barbarous area, hardly worth the attention of a civilized man."[9]

In the face of such evidence it seems more likely that news of Asian innovations in printing reached Europe, and the record of that news has been lost to us, than that no hint of these highly developed technologies traveled the well-worn routes of land and sea.

THE DEVELOPMENT OF PRINTING IN CHINA, AND ITS TRANSMISSION TO THE WEST

Before looking more closely at movable-type printing in Korea, we need to review the development of printing in China. Since early print technologies arose in Asia and traveled from there to the West, it seems a reasonable surmise, in the absence of evidence otherwise, that this process continued as printing developed.[10]

---

7 Tsien, 306–307.
8 His account completely confirms Marco Polo's — except that nowhere is Polo mentioned.
9 Morgan, 193.
10 The complex stories of the development and spread of ink and

Kublai Khan bestows a passport of safe passage to Marco Polo, by the Boucicaut master and workshop, ca. 1410–1412. France. Colors on vellum. *Bibliothèque Nationale de France.*

Paper

The earliest writing in China was usually on wood or bamboo; silk was also used. The invention of paper is attributed to Cai Lun, a Hunan official of the Han dynasty, in the year 105. Archaeologists have, however, discovered examples of paper dating from before the common era; there are also literary references to paper predating Cai Lun. Cai Lun's paper was made from silk rags, but many different fibers (notably bark and hemp) were later used.

Paper technology may have arisen from the process of felting. It seems logical that printing as a means of creating repeating patterns on textiles was a forerunner to printing on paper. "Whether European textile printing was influenced by the Chinese is not clear,"

---

glue technologies are beyond the scope of this essay.

Left: A government document, dated equivalent of 95 CE, written on bamboo strips and excavated at Juyan in Gansu province. *British Library*. Right: Silk banner decorated by printing, 8th to 9th c., found at cave 17 at Dunhuang. The roundel motif is of Persian origin. *British Museum*.

according to Tsien Tsuen-Hsuin, "but some patterns of Chinese origin, borrowed by Persian weavers, are said to have been transmitted to Western Europe, and certainly many Chinese decorative motifs had been successfully copied by European makers of figured fabrics before 1500."[11] Stamps similar to those for printing textiles were also used by the Chinese for seals and religious charms from an early date.

By the Tang dynasty (618–906) papers of the highest quality were being produced and sent to the capital as tribute. The paper industry was an enabling factor in the Chinese style of centralized government, with its bureaucracy making huge demands for paper.

---

11   Tsien, 313.

Cai Lun as the patron saint of papermaking, ca. 18th c.

Annual tax assessments alone required more than half a million sheets (each about twelve by eighteen inches) a year.[12]

Like other print-related technologies, papermaking was gradually transmitted from China to other regions. Papermaking spread throughout Central Asia by the end of the fourth century and to Korea apparently somewhat later. By the end of the eighth century

---

12   Twitchett, 12.

Kublai Khan paying for goods with paper currency as witnessed by Marco Polo, by the Boucicaut master and workshop, ca. 1410–1412. France. Colors on vellum. *Bibliothèque Nationale de France.*

paper was being produced in Baghdad. Although it reached Europe by the eleventh century, its use was still spotty at the time of Gutenberg, who printed some of his Bibles on parchment (an expensive process, requiring the skins of three hundred sheep for a single Bible).

In later dynastic China, Cai Lun was assimilated into the popular pantheon as the patron deity of papermaking.

Currency

Printed paper currency was developed in China in the eleventh century, in part to compensate for a shortage of copper coin in Szechwan, where the printing industry flourished.[13] The Mongol emperor Kublai Khan had a sophisticated understanding of paper currency. Rather than invalidate the existing Song currency — which would have devastated the Chinese economy — he

---

13 Twitchett, 43. By the end of the century problems of inflation and currency devaluation resulted from overprinting of currency.

allowed it, for a period of ten years, to be converted to a new currency that he standardized throughout his empire. "To facilitate trade and to promote the welfare of the merchants, Kublai initiated the use of paper currency throughout his domains," notes Morris Rossabi, adding that "Khubilai was the first Mongol ruler to seek a country-wide system of paper currency."[14]

The earliest existing European report of paper currency is a mention from 1255 by William of Ruysbroeck, a French missionary to the Mongol court.[15] The accounts of Marco Polo include a detailed description of the Chinese currency, which was briefly adopted by the Persian Ilkhanate. The Persian version was clearly based on the Chinese model, for it was called by the Chinese word *chao*, and it even included words printed in Chinese.[16] In the case of paper currency, as in other aspects of printing, the route of transmission was from China to the West.

Block with image reversed for printing, for a Mongol-period bank note, 1264–1340.

Playing cards

Printed playing cards were used in China from an early date, probably the ninth century. Cards were an early subject of printing because they were popular with all classes and as a result demanded reproduction in quantity, and they require standardized backs so that the contents of the face cannot be known. In Europe, too, cards were one of the

---

14 Rossabi, 123.
15 Tsien, 293.
16 Morgan, 165.

Left: Chinese playing card found near Turpan, ca. 1400. *Museum fur Volkerkunde, Berlin*. Right: Queen of Wild Men, ca. 1440, engraving by the Master of the Playing Cards, with whom Gutenberg is thought to have worked. *Kupferstichkabinett, Dresden*.

earliest applications of printing, "doubtless because of the early and widespread use in the East," in the judgment of Tsien Tsuen-Hsuin. "Probably they were brought to Europe by the Mongol armies, traders, and travellers."[17] Hellmut Lehmann-Haupt has produced evidence indicating that Gutenberg (who is said to have begun his career as a goldsmith) created copper engravings for playing cards prior to developing his printing press, apparently working in association with the artist known as the Master of the Playing Cards.

17   Tsien, 310.

Frontispiece of the earliest dated printed book, the Diamond Sutra, dated 868. China.

Woodblock book printing

In China a commercial book trade existed as early as the first century of the common era. Books were also commissioned by religious institutions and by the state. The earliest dated printed book was discovered in a cave temple at Dunhuang.[18] A scroll about sixteen feet long, it is a copy of the Buddhist Diamond Sutra, bearing a date equivalent to 868. The quality of the printing is remarkably high, suggesting an established print industry.

The entire Buddhist canon was printed by imperial decree around 1000, and it was reprinted several times in following centuries. One of these is the Jisha edition, named for the island where the monastery that commissioned the printing was located. The printing was begun

---

18 A printing of the Dharani sutra, discovered in Korea in 1966, is undated but must have been produced before 751. The development of Korean printing will be discussed below.

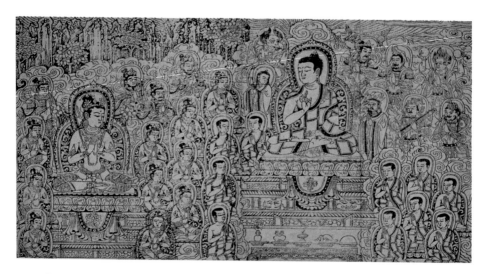

Chapter 2 of the Magical Charm Scripture of Great Splendor, 1231–1322, Yenshengyuan Monastery, Jisha, Suzhou, Jiangsu province. *Asian Art Museum, Gift of the Walter H. and Phyllis J. Shorenstein Foundation, 1991.208.*

in 1231 but completed under the Mongol rule of the Yuan dynasty. The complete edition consisted of 6,362 printed volumes containing 1,532 texts entailing the carving of more than 150,000 woodblocks.

Woodblock printing became popular in Europe in the fourteenth century. The blocks used were similar to Chinese woodblocks. Robert Curzon (1810–1873) was one of the first to pursue the similarity between Asian and European block books to its logical conclusion, arguing that "we must suppose that the process of printing them must have been copied from ancient Chinese specimens, brought from that country by some early travelers, whose names have not been handed down to our times." "Since all the technical processes are of Chinese rather than European tradition," adds Tsien Tsuen-Hsuin, "it seems that the European block printers must not only have seen Chinese samples, but perhaps had been taught by missionaries or others who had learned these un-European methods from Chinese printers during their residence in China."[19]

---

19   Tsien, 313.

The invention of movable type in China is attributed to the Song-dynasty inventor Bi Sheng (ca. 990–1051; spelled Pi Sheng in the Wade-Giles transliteration system used in the extract below) in the eleventh century. His process was described by Shen Kua (ca. 1031–1095). Bi's types were made of baked clay. They were set in an iron form, their position stabilized with heated resin and wax. After the printing was completed, the wax and resin were melted to release the type for later reuse, as Shen Kua explains:

> Pi Sheng, a man of unofficial position, made movable type. His method was as follows: he took sticky clay and cut in it characters as thin as the edge of a coin. Each character formed, as it were, a single type. He baked them in the fire to make them hard. He had previously prepared an iron plate and he had covered his plate with a mixture of pine resin, wax, and paper ashes. When he wished to print, he took an iron frame and set it on the iron plate. In this he placed the types, set close together. When the frame was full, the whole made one solid block of type. He then placed it near the fire to warm it. When the paste [at the back] was slightly melted, he took a smooth board and pressed it over the surface, so that the block of type became as even as a whetstone.
>
> If one were to print only two or three copies, this method would be neither simple nor easy. But for printing hundreds or thousands of copies, it was marvelously quick. As a rule he kept two formes going. While the impression was being made from the one forme, the type was being put in place on the other. When the printing of one forme was finished, the other was then ready. In this way the two formes alternated and the printing was done with great rapidity.
>
> For each character there were several types, and for certain common characters there were twenty or more types each, in order to be prepared for the repetition of characters on the same page. When the characters were not in use

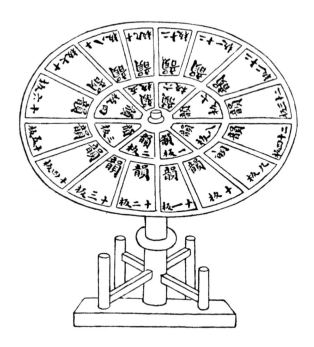

Revolving type table, from a book by Wang Zhen, 1313.

he had them arranged with paper labels, one label for each rhyme-group, and kept them in wooden cases.[20]

Shen Kua reports that "when Pi Sheng died, his font of type passed into the possession of my nephews," and Bi Sheng's type was still being used to print philological primers and neo-Confucian documents during the rule of the Mongol emperor Kublai Khan, by one of his personal councilors.[21]

A report by Wang Zhen in 1313 adds that tin type was also used. (The Chinese abandoned tin as a material for type because it would

---

20 Tsien, 201–202.
21 Tsien, 203.

Chinggis Khan pursuing enemies (detail), 1211, from Rashid al-Din's history. Persia. *Bibliothèque Nationale de France*

not hold the water-based Chinese ink.) Wang Zhen spent more than two years cutting sixty thousand type for use in his own wood-based movable-type printing. An illustration of his technique of laying type with a revolving table has survived.

CROSS-CULTURAL CURRENTS UNDER THE MONGOL EMPIRE

Under Chinggis Khan (prob. 1167–1227) the Mongols unified an enormous geographic territory — it is still history's largest contiguous empire — under central rule. To accomplish this the Mongol army was ruthless to the point of genocide. In this climate the opportunities for cultural and technological exchange must have been limited. But by the time of the rule of Chinggis's grandson Kublai Khan (r. 1260–1294) the situation had changed. Kublai Khan established the capital of his khanate in Beijing, where he

Kublai Khan, from an album of Yuan emperors, 1294. China. Ink and colors on silk. *National Palace Museum, Taipei.*

assumed the Chinese "mandate of heaven" and established the Yuan dynasty. Not viewing China merely as an opportunity for plunder by nomadic warriors, he saw the value of agriculture and urbanism, and he retained many Chinese traditions.

Beijing was not central enough for unified rule of the entire empire, and the Mongols were often troubled by contentious issues of succession, with the result that the empire was divided into regional khanates. But Kublai maintained good relations with his brother Hulegu, the Ilkhan of Persia. Hulagu, even more than Kublai, had in many respects assimilated into the culture of his subject people, and he had converted to Islam. The result was a lively exchange between West Asia and East Asia. It was this climate that encouraged contact between Europe and East Asia.

Muslim traders were active across much of the Mongol realm, including Korea. "Confucian Chinese officials had perceived commerce as demeaning and traders as parasites, but the Mongols did not share that attitude," notes Morris Rossabi. "Khubilai removed many of the previous limitations imposed on trade, paving the way for Eurasian merchants and for the first direct commercial contacts between Europe and East Asia."[22] The Uighur people of Central Asia — a Turkic people (whose language is believed to be related to both Turkish and Korean) who had governed a large empire in the eighth and ninth centuries — helped to facilitate this trade.

Kublai Khan sought to temper the influence of the native Han Chinese by peppering his court with Uighurs and other Muslims. Kublai enacted regulations giving a variety of special privileges to Muslims, such as exemption from taxation and the right to private ownership of weapons. "Small wonder, then," notes John D. Langlois, Jr., "that the Muslims were found in all regions of China in Yuan times."[23] Continuous Muslim settlement stretched from Central Asia across northern China. Muslim scholars founded a school in present-day Hopei, near the Yuan capital of Beijing. Muslim settlement extended to Korea, where historical records document the existence of established Muslim communities.

Centered along the Silk Road in Turfan in northwestern China, the Uighurs had been conquered by Chinggis Khan. He adopted the Uighur script for writing the Mongolian language. By this time

---

22 Berger, 32.
23 Langlois, 273.

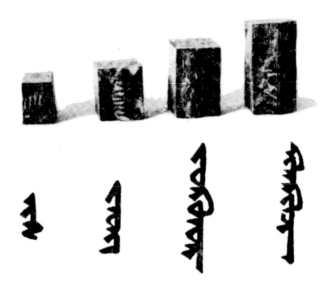

Wooden types and impressions in Uighur script, prob. early 14th c. (Tsien, 306).

many Uighurs had converted to Islam (some adopted Tibetan Buddhism). They included among their number a scholar class. Movable-type Uighur prints have been discovered in the Turfan area, along with wooden type fonts. The Uighurs were both ideally informed and ideally situated for transmitting information about printing from China and Korea to the Islamic territories of West Asia. "The introduction of printing farther to the west was probably accomplished by the Uighurs during the Mongol period," Tsien Tsuen-Hsuin maintains. "After the Mongol conquest of Turfan, a great number of Uighurs were recruited into the Mongol army; Uighur scholars served as Mongol brains, and Uighur culture became the initial basis of Mongol power. If there was any connection in the spread of printing between Asia and the West, the Uighurs who used both block printing and movable type had good opportunities to play an important role in this introduction."[24]

24 Tsien, 306.

Latin tombstone, 1342, from Yangzhou, China.

The most famous of the European travelers to Yuan China was Marco Polo, a teller of tales whose account is notable for its omissions and fabrications yet does restrain some of the more fantastic elements common to some other travel narratives of the Mongol period (that of John Mandeville, for example). Polo claimed — how truthfully it is difficult to say — to have had an audience with Kublai himself. However that may be, it is certain that European travelers visited the Yuan court in Beijing. There they would have been well situated to learn of Korea's perfection of printing with movable metal type.

CAST-TYPE PRINTING IN KOREA'S GORYEO DYNASTY (918–1392)

The Goryeo dynasty (from which the name "Korea" comes) was founded by Wang Geon, who unified the country in 918 and established Buddhism as its state religion. Because China was in transition after the collapse of its Tang dynasty in 906, Goryeo was able initially to flourish without undue concern about external affairs. A Song dynasty envoy from China, Xu Jing, produced a travel account in 1123 that depicted Goryeo as a sophisticated and well-managed society. Already, however, the country found itself forced to respond to threats from Central Asian peoples. Finally, in 1231, Mongol forces invaded. They were repulsed but launched five more attacks over the next three decades, forcing the Goryeo court to withdraw to the island of Ganghwa. In 1270 the Goryeo king formally surrendered, and Mongols assumed control of Korea. Many native Koreans continued to oppose the Mongol occupiers, however, and since military resistance had failed, spiritual power was summoned through the printing of Buddhist texts.

Korea had a long and distinguished woodblock printing tradition. According to Kumja Paik Kim, "the oldest extant woodblock printed text on paper in East Asia is the Dharani sutra discovered in the Seokka-tap (Shakyamuni pagoda) in 1966 in Bulguk-sa Monastery in Gyeongju. Since this pagoda was completed in 751, the printed sutra placed within has the terminal date of 751."[25] Kim also notes the remarkable Goryeo dedication to reproducing the Tripitaka, leading up to the first printing with movable metal type:

> This period is especially famous for carrying out monumental projects of carved woodblocks containing the complete set of Buddhist canon, the Tripitaka (sutras, laws, and treatises), not just once but twice. The first set, which was burned during the Mongol invasion in 1232, had been completed in

---

25 Kim, Kumja Paik (2003).

Haeinsa Temple in Hapchon County, North Kyongsang province, is home to the most complete and best-preserved woodblocks of the Buddhist Tripitaka. *Photo by Arian Zwegers, http://bit.ly/1miiHw3.*

1087 to expel the invading Khitans through prayers to Buddhas. The second set, known today as Tripitaka Koreana, was completed in 1251 as prayers to the power of Buddhas for the protection of the nation from the invading Mongols. The second Tripitaka set, containing more than 8,000 woodblocks, is now housed in the repository in Haein-sa Monastery near Daegu. Goryeo is also credited with inventing movable metal type in the first half of the thirteenth century to meet the heavy demands for various types of books, both religious and secular. *Prescribed Ritual Texts of the Past and Present* (Sangjong Gogeum Yemun) was printed with the movable metal type in 1234.[26]

---

26 Kim, Kumja Paik (2003), 13.

Under Mongol rule "Korea and China also grew closer, as the Mongol-enforced peace throughout their conquered territory allowed envoys and traders to move freely between the two countries. Goryeo officials served in the Yuan government, where because of their literary skill and knowledge of Confucian statecraft, they made contributions to governance."[27] There was also a sea trade that connected Korea to China and points beyond (when Giovanni di Marignolli arrived at the port of Zhengzhou in 1346 he found a depot for European traders ready to receive him). Wang Geon served as an admiral in the Korean navy. Fifty-seven official diplomatic sea voyages to Song-dynasty China, each carrying 100–300 emissaries, were recorded in the 160 years following the establishment of the dynasty. For a joint Goryeo-Mongol expedition to Japan in 1274 the Koreans built an armada of 900 ships in four and a half months.[28] Under Goryeo rule private merchants actively traded by sea with mainland ports — several arrivals of West Asian trading ships were recorded during the eleventh century.[29] Consequently all of the conditions existed for the transmission of significant technological information from Korea to Europe.

While the development of Korean metal type anticipated or responded to the need to replace documents abandoned or destroyed during the Mongol invasions, a contributing factor was the relative scarcity of appropriate hardwoods comparable to the pear wood and jujube used in China. The Korean mold-casting method of producing fonts was probably based on their experience with bronze coins; Koreans were also accomplished in bronze casting of bells and statues. The "excellent workmanship," "dignified form," and "clear and even characters" of Korean coins were admired by Song-dynasty Chinese scholars.[30] A fifteenth-century description of the Korean font casting process was recorded by Song Hyon:

---

27 Edward Shultz, "Cultural History of Goryeo," in Kim (2003), 30.
28 Young, 18.
29 Kim (2003), 19f2.
30 Sohn, 100.

At first, one cuts letters in beech wood. One fills a trough level with fine sandy [clay] of the reed-growing seashore. Wood-cut letters are pressed into the sand, then the impressions become negative and form letters [molds]. At this step, placing one trough together with another, one pours the molten bronze down into an opening. The fluid flows in, filling these negative molds, one by one becoming type. Lastly, one scrapes and files off the irregularities, and piles them up to be arranged.

Much of our knowledge of Goryeo printing is based on written records, as Korea's turbulent history has prevented many works from surviving. But one surviving book, the *Pulcho chikchi simch'e yojol* (Selected teachings of Buddhist sages and Son masters) contains a date equivalent to 1377, making it the earliest extant book printed with movable metal type. It was printed at Hungdok-sa Temple near Chongju (the ruins of the temple, including a type-casting foundry, were discovered during building excavation in 1985). The book was clearly printed using metal type, for, among other telling features, some characters were printed upside down, their alignment is not always straight, and the inking is uneven in a manner not characteristic of block printing.[31]

It might surprise the heirs of Gutenberg to learn that a wood-block version of this same book was printed just a year after the metal type edition. Today we are accustomed to think of movable-type printing with metal type as dramatically superior to woodblock printing, and certainly the European alphabets are ideally suited to this technique. But in East Asia the advantages were less clear-cut. The Jesuit missionary Matteo Ricci noted in the early seventeenth century that Chinese cutters could produce wood blocks as quickly as European typesetters could make up their pages. What's more, the wood blocks could be stored for later use, unlike the printers' forms used in the West, which

---

31 Ch'on, 20.

Printing plates from *Song of the Moon's Reflection on a Thousand Rivers and Episodes from the Life of the Buddha* (Worin ch'on-gang chi kok), Korea, Joseon dynasty. In the fifteenth century, during the Joseon dynasty that succeeded the Goryeo, a new system of writing Korean was introduced, which was better suited to movable type than the Chinese character system used during the Goryeo period (Park Seung-U, *Koreana* 7, no. 2, 27).

were disassembled and the type returned to its cases when printing was completed. Woodblock technology also facilitated book illustration, which was more advanced, and more common, in East Asia than in the West.

Movable-type printing, as Shen Kun had already noted in the eleventh century, was of most value when a large number of copies were desired. The practicality of woodblock printing meant that in East Asia books could be produced in very limited runs, while the adoption of movable-type printing in the West meant that only commercial or underwritten publications could be published without great difficulty (a situation that has endured to this day). As a result, in the West printing to some extent contributed to "an impoverishment of the written tradition," in the view of Jacques Gernet, "because publishers could not take the risk of bringing out works which were not assured of a fairly large sale."[32]

But being a latecomer to printing was also a kind of blessing for Europe. The entire development of printing was highly compressed: Europe adopted paper in the eleventh and twelfth centuries; by the thirteenth century good-quality paper was being made in Italy. In the fourteenth century woodblock printing was widely adopted, and the following century saw the development of typographical printing, which spread with astounding rapidity. By contrast, China had used paper as the principal material for writing since the Han period, and the proto printing techniques of stamping and rubbing were also widely used during the Han. Woodblock printing was employed at least from the eighth century. All of these technologies were a routine part of East Asian culture by the end of the first millennium, so printing did not carry the shock of the new for East Asia as it did for Europe. Put another way, the impact of printing in East Asia, though in its way just as dramatic as in Europe, had long since occurred, contributing to the result that East Asian culture was in many respects more advanced than that of Europe; the Gutenberg boom amounted to a kind of catching up with the East.

So was Gutenberg influenced or inspired, directly or indirectly, by Asian printing? As Eva-Maria Hanebutt-Benz properly observes, "We do not know if Johannes Gutenberg had any kind of knowledge of the fact that long before his invention printing with moveable type was done in East-Asia."[33] Still, as new information is discovered, "the notion that knowledge of printing in the Far East could have found its way to Strasbourg or Mainz," in the view of one Western scholar of printing, "becomes more insistent and

---

32 Gernet, 336.
33 Hanebutt-Benz, 41.

persuasive."[34] While there is no "smoking gun" to establish a direct connection, there is plenty of circumstantial evidence suggesting that East Asian printing influenced early Renaissance Europe (not, apparently, as a direct technological transmission but rather as a conceptual model to be reverse-engineered by the Europeans), and we may ask why movable-type technology should have differed from other print technologies in its development. While the continuous line of transmission from East Asia to Europe was for a time interrupted, under the mature Mongol empire widespread trade and exchange resumed, and this occurred around the same time that Korea perfected movable-type printing. The continuous line of cultural connection that existed between Korea and Europe through the fourteenth century would have enabled this technology to follow a similar route of transmission as those that preceded it.

34 Kapr, 109.

Berger, Patricia, and Terese Tse Bartholomew. *Mongolia: The Legacy of Chinggis Khan.* San Francisco: Asian Art Museum, 1995.

Ch'on Hye-bong. "Pulcho chikchi simch'e yojol." *Korea Journal* 3:7 (July 1963): 20–21.

———. "Typography in Korea: Birthplace of Moveable Metal Type." *Korea Journal* 3:7 (July 1963): 10–19.

Gernet, Jacques. *A History of Chinese Civilization.* Trans. J. R. Foster and Charles Hartman. Cambridge: Cambridge University Press, 1982, 1996 (2nd ed.).

Hanebutt-Benz, Eva-Maria. "Gutenberg's Metal Type." *Printing and Publishing Culture: Proceedings of the Third International Symposium.* Chungbuk-do, Korea: Cheongju Early Printing Museum, 2000.

Kahn, Paul. *The Secret History of the Mongols: The Origin of Chingis Khan.* "Based on the English translation of F. W. Cleaves." Berkeley: North Point Press, 1984.

Kapr, Albert. *Johannes Gutenberg: The Man and His Invention.* George Martin tr. Brookfield, VT: Scolar, 1996.

Kim, Doo-jong. "History of Korean Printing." *Korea Journal* 3:7 (July 1963): 22–26.

Kim, Joo-young. "The Tripitika Koreana and Changgyonggak at Haein-sa Temple." *Koreana* 7, no. 2 (Summer 1993), 32–37.

Kim, Kumja Paik. *The Art of Korea: Highlights from the Collection of San Francisco's Asian Art Museum.* San Francisco: Asian Art Museum, 2006.

———. *Goryeo Dynasty: Korea's Age of Enlightenment, 918–1392.* San Francisco: Asian Art Museum, 2003.

Langlois, John D., Jr. *China under Mongol Rule.* Princeton: Princeton University Press, 1981.

Lee, Jae-jun. "Hungdok-sa Temple Site in Ch'ongju." *Koreana* 7, no. 2 (Summer 1993), 22–27.

Lehmann-Haupt, Hellmut. *Gutenberg and the Master of the Playing Cards.* New Haven: Yale University Press, 1966.

Marcou, David J. "Korea: The Cradle of Movable Metal Type." *Korean Culture* 13:1 (Spring 1992): 4–7.

McLuhan, Marshall. *The Gutenberg Galaxy.* Toronto: University of Toronto Press, 1962.

Morgan, David. *The Mongols.* New York: Basil Blackwell, 1986.

Printing and Publishing Culture: Proceedings of the Third International Symposium. Cheongju: Cheongju Early Printing Museum, 2000.

Rossabi, Morris. *Khubilai Khan: His Life and Times.* Berkeley: University of California Press, 1988.

Sohn, Pow-Key. "Early Korean Printing." *Journal of the American Oriental Society* 79, 2 (Apr.–June, 1959), 96–103.

———. "Printing Since the 8th Century in Korea." *Koreana* 7, no. 2 (Summer 1993), 4–9.

Tsien Tsuen-Hsuin. "Paper and Printing," part one of vol. 5 in Joseph Needham, *Science and Civilisation in China.* Cambridge: Cambridge University Press, 1985.

Twitchett, Denis. *Printing and Publishing in Medieval China.* New York: Frederic C. Beil, 1983.

Young, Myung-chui, "Korea's Sphere of Maritime Influence," *Koreana* 20, no. 2 (Summer 2006).

The Art of Tao

~~~

Great understanding is broad and unhurried;
small understanding is cramped and busy.

Great words are bright and open;
small words are chit and chat.
— from *Chuang Tzu: The Inner Chapters* (tr. David Hinton)

How can we understand Taoism? It appears at first to be a school
of philosophy, but then we learn that ordained Taoist priests,
wearing formal robes, perform prescribed rituals before precisely
laid-out altars. It seems firmly rooted in humanism, but then we
discover that it boasts an extensive pantheon of deities who popu-
late an elaborate network of heavens. It seems to address in the
broadest terms the most general questions, but then we find that
its theories are detailed in volumes of painstaking minutia. It may
appear as a religion, but then it manifests as a system of alchemy,
of medicine, of geomancy, of astrology, or in any number of bewildering forms.

Somewhere the ancient Taoist sages are laughing at our confusion. "We look but don't see it," says Laozi, "and call it indistinct"
(*Daode jing*, verse 14).

Imagine a nebulous thing
here before Heaven and Earth
silent and elusive
it stands alone not wavering
it travels everywhere unharmed
it could be the mother of us all
not knowing its name
I call it the Tao
— *Daode jing*, verse 11 (tr. Red Pine)

◀ Celestial Deity of the Purple Realm accompanied by a demon
(detail), ca. 1600. China. Ink and colors on silk. *Paris, Musée des
Arts Asiatiques Guimet*, EO 751. A dizzying array of Taoist deities,
typically portrayed amid swirling clouds, patrols the heavens.

Let's try to see. Let's review the roots of Taoism in the ancient classics, consider key Taoist concepts, and then turn our gaze to religious Taoism. The story begins in the late Bronze Age, with Laozi.

PROGENITORS

Laozi and the Daode jing

> Thirty spokes converge on a hub
> but it's the emptiness
> that makes a wheel work
> pots are fashioned from clay
> but it's the hollow
> that makes a pot work
> windows and doors are carved for a house
> but it's the spaces
> that make a house work
> existence makes something useful
> but nonexistence makes it work
> — *Daode jing,* verse 11 (tr. Red Pine)

ABOVE: Laozi meets Yin Xi, the Warden of the Pass, at Hangu Pass (detail), by Jiang Xun (1764–1821). China. Album painting; ink and colors on silk. *Paris, Musée des Arts Asiatiques Guimet*, MG 22764.

OPPOSITE: Laozi on an ox, mid-16th c., by Zhang Lu (ca. 1490–1563). China. Hanging scroll; ink on paper. *National Palace Museum, Taipei.* Laozi is said to have been traveling in the company of an ox and a servant boy when he dictated the *Daode jing.*

It is written in the *Daode jing* (The way and virtue), the small classic that lies at the heart of Taoism and whose authorship is attributed to Laozi sometime around the sixth century BCE, that "nonexistence makes it work." How appropriate, then, that Laozi's own existence has long been the subject of lively debate.

According to Sima Qian (146–86 BCE) in his *Shi ji* (Records of the grand historian), Laozi was a custodian of the imperial archives, an older contemporary of Confucius (some say the *Lao* in Laozi means "old," while others regard it simply as a family name), who retired to the west in his old age. At Hangu Pass between the Yellow River and the Chungnan Mountains, Laozi met Yin Xi, the Warden of the Pass, and revealed to him the text of the *Daode jing*.

But the *Shi ji* also alludes to a son of Laozi who served as a general of Wei in 273 BCE. The father of this man could not have been a contemporary of Confucius (551–479). Some scholars, particularly in mainland China, have dated Laozi in the fourth or third century BCE; others have held to the traditional dates (usually given as 604–531); and still others (especially in the West) have insisted that Laozi is a purely legendary figure who never existed at all. "What has been transmitted through the ages about Laozi is of a purely legendary nature," according to Kristofer Schipper in the catalogue accompanying an exhibition organized by Stephen Little at the Chicago Art Institute, entitled *Taoism and the Arts of China*. But Wing-tsit Chan, in his *Source Book in Chinese Philosophy,* says that "the theory that Lao Tzu [Laozi] never existed or is merely a legend compounded of ... different accounts is no longer seriously entertained."

Whoever Laozi may have been, "Chinese civilization and the Chinese character would have been utterly different if the book *Lao Tzu* [Laozi; the *Daode jing* is often referred to by this name] had never been written," Wing-tsit Chan asserts. "No one can hope to understand Chinese philosophy, religion, government, art, medicine — or even cooking — without a real appreciation of the profound philosophy taught by this little book."

What accounts for the extraordinary influence of this terse classic of five thousand words (about the length of this essay)? By promoting ideals of nonconformity, individualism, tranquillity, acceptance, rela-

Daode jing of Laozi, Upper Roll, 8th c., Dunhuang, Gansu province. Handscroll; ink on paper. *Bibliotèque Nationale de France.*

tivity, transcendence, and the primacy of the natural world, Taoism provided a counterpoint and corrective to Confucianism, with its emphasis on social responsibility and hierarchies of authority. The *Daode jing*'s open-ended, suggestive style leaves much open to interpretation (the curmudgeonly British literary historian Herbert Giles wrote that from it "little meaning can be extracted except by enthusiasts who curiously enough disagree absolutely among themselves"). In the Chinese tradition, the book is usually read with the help of some of the many commentaries that have been appended to it over the centuries.

The *Daode jing* is a deep, still pool from which the key tenets of Taoism are drawn. It is a mirror to the reader, in which one can find the individual truths most corresponding to one's personal search.

> The best are like water
> bringing help to all
> without competing
> choosing what others avoid
> hence approaching the Tao
> — *Daode jing,* verse 8 (tr. Bill Porter)

Zhuangzi

> Long ago, a certain Chuang Tzu [Zhuangzi] dreamt he was a butterfly — a butterfly fluttering here and there on a whim, happy and carefree, knowing nothing of Chuang Tzu. Then all of a sudden he woke to find that he was, beyond all doubt, Chuang Tzu. Who knows if it was Chuang Tzu dreaming of a butterfly, or a butterfly dreaming of Chuang Tzu? Chuang Tzu and butterfly: clearly there's a difference. This is called the transformation of things.
>
> — *Chuang Tzu: The Inner Chapters* (tr. David Hinton)

We are on firmer ground in speaking of the second great figure of early Taoism — his uncertainties about his butterfly nature notwithstanding — than we are with Laozi. It is generally agreed that Zhuangzi was a historical figure whose life probably spanned much of the fourth century BCE; he is said to have been a cleric in a lacquer workshop. According to Sima Qian, after working as a minor official, he somehow obtained the opportunity to become a prime minister but declined the offer. Only the first seven chapters of the book bearing his name, however, are believed likely to have been written by him; they are known as "the inner chapters."

Today, for Taoists and non-Taoists alike, Laozi and Zhuangzi are considered a paired set ("Lao-Zhuang"), the twin progenitors of Taoism. But it was not until several hundred years after Zhuang's lifetime, in the fourth century CE, that the two began to be joined. In retrospect, the association seems inevitable, for despite their differences they share many attitudes, and both can be viewed in counterpoint to Confucianism.

Zhuangzi was as much a literary stylist as a philosopher. While Laozi's *Daode jing* is philosophical in tone and telegraphic and evocative in style, Zhuangzi's work is composed of what translator David Hinton calls a "collage technique," making use of many tones and literary modes. In general it is lively, humorous, informal, and at times a bit sarcastic, especially when dealing with the shortcomings of competing Confucian attitudes.

Zhuangzi Dreaming of a Butterfly, mid-16th c., by Lu Zhi (1496–1576). China. Leaf from an album of ten leaves; ink on silk. *Palace Museum, Beijing.* This painting, by one of the finest Wu school artists of the sixteenth century, depicts a famous scene from the *Zhuangzi.*

"In Chuang Tzu [Zhuangzi]," writes Wing-tsit Chan, "differences between Confucianism and Taoism become much sharper [than with Laozi]. The Confucianists teach full development of one's nature, fulfillment of one's destiny, and participation in the creative work of nature. Chuang Tzu, on the other hand, believes in nourishing nature, returning to destiny, and enjoying Nature. The Confucianists want people transformed through education, but Chuang Tzu leaves transformation to things themselves."

Zhuangzi is above all a relativist (and relativism is anathema to Confucianism). Does he dream of the butterfly, or is it the butterfly that dreams of him? Once Zhuangzi was walking by a river with the Confucian philosopher Huizi, and he remarked on the happiness of the fish sporting in the river. Huizi challenged Zhuangzi: "You are not a fish. How can you know the happiness of fishes?" "I know it," Zhuangzi replied, "through the river." Stephen Little explains: "According to Zhuangzi, true understanding should be acquired

The Pleasures of Fishes (detail), 1291, by Zhou Dongqing. China. Handscroll, ink and light colors on paper. *The Metropolitan Museum of Art, New York, Purchase, Fletcher Fund,* 47.18.10. Zhuangzi's famous exchange with the Confucian philosopher Huizi on the pleasures of fishes was fodder for Zhou Dongqing, who specialized in paintings of fish.

intuitively, without the need for explication. Huizi, a man obsessed with logical explanations, is unable to grasp this point."

Zhuangzi as much as Laozi sets the tone and the agenda for Taoism. "Just as Mencius did not merely elaborate on Confucius' doctrines but presented something new, so Chuang Tzu definitely advanced beyond Lao Tzu," says Wing-tsit Chan. In the concluding passage of the Inner Chapters, Zhuangzi offers a parable on the transformative powers of opposites. This process will be given shape in the familiar Taoist taiji symbol in which yin and yang, each containing the germ of the other, continually engulf one another in an ongoing process of transformation. At the same time, with a nudge to the social activism of the Confucianists, Zhuangzi reminds us of the value of leaving well enough alone — and the danger of being caught in the middle:

> At the origin of things there was Thunder (Shu), ruler of
> the Southern Ocean, and Bolt (Hu), ruler of the Northern

Pavillions in the Mountains of the Immortals, 1550, by Qiu Ying (1494–1552). China. Hanging scroll; ink and colors on paper. *National Palace Museum, Taipei*, 000033. The text at the top describes a land, peopled with immortals, that is always lush and green. For Taoists, towering mountains reaching up to the heavens were touchpoints to the cosmic. They represented the most impressive physical manifestation of *qi*. There too the mushrooms of immortality grew. Taoists who had achieved the goal of everlasting life would naturally wish to reside among the peaks.

Ocean. And in the Middle Realm, PrimalDark (Hun Tun) ruled. Thunder and Bolt often met together in the lands of PrimalDark, and PrimalDark was always a most gracious host. Eventually, Thunder and Bolt tried to think of a way to repay PrimalDark's kindness. They said: "People all have seven holes so they can see and hear, eat and breathe. Only PrimalDark is without them. Why don't we try cutting some for her?"

So ThunderBolt began cutting holes, one each day. On the seventh day, PrimalDark was dead.

— *Chuang Tzu: The Inner Chapters* (tr. David Hinton)

CONCEPTS

The Tao

The Warring States period of the Western Zhou dynasty, when Zhuangzi lived, was a time of political turmoil but also a golden age of Chinese philosophy characterized by a "Hundred Schools of Thought." Each school had its own tao, or "way." The word *tao* refers to a road or path (as in such English words as driveway, pathway, roadway, byway), and by extension, a way of doing something or regarding something (if it were not a familiar English word based on an earlier system of transliteration it would be spelled as it is pronounced, *dao*).

Why were the teachings of Laozi and Zhuangzi so powerful that Taoism was able to co-opt such a common word to define its own system of belief? Wing-tsit Chan explains:

> Whereas in other schools Tao means a system or moral truth, in this it is the One, which is natural, eternal, spontaneous, nameless, and indescribable. It is at once the beginning of all things and the way in which all things pursue their course. When this Tao is possessed by individual things, it becomes its character or virtue [*de*]. The ideal life for the individual, the ideal order for society, and the ideal type of government are all based on it and guided by it. As the way of life, it

denotes simplicity, spontaneity, tranquillity, weakness, and most important of all, non-action (*wu-wei*). By the latter is not meant literally "inactivity" but rather "taking no action that is contrary to nature" — in other words, letting Nature take its course.

For Taoists, the Tao is the undifferentiated primal void that underlies and pervades all being. It is the unspeakable and unknowable that lies beyond human understanding.

> The way that becomes a way
> is not the Immortal Way
> the name that becomes a name
> is not the Immortal Name
> — *Daode jing,* verse 1 (tr. Red Pine)

Qi, the Vital Energy

"In the Taoist vision of cosmogenesis, there was first the Tao, empty and still," writes Stephen Little. "Then, gradually, primal energy (*yuan qi*) was spontaneously generated out of the Tao."

The primal energy, qi (pronounced "chee") is always in a state of flux — in fact the only constant in the universe is the persistence of change. The material world is but a manifestation of the operations of qi, as the Taoists anticipated quantum physics in exploring the nexus of energy and matter. Qi was considered to manifest itself particularly strongly in certain areas, such as mountains and caves. Feng shui is essentially the art of directing qi, or at least of responding to its directions.

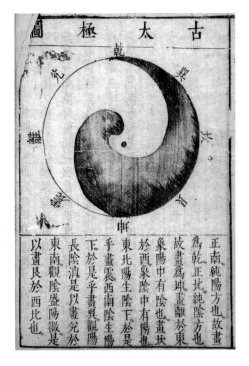

Diagram of the Supreme Ultimate, from the *Compendium of Diagrams,* 1623, by Zhang Huang. China. Woodblock printed book; ink on paper. *The University of Chicago Library, East Asian Collection.* Taiji ("supreme ultimate") diagrams such as this one symbolize the interplay of yin and yang within the Tao; each contains the germ of the other.

Illustration of Inner Circulation, 19th c. China. Wood engraving; ink on paper, *Richard Rosenblum Family Collection, Newton Center, Massachusetts.* This print expresses the Taoist notion of the transformation of things, for the same forces that manifest themselves as mountains, rivers, celestial bodies, animals, and plants are also viewed as operating within the microcosm of the human body. "The entire diagram is framed on the right by the spinal cord, which connects the lower torso with the cranial cavity, says Taoism specialist Shawn Eichman. "Within the three major sections of the body — the head, the upper torso, and the lower torso, the areas of the three 'cinnabar fields' (*dantian*) — complementary images of yin and yang energy are shown intermingling."

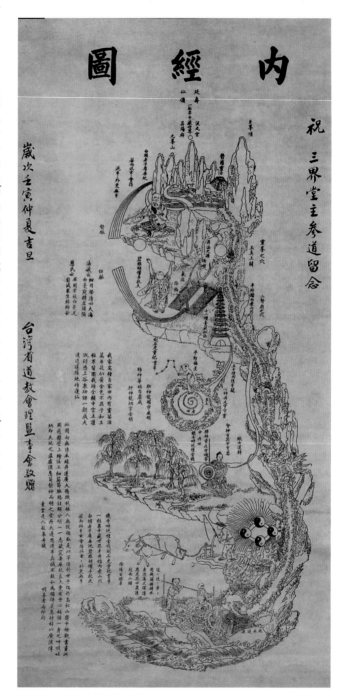

In terms of the inner alchemy of the human body, qi was seen as governed by the vital force of breath. This is analogous to the Western concept of inspiration, which also derives from the concept of breathing. Traditional Chinese medicine views illness as caused by blockages in the flow of qi. Acupuncture is one technique for removing such blockages and releasing the backed-up qi, thereby restoring the balance of yin and yang.

Yin/Yang

> The Tao gives birth to one
> one gives birth to two
> two gives birth to three
> three gives birth to ten thousand things
> ten thousand things with yin at their backs
> and yang in their embrace
> and breath between for harmony
>   — *Daode jing,* verse 42 (tr. Red Pine)

According to Taoist belief, the vital force, qi, initially manifested itself in a kind of undifferentiated noumenon called *hundun* (what David Hinton rendered as "PrimalDark" in his translation of Zhuangzi's parable, above). Out of this vague, swirling, massless mass, yin and yang emerged, like substances separated in a centrifuge. The interplay of these two opposing qualities gave birth to the material world in all its many forms.

Yin is dark, female, and subtle; yang is bright, male, and overt. Winter is yin, summer is yang; the moon is yin, the sun is yang. In a commentary on the *Daode jing* presented to the emperor in 1078, Lu Huiqing wrote of the verses quoted above: "Dark and unfathomable is yin. Bright and perceptible is yang. As soon as we are born, we all turn our backs on the dark and unfathomable yin and turn toward the bright and perceptible yang. Fortunately, we keep ourselves in harmony with the breath between." To some extent, Taoism can be viewed as championing the virtues of yin in the face of Confucianism's emphasis on yang.

The Taoist deity Magu, ca. 1800–1900. China. Hanging scroll; colors on silk. *Asian Art Museum, Gift of Hillary and D. G. Dumas,* F2005.74.2.

Magu, Taoist Goddess of Longevity, was also a protector of women. Her name is an amalgam of *Ma* (hemp, cannabis) + *gu* (lady, aunt, maiden). She was associated with prosperity and long life. Here she presents a tray bearing the peaches of longevity, lingzhi fungus (mushrooms reputed to have extraordinary medicinal qualities), and narcissus (a symbol of prosperity; the Chinese word for narcissus, *shuixianhua,* contains the word for immortal, *xian*). Additional symbols such as bats, bamboo, and orchids also are associated with immortality.

Among Magu's garments is a shawl made up of leaves, testifying to her association with the plant world. A wine gourd hangs from her waist. Joseph Needham believed early Taoists burnt cannabis in incense burners. "The incense-burner remained the centre of changes and transformations associated with worship, sacrifice, ascending perfume of sweet savour, fire, combustion, disintegration, transformation, vision, communication with spiritual beings, and assurances of immortality. Wai tan and nei tan [outer alchemy and inner alchemy] met around the incense-burner," Needham says, adding, "Might one not indeed think of it as their point of origin?"

Today the symbol of yin/yang is the taiji diagram (p. 81), but it did not appear in a Taoist context until the Song dynasty (960–1279). Before that time, yin was often represented by the tiger and yang by the dragon; this convention dates at least from the Zhou dynasty (ca. 1050–256 BCE) and probably from the Neolithic. The tiger and dragon are often found as a paired motif in Taoist iconography. "In addition to symbolizing yin and yang, the tiger and dragon also symbolize west and east, and the elements (or phases) fire and metal," says Stephen Little. "In Taoist chemical alchemy (*waidan,* or 'Outer Alchemy'), the tiger and dragon also represent two of the most powerful elixir ingredients known, lead and mercury, while in the Inner Alchemy (*neidan*) tradition, the two animals symbolize yin and yang as they are brought together in the inner (human) body through visualization and transformed to create a divine embryonic form of the practitioner."

RELIGIOUS TAOISM

From its ancient beginnings as a philosophy, a guide to conduct, and a commentary on governance and ritual, Taoism developed over the centuries into an organized religion, changing significantly in the process.

Under Emperor Wu (r. 140–87 BCE) of the Han dynasty (206 BCE–220 CE), Confucianism began its long tenure as China's official state ideology. But Taoist ideals remained strong, particularly among commoners. In 142 CE, a Taoist hermit named Zhang Daoing (or Zhang Ling) was visited by a vision of Laozi. Laozi, now calling himself the "Celestial Master," revealed to the devout hermit a "new testament," prohibiting sacrifice and rejecting the old gods and spirits who accepted sacrifices. In their place, Laozi presented Three Heavens. "The Three Heavens each contained one cosmic energy (*qi*), called, respectively, 'Mystery,' 'Principle,' and 'Origin' (*xuan, yuan,* and *shi*). They had three colors — blue, yellow, and white — and constituted the roots of Heaven, Earth, and Water. Each had its own virtue: Heaven (in the sense of the sky) gave forth blessings; Earth forgave sins; and Water averted calamities. Three

The Dipper Mother, 18th c. China. Dehua porcelain. *Asian Art Museum, The Avery Brundage Collection*, B60P1362. The Dipper Mother is the mother of the stars of Ursa Major, the Big Dipper. Thought to derive from one of the devas (inhabitants of the heavenly realms) of Buddhism, she is associated with healing and childbirth. Here she is sitting on a lotus throne and wearing a crown. She has a third eye in her forehead, and her eighteen arms hold a variety of sacred weapons and vessels.

officials (*Sanguan*), pure emanations of the Tao, performed these functions," says Kristofer Schipper, adding that "here we find for the first time a true Taoist pantheon ... distinct from the ephemeral gods, spirits, and ancestors of ancient China."

Zhang Daoling is credited with establishing the first organized Taoist communities, although it was not until the period of the Northern and Southern dynasties (420–589) that Taoism became fully formed as a religion. As the religion developed, Laozi became deified and a new pantheon of gods, goddesses, and immortals emerged, among them Taiyi (Supreme Ultimate), Queen Mother of the West (Xiwangmu), Celestial Worthy of Primordial Beginning, Marshal Wen, the Dipper Mother, Zhongli Quan, and countless more; even Buddhist figures such as Guan Yin were welcomed into the Taost pantheon. Still, "the high gods of Taoism," according to Stephen Little, "are ultimately mere pneuma who exist to put a recognizable face on the Tao itself."

Little describes a typical Taoist ritual:

> Taoist ritual is a public event, designed to serve the needs of a community. The central figure in any Taoist ritual is the priest (*daoshi*), who petitions the gods on behalf of the community he serves. Incorporating words, music, and dance, Taoist ritual is a performance closely linked to theater

Zhang Daoling, regarded as the founder of religious Taoism, seated on a tiger, nd. China. From *La Voie du Tao: Un Autre Chemin de l'Être*, by Catherine Delacour, ed., *Galeries nationales du Grand Palais, Paris.* The tiger and dragon are ancient symbols of the forces of yin and yang respectively.

and may last from several hours to several days. In the course of a ritual, the priest visualizes his own return to the Tao, the source of all things. Among the sacred dance forms in Taoist ritual is the symbolic pacing of the stars of the Northern Dipper (the Big Dipper), the seat of the celestial bureaucracy of the gods.

The Taoist ritual space, or altar (*daochang* or *daotan*), reflects the structure of the cosmos, and is visualized as a sacred mountain connecting the human and divine realms. The altar may be installed anywhere, and is taken apart when the ritual is complete.

~

For artists, Taoism offered not just a repertoire of subjects but also a way of seeing, and a way of doing: a tao of art. The first of the "six laws of painting" set down by the scholar Xie He in the early sixth century CE reads *qiyun shendong*: "convey movement through harmony of spirit." Taoist artists, understanding that existence is fluid, created lively works full of movement, as they sought to transmit the essence of their vision by serving as vehicles for the expression of qi. The result is a marvel: we need only to look — and to see.

who trusts his vision
lives beyond death
this is the Hidden Immortal
— *Daode jing,* verse 52 (tr. Red Pine)

Taoist Ritual at the Imperial Court, ca. 1723–1726, by Jing Bingzhen. China, Qing dynasty (1644–1911). Hanging scroll; ink and colors on silk. *Arthur M. Sackler Gallery, Smithsonian Institution, Washington, DC; Purchase Smithsonian Collections Acquisitions Program, and Partial Gift of Richard G. Pritzslaff,* S1991.99. This painting depicts a Taoist ritual being performed on an altar made of three stacked tables. The verticality of the altar is probably a metaphor for the mountain, considered a sacred space where qi is manifested.

Primary sources for this essay, originally written on the occasion of an exhibition organized by the Art Institute of Chicago in 2004 (though here revised), entitled *Taoism and the Arts of China,* include Hinton, David, ed. and tr., *Chuang Tzu: The Inner Chapters* (Berkeley: Counterpoint, 1997); Little, Stephen, ed., *Taoism and the Arts of China* (Berkeley: University of California Press, 2000); Pine, Red., ed. and tr., *Lao-tzu's Taoteching* (San Francisco: Mercury House, 1996; reprinted Port Townsend, WA: Copper Canyon Press, 2009); and Wing-tsit Chan, *A Source Book in Chinese Philosophy* (Princeton, NJ: Princeton University Press, 1963, 1972).

Before History

WHAT RECENT ARCHAEOLOGY REVEALS
ABOUT CHINA'S ANCIENT PAST

∾∾∾

China is a land rich in history, and in historians. Chief among the ancient historians is Sima Qian, whose *Shi ji* (Records of the grand historian) dates from near the beginning of the Han dynasty (206 BCE–220 CE). A monumental work of 130 chapters — a full translation would total more than three thousand pages — it is but one of many historical texts, commentaries, and annotations preserved by generations of Chinese scholars. The legacy of these historians is a vast trove of information, which has often proven remarkably reliable.

But history has its limits. Chinese civilization, the historians assured us, arose in the Yellow River valley. From there it developed through a generally linear succession of dynasties — Xia, Shang, Zhou, Qin, Han, and so on — all the way to the creation of the Republic in the early twentieth century. The First Emperor, though criticized by historians of the Han dynasty, was still credited with unifying China, which subsequently grew to encompass additional territories that had been occupied, it was said, by semi-barbaric peoples.

Faced with this narrative, early twentieth-century archaeologists focused on the region identified by the historians as having given birth to Chinese civilization. But in the past few decades, archaeologists have cast a wider net, devoting considerably more resources than previously to other areas. The surprising results have turned conventional notions of the origins of Chinese civilization on their head. While many of the discoveries remain enigmatic — archaeology has its own limitations — it now appears that civilization developed in multiple regions in China, and the

◀ According to Chinese tradition, the first dynasty, the Xia, spanned hundreds of years in the second millennium BCE, but many scholars — especially in the West — have considered it legendary. Discoveries made at the Erlitou archaeological site at Yanshi in China's Henan province, such as this turquoise-inlaid bronze animal mask, ca. 1900–1350 BCE, have led some to suggest that the Erlitou culture might correspond to the Xia. *Photo by Daderot, http://bit. ly/1l3jBMZ.*

In the 1980s, archaeologists were stunned when they uncovered pits in Sanxingdui, Guanghan, Sichuan province, China, that were filled with ivory tusks, animal bones, and ceramics. But the most extraordinary discoveries at Sanxingdui were Bronze Age works in an unprecedented style, such as the more than eight-foot-tall bronze standing figure on the facing page (ca. 1300–1100 BCE, Pit 2), and the bronze human heads with gold leaf (ca. 1300–1000 BCE, Pit 2), above. *Photos by kudumomo, http://bit.ly/1ffKW7q.*

beginnings of the long dynastic period were as much a process of the complex interacting and coalescing of multiple cultures as the expansion of a single ur-culture.

Few texts remain from pre-Confucian China. But some art objects unearthed in recent archaeological discoveries date from 5000 BCE. In the seven thousand years since that time, no period has more dramatically expanded our knowledge of ancient China than the past few decades. Many Chinese artists and patrons since the Song dynasty have possessed an antiquarian temperament, and there has long been a keen interest in ancient works and styles. Yet modern field archaeology in China did not begin until the twentieth century, well after significant archaeological works had been undertaken around the Mediterranean. After Torii Ryuzo of Japan uncovered Neolithic artifacts in northeast China, American, English, French, German, Russian, and

Swedish explorers followed (among them was Aurel Stein, who removed more than ten thousand valuable works to the British Museum and the British Library).

During the Japanese occupation and the civil war, archaeological excavations were suspended, but since 1950 Chinese archaeology has been an enterprise regulated and supported by the state, and it has made consistent strides in illuminating the Chinese past. The real explosion in archaeological research, however, took place after the demise of the Cultural Revolution in 1976, when greater resources were made available to archaeologists and scien-

tific chronometric (radiocarbon and carbon-14) dating techniques were consistently employed for the first time. In recent decades, excavations have been made virtually throughout the geographically and ethnically diverse expanse of China.

NEOLITHIC PERIOD (5000–2000 BCE)

The most significant reassessment resulting from recent archaeological discoveries is that ancient China was a much more diverse place than the dynastic historians would have us believe.

Only a few millennia after the retreat of the last Ice Age, around

Painted ceramic vessel, 3100–2700 BCE. China; Majiayao culture. *Shanghai Museum. Photo by Charles W. Clark, http://bit. ly/1lmZA3K.*

8000 BCE, human agricultural settlements began to arise in several parts of the world. Among the earliest were sites in the watersheds of the Yellow and Yangzi rivers and in northeastern China. These cultures were some of the first to use pottery, develop the potter's wheel, employ plowing in agriculture, and practice metallurgy.

Although areas in the Yellow River region, where dynastic China would later arise, were thought to have been the wellspring of all subsequent Chinese civilization, we now know that at least half a dozen Chinese cultures evolved concurrently during the Neolithic period. We are also learning that more extensive contact and exchange took place during the period than was previously suspected.

Middle and Upper Yellow River Basin Cultures

The earliest Chinese sites uncovered by archaeologists date from 10,000 BCE, give or take a few centuries. We begin to see the most substantial Chinese settlements around 5000 BCE — two thousand years before the first Egyptian dynasties. A group of such settlements, located in the middle and upper reaches of the Yellow River watershed (including the Wei River), known collectively as the Yangshao culture (ca. 5000–3000), established agriculture-based villages whose staple crop was millet.

Both of China's great rivers, the Yellow and the Yangzi, flow from sources in the high, arid: mountain plateaus of Eastern China — the Bayankala Mountains separate the Yellow River to the north and the Yangzi River to the south. The Yellow River, the most heavily silt-laden river in the world, gets the muddy color that gives it its name from the large amount of sediment it carries. When the river flooded, this sediment enriched the surrounding soil, creating favorable conditions for agriculture. The Yangshao communities depended on the river for their nourishment. It provided fish and waterfowl, offered a means of transportation, gave water for drinking and irrigation, and yielded clay for pottery. Grasses along the river were suitable for grazing domesticated animals such as pigs.

As they developed during the late Neolithic period, the villages came to consist of thatched-roof houses, made of wattle and daub, aligned around an open commons and surrounded by a ditch. Outside this central area were slash-and-burn fields, where millet and vegetables were grown, and also burial sites and pottery kilns. Such kilns, found at all major sites, appear to have been heavily used. A major site at Banpo near Xi'an has yielded polychrome painted pottery in which black pigment was applied to a reddish base. Later in this same area, the Taosi Longshan culture came up with a more colorful palate, and also left a rich legacy of jadework.[1] In the Upper Yellow River basin, a related culture, the Majiayao (ca. 3200–2800), produced some of the earliest Chinese coppers and bronzes. They also developed an exceptional ceramic tradition distinguished by a great variety of shapes of vessels of remarkable elegance. The straw color of their ceramics contrasts with the redder color of pottery downriver.

Lower Yellow River Basin Cultures

Two pre–Bronze Age cultures, the Dawenkou (ca. 4150–2650) and the Shandong Longshan (ca. 2600–1900), occupied the lower Yellow River. For them, as for the upriver cultures, millet was the staple crop.

The Dawenkou, who often lived in houses built partially below ground level, made use of bone, tooth, and shell sickles and stone axes and hoes. They produced pottery in several colors (especially red) and

---

1 Things tend to become confused when talking about the Longshan culture because it is actually several related cultures inhabiting both the upper and the lower Yellow River, with such distinctions as Shaanxi Longshan, ca. 2300–2000; Henan Longshan, 2600–2000; and Taosi Longshan, 2500–1900, in the middle river region alone.

Gui-style ceramic with twisted handle, ca. 2400–2000 BCE. China; Shandong Longshan culture. *Photo by Christopher, Tania, and Isabelle Luna, http://bit.ly/1dP2dl9.*

excelled at carving ivory and bone. Seemingly fond of ornamentation, they wore hairpins, necklaces, and bracelets made of jade, stone, bone, tooth, ivory, and ceramic.

Their successors, the Shandong Longshan, built towns surrounded by pounded-earth walls and made use of copper and bronze tools. Their accomplished pottery work is typified by high-stemmed, eggshell-thin goblets, while their jade work is elaborate and sophisticated. In part because Longshan burial sites show different levels of elaboration, archaeologists surmise that a distinction among social classes may have played a significant role in the culture's social organization.

Hongshan Culture, Northeast China
Northeast of the Yellow River cultures, in the far north of China at present-day western Liaoning province and southeastern Inner Mongolia, lived a culture known as the Hongshan (ca. 4700–2920). Early archaeological research in this area yielded enigmatic results, and it was not until the 1950s that the Hongshan began to be considered a distinct culture. In the late 1970s and 1980s, however, a series of startling discoveries revealed the extent and richness of the Hongshan. Today more than five hundred sites have been excavated.

The Hongshan appear to have been at least as interested in hunting as farming; at any rate, their agricultural implements are simple and basic, while their hunting tools are crafted with precision. Hongshan sites, which are often located on hillsides, show an abundance of both wild and domestic animal bones, suggesting that they may have been semi-nomadic. Still, six pottery kilns have been found, along with both painted and unpainted pottery.

The head of this C-shaped Hongshan dragon with a piglike snout, probably made before 5000 BCE, is excised with fine lines. Edges have been ground to the sharpness of knife blades, and a hole bored for suspension. The earliest known Chinese jade dragon, it is celebrated as "The First Dragon of China." Hongshan culture. Excavated in 1971 from Sanxingtalacun, Ongniud Banner, Inner Mongolia Autonomous Region. *Photo by Jun Wang, http://bit.ly/1fqHqJi.*

But jade appears to have been more prized by the Hongshan than pottery, as it appears in greater abundance in the larger tomb sites. Hongshan jades are simple and relatively plain, yet they display the affinity for the animal world that often develops among hunting peoples. Among them appear dragonlike creatures with piglike snouts, rendered in a coiled form similar to that of the earliest dragons of the Shang dynasty. But the extent of Hongshan influence on the development of Chinese civilization is debated.

Liangzhu Culture, Lower Yangzi River Basin

The Yangzi, which originates in western Qinghai province and flows into the East China Sea at Shanghai, is the third longest river in the

Archaeology has its limits. This Liangzhu culture jade cong (ca. 3400–2200 BCE) is superbly crafted, with a monsterlike face ground in relief on each of its four corners. But the function of such congs — tubes that, in section, are square on the outside and round on the inside — remains a subject of speculation. *Asian Art Museum, The Avery Brundage Collection*, B60J603.

world, after the Amazon and the Nile. Its watershed includes nearly one-fifth of China, much of it suitable for cultivation. In the middle and lower reaches its climate is hot and humid, and its early cultures developed the cultivation of rice rather than millet as in the north. Recently I heard a presentation by Tianlong Jiao, chief curator of the Hong Kong Maritime Museum, on the subject of the Liangzhu, who thrived for about a millennium, from 3300 to 2200 BCE, in the lower Yangzi. At their base near present Shanghai they had a population of 100,000 where now live 45,000. Their double-moated capital city covered 2.9 million square meters. They appear to have had a sophisticated maritime capability. And their production of jade objects was extraordinary: just eleven burial sites have yielded more than 3,500 jades. Yet all recollection of the Liangzhu seems to have been lost by the time of the early histories, and their existence was only uncovered through excavations in the 1930s (further excavations in 1999 increased understanding of the Liangzhu). Dr. Jiao believes the Liangzhu were displaced by an inland culture, the Guangfulin. Aspects of Liangzhu culture, such as their near-obsession with jade, may have been appropriated by subsequent cultures. And they may have been ancestors of modern Polynesians, Melanesians, Micronesians, and indigenous people on the islands of Southeast Asia.

Modern archaeological excavations have demonstrated that the elements of a developed Chinese civilization arose not in a single location but in many regions that had contacts and mutual influences. Collectively, they laid the groundwork for the three dynasties — the Xia, Shang, and Zhou — of Bronze Age China.

BRONZE AGE CHINA

> At first the sky and the earth were a single blurry thing, like an egg. Out of that Pangu was born. After eighteen thousand years, the sky had separated from the earth — the yang, which was light and pure, rose to become the sky, and the yin, which was heavy and murky, sank to form the earth. Between them was Pangu, who went through nine changes every day. His wisdom was greater than that of the sky and his ability was greater than that of the earth. Every day the sky rose ten feet higher, the earth became ten feet thicker, and Pangu grew ten feet taller. By the end of another eighteen thousand years there was an extremely high sky, an extremely thick earth, and an extremely tall Pangu. Then came the Three Emperors....
> —from the *Yi Wen Lei Ju* (Collection of literature arranged by categories), by Ouyang Xun, ca. 604 CE

Literary accounts such as the Tang-dynasty encyclopedia the *Yi Wen Lei Ju* and historical classics such as Sima Qian's Han dynasty *Shi ji* seem ancient from our perspective, yet they are nearly as close in time to our twenty-first century CE as to the twenty-first century BCE when the Xia dynasty — until recently considered legendary by many scholars and still a subject of controversy — was said to have been founded. "The traditional and orthodox histories of China present a comparatively clear and consistent account of the origin and early development of the Chinese civilisation," observed British sinologist C. P. Fitzgerald thirty years ago. But, he continued, "this is no longer accepted by modern scholarship as history. Any study of the early Chinese culture to-day is based rather on the evidence of archaeological research than on these traditional literary sources."

Pangu, the Chinese accounts tell us, was followed by the Twelve Emperors of Heaven, each of whom reigned for eighteen thousand years, then by the Twelve Emperors of Earth, who reigned for an equal term. They were followed by the Nine Emperors of Mankind, then the Sixteen Sovereigns, and so on, down to the Yellow Emperor who founded Chinese civilization, and on to the Great Yu, the Regulator of Floods, who founded the Xia dynasty, the first of the historical dynasties according to Chinese tradition (the first three dynasties, the Xia, Shang, and Zhou, are often grouped together under the rubric "The Three Dynasties").

Xia Dynasty (ca. 2100–ca. 1600 BCE)
While Western historians have generally questioned the reliability of the ancient Chinese texts, Chinese scholars have recognized that the traditional accounts have often proved surprisingly accurate. Those accounts tell us that the capital of the Xia dynasty was in what is now western Henan province, in the Yellow River basin, and that it was founded around the beginning of the second millennium BCE. Armed with this information, Chinese archaeologists since the 1950s have conducted fieldwork at sites near Yanchi in Henan. These excavations have produced evidence of a pre–Shang dynasty culture called the Erlitou culture. Because the time and place coincide with the historical accounts, and based on the presence of "palaces" filled with impressive artifacts, most Chinese authorities have concluded that the excavations have indeed uncovered the remains of the Xia, the ancient culture that began the Chinese dynastic history that continued until modern times — according to Chinese scholar Zou Heng, "Erlitou" and "Xia" may now be used interchangeably.

The Erlitou sites have yielded a great deal of gray pottery that can be dated to between the Neolithic and the early Shang periods. They have also produced a dozen pounded-earth foundations that suggest "palaces" similar to those of later Chinese practice.

Excavations near where the Neolithic Hongshan culture was uncovered have also produced evidence of a culture called the Xiajiadian that was approximately contemporaneous with Erlitou. Its artifacts provide evidence of connections to other Bronze Age cultures, both in the Yellow River basin and in Western Central Asia. The Xiajiadian sites, which feature pounded earth or stone defensive walls, are found, often in pairs or clusters, in the table lands above rivers. Traditional accounts that ascribe to the Great Yu the regulation of floods throughout China express the reality that Chinese cultures in this period were beginning to deal in a systematic way with the river system that was their lifeblood.

Tripod jar (li), ca. 2200–1600 BCE. China; Lower Xiajiadian culture. Gray earthenware. The three-legged form allows placing the jar directly in the fire. *Photo by ellenm1, http://bit. ly/1ffUHSH.*

Shang Dynasty (ca. 1600–1050)

According to traditional histories, the Xia dynasty came to an end as a result of the excesses of its final ruler, Jie, a tyrant who is supposed to have made thousands of naked men and women engage in amorous performances for his amusement as he sailed with his queen in a lake filled with wine (it has been suggested that faint memories of ancient fertility rites may contribute to this story). King Tang put an end to such indignities sometime before 1500 BCE, when he overthrew Jie and founded the Shang dynasty, which would endure for more than half a millennium.

With the arrival of the Shang dynasty we approach the intersection

Bo (musical instrument) with four tigers, early 9th century–771 BCE. China; Western Zhou dynasty. Bronze. *Photo by Charles W. Clark, http://bit.ly/1fl8GIA.*

of archaeology and history. The Shang made inscriptions on tortoise shell and ox bone, and later on bronze. The earliest site with written inscriptions that connects with the later written record is Anyang, which was one of the first excavated. Oracle bones had been reported in the region since at least the nineteenth century, and in 1928 major excavations were begun; further digs in 1991 yielded fresh discoveries. They reveal an extensive city of buildings with stamped-earth foundations, as well as jades, bronzes, and around 150,000 oracle bones. Shang inscriptions identify nine rulers by name.

The richest Anyang discovery, in 1976, was the tomb of Fu Hao, one of the wives or consorts of Wu Ding, who reigned around 1200 BCE. Fu Hao was also a priestess and a general — perhaps the most powerful of her time. The inscriptions record many victorious military campaigns in which she led thousands of troops, and her tomb has yielded more than 100 weapons, unusual for a woman's tomb. She was well equipped for her afterlife in other ways as well: the tomb was stocked with more than 200 bronze ritual vessels and 250 other bronze objects (totaling 116 metric tons), including bells, tools, and weapons, along with some 750 jades, more than 100 stone and semi-precious stone carvings, more than 560 bone carvings, 3 ivory goblets, 11 ceramics, and 6,800 cowries.

The value of the written records in identifying figures like Fu Hao cannot be overstated. Yet the written record can also be misleading. Because the Shang people possessed writing, they controlled the historical record. The impression was created that Shang was the dominant culture of its time, which seemed to make sense because of the later historical importance of the region. But the discovery in 1986, in the remote southwestern province of Sichuan, of the Sanxingdui pits (see pp. 92–93) shook up the accepted view of the Shang period. Here was a major site, discovered by accident, that showed a comparable civilization producing artworks that resemble nothing else from other Bronze Age cultures in China. Another accidental discovery, Xin'gan, a site in the Yanzi region, was excavated in 1989. It yielded the second richest burial from the period after Fu Hao's tomb. These cultures have received less archaeological attention than Anyang, and one can only guess what remains to be found. (Jay Xu, director of the Asian Art Museum, in a lecture available on iTunesU at bit.ly/1qcxC9W, traces evidence of cultural interactions among the cultures.) Archaeology has corrected the historical record, and it is now clear that the Shang dynasty was just one of several fairly equally matched cultures that coexisted during China's Bronze Age.

Western Zhou Dynasty (ca. 1050–770 BCE)

The last ruler of the Shang, the histories tell us, was overthrown when he repeated the excesses of Jie, the last Xia ruler. The new dynasty, the Zhou, would be the longest lived in Chinese history. It would become a sort of golden age, in the arts if not in politics, during which Confucius (551–479), Laozi (500s?), Mozi (499–420?), Zhuangzi (399–295?), Mencius (371–289?), and other philosophers flourished, and such classics as the *I jing* (Book of changes), *Shi jing* (Book of songs), *Daode jing* (The way and virtue), *Li ji* (Book of rites), and *Chun qiu* (Spring and autumn annals) were assembled.

But most of those literary and philosophical accomplishments were recorded in the later Zhou. The earlier period of the Zhou dynasty, which is considered part of Bronze Age China, is referred to as the "Western Zhou." It endured to about 770 BCE, when the capital was moved to the east and lost much of its power, as the kingdom devolved into a more fragmented and independent array of feudal fiefdoms. During the 330 years of the Western Zhou, an effort was made to expand and consolidate power by granting regional authority to members of the royal family and government officials. The government of this tenuous federation was situated in Shaanxi province, but the vassal fiefdoms grew increasingly independent. Archaeological excavations have provided insights into many of them, especially the Zhou states of Guo, Jin, Yan, Qufu, and Qi.

Some of these excavations have shed light on long-standing historical controversies. For example, whereas the Eastern Zhou historians Ban Gu (32–92) and Zheng Xuan (127–200) situated the capital of the state of Jin near present-day Taiyuan in Shanxi province, the Ming-dynasty historian Gu Yanwu (1613–1682), basing his argument on other historical documents, proposed a site further south in Shanxi. In the late 1970s, archaeologists discovered the rich Tianma-Qucun site, containing residential remains and numerous Jin state tombs, which appears to confirm Gu Yanwu's position. In this way China's previously hazy Three Dynasties period—which only a few decades ago was known only through much later written accounts—is being brought into focus.

CHU CULTURE

> Grasping our great shields and wearing our hide armour,
> Wheel-hub to wheel-hub locked, we battle hand in hand.
> Our banners darken the sky; the enemy teem like clouds:
> Through the hail of arrows the warriors press forward.
> They dash on our lines; they trample our ranks down.
> The left horse has fallen, the right one is wounded.
> Bury the wheels in; tie up the horses!
> Seize the jade drumstick and beat the sounding drum!
> The time is against us: the gods are angry.
> Now all lie dead, left on the field of battle.
> They went out never more to return:
> Far, far away they lie, on the level plain,
> Their long swords at their belts, clasping their elmwood bows.
> Head from body sundered: but their hearts could not be vanquished.
> Both truly brave, and also truly noble;
> Strong to the last, they could not be dishonoured.
> Their bodies may have died, but their souls are living:
> Heroes among the shades their valiant souls will be.
> — From the *Chu ci* (*Songs of Chu,* tr. David Hawkes)

With the Eastern Zhou period (ca. 771 to 255), we enter the beginnings of the Iron Age, a time of both great political turmoil and great achievement in art, literature, and philosophy, earning it the sobriquets "Hundred Schools of Thought Contending" (*baijia zhengming*) and "Hundred Flowers Blooming" (*baihua qifang*). It is usually divided into two phases, called the Spring and Autumn Period (771–480) and the Warring States Period (480–221).

During the Spring and Autumn period (which takes its name from the title of a classical history of the time), the Zhou king had become a figurehead, as a feudal city-state system replaced the more centralized rule of the Western Zhou. The rulers of these states prided themselves on a code of chivalry, pageantry, and ritual. It was an unstable period, in which hegemony shifted among the states of Zheng, Qi, Song, Jin, Chu, Wu, and Yue; it ends around the time of the death of Confucius.

The struggles continued during the Warring States Period, when Qi, Chu, Qin, and other states fought unremittingly to control all of China. They continued the pattern of the Spring and Autumn period, but now on a much larger scale, as small conflicts were replaced by clashes of large armies boasting at least some weapons made of iron. Rather than battles between small cities and towns, Chinese warfare was now large-scale conflict engulfing entire societies and employing professional soldiers.

One of the warring states, the state of Chu in southern China, is of particular archaeological interest. The Chu culture's richness is manifest in literature such as the *Chu ci* (Songs of Chu), an anthology that dates to the Late Warring States and the Han periods, and in extraordinary lacquers, bronzes, and textiles. Often Chu objects hark back to earlier forms, for while the Yellow River cultures by and large favored Confucianism, for the Chu Taoism and Shamanism were more important. Shamanism continued in the Chu region long after it had faded in the north. The imaginary figures and animal creatures made of lacquered wood from the Warring States Chu tombs are an artistic reflection of the importance of the shaman.

Assaults and battles every day arose,
And blood flowed on the plains,
As it had since earliest antiquity.
For generations past all count
Till the time of the Five Emperors
None could forbid it and make it stop.
Not until now, when this our emperor
Has made the world one family,
And weapons of warfare are lifted up no longer.
— Inscription on the summit of Mount Yi

The Eastern Zhou can be viewed as a succession of efforts to unify China. This was finally achieved in 221 BCE by King Zheng (r. 246–210), posthumously known as Shihuangdi, the "First Emperor." To Zheng is attributed the destruction of the records of the previous periods, casting the Three Dynasties into a haze from which they are only now emerging, thanks to the recent archaeological discoveries I have been describing. He has been called one of the great destroyers of history, but he also forged a new age and laid the groundwork for one of history's most enduring political systems. He was conventionally credited with having initiated the Chinese dynastic monarchy that endured until 1911, when another revolution as momentous as his own again irrevocably changed the course of Chinese history. The written record of early imperial China, though voluminous, says relatively little about its art and aesthetics, whose history has largely been left for archaeologists to expose. Notable discoveries include the tomb of Liu Sheng, which contained his famous jade shroud; the tomb of the king of Nanyue, which reveals the effect of foreign influences on Chinese art; the Famen Monastery pagoda, which has yielded fascinating early Buddhist imagery; and Tang-dynasty sites, which demonstrate the integration of Chinese and foreign styles. "The art of imperial China," observes Xiaoneng Yang, "embodies a distinctively humanistic, even modern sensibility. Art that was primarily sacred, religious, practical, and imaginary in its early stages is transformed here into a secular, realistic, practical, and ultimately human aesthetic."

No archaeological discovery from early imperial China was more unexpected or more dramatic than that of the First Emperor's underground army. The existence of the army was unsuspected from historical documents. Sima Qian reported that the imperial complex was destroyed in a fire set by invading troops in 208 BCE. The capital was said to have burned for months, and with the destruction of his capital, knowledge of the emperor's hidden treasures vanished.

Until, that is, March 1974, when farmers digging a well in the village of Xiyang in Lintong, Shaanxi province, unearthed large fragments of terra-cotta. Excavations on the site revealed an immense army of life-size terra-cotta warriors in pre-battle formation, no doubt intended to protect the emperor in his quest for immortality. Besides thousands of infantrymen, the army included cavalry, officers, and war chariots. Also uncovered were offices, halls, stables, palaces, a theater, even a zoo. (The emperor's tomb remains unopened at this time.)

Most of what we knew about the First Emperor had come to us from Sima Qian, who, we must remember, was the grand historian of the victorious Han. His account proves the adage that history is written by the victors. Did the atrocities attributed to the emperor by Sima Qian really happen? I wouldn't doubt it, but it is hard to be certain. In any case, the "controversy" about

Mythological creature (usually described as an antlered crane), before 433 BCE, excavated from the tomb of Marquis Yi of Zeng. China; Hubei province (Chu culture). Bronze. *Photo by Wmpearl, http://bit.ly/1ffhEWn.*

whether the emperor was a tyrant, who burned books and buried scholars alive, or a hero who unified China (the word "China" derives from his name, Qin, which is pronounced "chin"), standardizing writing, weights, measures, and currency, and establishing the rule of law, is a silly one. We need neither historians nor archaeologists to know that the set of rulers who establish vast empires does not much overlap with that of the sweetest people ever. But we also know that in the past few decades modern archaeologists have shed as much light on the emperor and the ancient China from which he arose as did the parade of dynastic historians whose accounts had defined him for millennia. Their excavations make it clear that Chinese civilization did not develop outward from a single source, as centuries of Chinese historians would have had us believe, but rather was a process of coalescing of many separate (though interconnected) cultures. Only after many centuries, when these cultures had been largely brought together, was the First Emperor able to unify China and inaugurate its long imperial history.

▲▶ Terra-cotta warriors from the First Emperor's underground army on display at the Asian Art Museum, San Francisco. *Photos by T. Christensen.*

SOUTH ASIA,
HIMALAYAS

The Temple across the Valley

THREE HUNDRED YEARS OF THE KHALSA

For many years now, I have lived in an unfashionable, semi-rural, largely working-class suburb in the East Bay of the San Francisco Bay Area. It's not so bad. For a long time I thought the worst thing was that there is not much here; now I think that the best thing is that there is not much here. Halfway up a south-facing hill, my property is screened off from my neighbors. The only view it affords beyond our own backlot garden is Wildcat Canyon on the opposite side of the valley where trains once carried weekend picknickers from Richmond but which is now a drag of liquor stores and filling stations.

The most arresting feature on that opposite hillside is a large Sikh gurdwara. (Sikh temples are called *gurdwaras,* "doorways to the gurus.") Called the Gurdwara Sahib, it is one of fourteen gurdwaras in California, and the closest to San Francisco. In my town Sikh men

▲ Gurdwara Sahib, El Sobrante, CA. *Photo by Coro, http://bit. ly/1rM8k6j.*

◀ "A Sikh," from *The Costumes of the Peoples of India,* by Captain W. W. Hooper and Surgeon G. Western, 1860–1870. Albumen print. *Victoria and Albert Museum,* 0932:5(IS).

walk the street in their distinctive turbans. They are often mistaken for Muslims (their traditional rivals), and are sometimes harassed by local rednecks. Among the Sikh kids in our high school was a friend of one of my daughters who shocked everyone by cutting his hair for prom. He did it to please his Chinese-American girlfriend, people said. But today, working at a tech start-up, he still wears his hair short.

Sikhs came in numbers to North America more than a century ago. The first Sikh gurdwara on this continent opened in British Columbia in 1908. A second opened in Stockton, California, a year later. The Sikh communities remained extremely small until the 1950s and '60s, when changes in U.S. immigration laws (following the independence of India in 1947) enabled more Sikhs to relocate here.

BIRTH OF THE GURU

The Sikh story, of course, begins much longer ago. In 1469, Europe was experiencing its Renaissance. The birth of Niccolò Machiavelli heralded an age of unbridled political aspiration, and the birth of explorer Vasco da Gama, discoverer of the sea route to India, presaged the worldwide European empire that would eventually result. Across the Atlantic, Aztec priests were seeking portents in the death of the empire's first great ruler, Moctezuma I. Before the century was out their darkest prophesies proved true, as Europeans would begin their conquest of the Americas, while in Africa, they were beginning the process of colonization. In East Asia Japan was torn by civil war, Ming China was turning inward, and Korea's young Confucian dynasty, the Joseon, was setting off in new directions that would move away from Chinese models.

Islam continued to expand. Only a decade before, the Ottomans had conquered Constantinople and destroyed the Byzantine empire. And in South Asia, Mughal Muslims were making inroads into formerly Hindu areas. In one of those areas, the northern Indian region of Punjab, a Hindu infant was born. He was Guru Nanak, and the religion he would found, Sikhism, would eventually spread around the world, even to my valley in the San Francisco Bay Area.

In South Asia, Sikhs created a cosmopolitan kingdom that ruled not only Punjab but also the whole of Kashmir, and into Ladakh in the Himalayas. The kingdom endured almost four hundred years after the birth of Guru Nanak. Then a European colonial power succeeded in conquering the Sikh kingdoms, when the English annexed Punjab in 1847. Following their victory, the English predicted the demise of Sikhism, only to be surprised by its astonishing revival and growth.

PUNJAB: SIKH HOMELAND

> Stand up like a cypress
> On your own feet,
> and firm on your roots;
> See, on the high top of your heart, stars hanging;
> The moon, hiding, plays behind your height,
> and the beauty of the world, diving
> In your heart, comes out washed in brightness.
> — Puran Singh (tr. Surjit Singh Dulai)

"Of all the regions of India," author Shiva Naipaul has written, "the Punjab is the most evocative." (In 1947, the region was divided, so that part now lies in Pakistan.) Its history extends to ancient times. The gateway to India for travelers through the Khyber Pass — the long, narrow passage through the snow-covered mountains of the Hindu Kush on the border of Afghanistan and Pakistan — it was a center of the ancient Indus Valley Civilization (2500–1500 BCE), the largest and in some respects the most advanced of the four great ancient civilizations (the others were Egypt, Mesopotamia, and China).

A broad, flat plain sloping slowly away from the western mountains, Punjab seems at first an inhospitable region for such a civilization. Its climate ranges from extreme cold to extreme heat, from desperate drought to furious monsoons. Guru Nanak described the hot, dry early part of the year: "The sun scorches ... the earth burns like an oven. The waters give up their vapors, yet it burns and scorches relentlessly."

From this heat the monsoons provide relief. Indian writer Khushwant Singh has described their arrival:

> The blazing inferno lasts from the end of April to the end of June. Then come the rains. The monsoon makes a spectacular entry. It is heralded by the monsoon bird which fills the dusty plains with its plaintive cries. The colorless grey sky suddenly fills with dense masses of black clouds. There are flashes of lightning and the earth shakes with the rumble of thunder. The first big drops of rain are swallowed by the dust and a heavenly fragrance rises from the earth. Then it comes in torrents, sheet upon sheet, and continues for several hours. Thereafter the skies are frequently overcast; clouds and sunshine contend for dominion; rainbows span rainwashed landscape; and the setting sun fires the bulbous clouds in hues of red and purple. Two months of incessant downpour turn land into a vast swamp. Rivers fill up and become a mass of swirling muddy waters.

Those rivers give Punjab its name, which means "Five Rivers" (they are the Jhelum, Chenab, Ravi, Sutlej, and Beas). Five is a significant number for Sikhs. Most observe the "five Ks" of uncut hair (*kesh*), dagger (*kirpan*), steel bangle (*kada*), short pants (*kachha*), and comb (*kangha*). Many Sikh congregations elect five members as their representatives.

Despite the danger of flooding, water has made Punjab India's most prosperous state. Crisscrossed with irrigation canals and dotted with wells, it produces more than half of India's grain.

GURU NANAK

Guru Nanak was the first of the ten gurus who guided the Sikh community until the death of Guru Gobind Singh in 1708. His story is told in the *Janam Sakhi,* the traditional narrative of his life. Born to a simple Hindu family in what is now Pakistan, he

quickly revealed a thirst for knowledge and understanding, studying
Hindi, Persian, and Arabic. He wore
a mix of Hindu and Muslim dress and
in his teachings sought to bridge the
differences between the two religions
(yet Sikhism should be viewed as a
new religion, and not a blend of prior
ones). He wrote:

> Accept all humans as your equals
> and let them be your only sect.

Following Guru Nanak's teachings,
Guru Arjun, the fifth Guru, included
writings from Hindu and Muslim saints
in the Sikh holy scriptures, and a Muslim saint is said to have laid the foundation stone of the Sikh's Golden Temple
in Amristar.

Guru Nanak traveled widely to
spread his vision — he is said to have
journeyed as far as Sri Lanka and Tibet.
He taught that there is one God, cre-

Order of Merit, ca. 1838. Pakistan;
Lahore. Enameled gold set with emer-
alds and diamonds, *Collection of Gursharan and Elvira Sidhu.* The five wide
and thin elements that project from this
medal probably reflect the importance
of the number five in Sikhism. Ranjit
Singh's Order of Merit characteristi-
cally shows the aging maharaja in profile, clothed in white.

ator of all things, who is manifested in the world through his Word
(*nam*): "There is but One God, His name is Truth, He is the Creator.... He was True in the beginning, He was True when the ages
commenced and has ever been True, He is also True now." Guru
Nanak taught that spiritual wisdom was found through contempla-
tion and inward meditation rather than outward action or ritual:

> The one is supreme, the whole cosmos is under its sway,
> why revere feats and miracles which lead you astray?

and

Within the mind itself
Lie all kinds of jewels, rubies, and pearls

and

Divine music is heard in every soul;
Resonant, continuous, self-sustained, a revelation

Guru Nanak taught that heavenly light exists in every human being ("God is formless, colorless, markless; He is casteless, classless, creedless"), and therefore he advocated a casteless society ("Everyone says there are four castes, but it is from God that everyone comes") and spoke on behalf of the rights of women ("Without woman there is none"). Sikh gurdwaras are open to all, regardless of caste, creed, color, race, sex, or nationality.

Despite his insistence on the importance of meditation, Guru Nanak did not withdraw from society but participated fully, marrying and raising a family. Following his example, Sikhism places a high importance on family life and social involvement.

The first Mughal emperor, Babur, reigned during Guru Nanak's lifetime. Although the Mughals were relatively tolerant of non-Muslims in their empire (where the majority of the population was Hindu), Guru Nanak suffered Mughal persecution. As the Sikh community grew, so did the persecution. V. S. Naipaul considers this a key factor in Sikhism's early development:

> People within the Hindu fold had always been rebelling against brahmin orthodoxy.... Buddha had rebelled; Guru Nanak, the first Guru of the Sikhs, had rebelled. Two thousand years separated the rebellions, and they had different causes. Buddha's rebellion had been prompted by his meditation on the frailty of flesh. Guru Nanak's rebellion or breaking away had been prompted by the horrors of the Muslim invasions — the horrors to which no one could see an end.
>
> Guru Nanak's illumination was the quietest one that there was a middle way: that there was no Hindu and no

Guru Nanak, ca. 1770. India; Lucknow, Uttar Pradesh state. Colors and gold on paper, *Asian Art Museum, Gift of the Kapany Collection,* 1998.60. This late-eighteenth-century portrait of Guru Nanak (1469–1529), executed in Mughal courtly style, portrays Nanak as an elderly man engaged in study.

Guru Gobind Singh on Horseback, ca. 1830. India; Guler, Himachal Pradesh state. Colors on paper, *Collection of Gursharan and Elvira Sidhu*. Guru Gobind Singh (Guru 1675–1708), the tenth and last of the Sikh gurus, founded the Khalsa, or Order of the Pure, in 1699. Devoid of caste divisions, the order vowed to protect the faith and take up arms against injustice.

Muslim, that there could be a blending of the faiths. Islam had its fixed articles of faith, however, its fixed, pervasive rules — no room there for Nanak-like speculation and compromise [and] one hundred years later, at the time of the fifth Sikh Guru, the persecutions and martyrdoms at the hands of the Mughals began. Nearly 100 years after that, at the time of the tenth and last human Guru, the religion was given its final form, and Sikhs were given their distinctive appearance … so that every day, with these intimate emblems, a man would be reminded of what he was.

GURU GOBIND SINGH AND THE KHALSA

The year 1999, when I drafted the first version of this essay, marked the three hundredth anniversary of the Khalsa, or the "pure ones," a sacred order of men and women from all castes created in 1699 by Guru Gobind Singh, the tenth and last Sikh Guru. Sikhs believe that the Gurus transmitted the Word of God, and that all ten Gurus, though living at different times, had the same message and the same mission.

Following the death of Guru Nanak, the Sikh community grew

Sikh helmet with chain-mail neckguard, 1820–1840. India or Pakistan; Punjab. Brass and iron with gold overlay. For Sikhs, uncut hair is a symbol of devotion. The shape of this helmet enabled the wearer's hair to be contained in a topknot. In addition to a helmet with chain mail attached, a typical suit of Sikh armor contained a body suit of chain mail, shields around the chest area, and arm defenses. *Asian Art Museum, Gift of the Kapany Collection, 1998.69. Photo by Marshall Astor, http://bit.ly/1z5dTi2.*

rapidly, and it faced increasing repression from the Mughal rulers of Punjab. The fifth Guru, Guru Arjun, who compiled the Sikh sacred scripture, the Adi Granth, and established the Golden Temple at Amritsar as a sacred center for Sikhs, died in Mughal custody. He advised his son Hargobind, the sixth Guru, to arm himself, and Hargobind took up two swords, one representing spiritual and the other temporal authority.

▲ Maharaja Gulab Singh (detail), 1855, by William Carpenter. Watercolor on paper. *Victoria and Albert Museum*, IS 153-1882. Another
portrait of Gulab Singh, here by an Englishman, William Carpenter. Carpenter depicts his subject in 1955, some six years after Punjab has been annexed by the British.

◀ Maharaja Gulab Singh of Jammu and Kashmir, ca. 1846. Colors
on paper. *Victoria and Albert Museum*, IS 194-1951. At the death
of Ranjit Singh in 1839, his empire began to collapse, until it
was finally annexed by the British in 1849. Other maharajas of
the Punjab region attempted to emerge as strong rulers. Maharaja Gulab Singh of Jammu and Kashmir was a close associate
of Ranjit Singh.

By the time of Gobind Singh (who was born about two hundred years after Guru Nanak), relations between Sikhs and Mughals had irrevocably deteriorated. In 1675, the ninth Guru, Gobind Singh's father, was executed. In 1699, Gobind Singh, having grown old enough to lead, took the extraordinary step of inaugurating the Khalsa, which established many of the traditions that most Sikhs observe today, such as the "five Ks" and the rite of baptism. Guru Gobind Singh gave the Khalsa responsibility for defending the principles of religious freedom and justice, as taught two centuries earlier by Guru Nanak, the first Sikh Guru. While Guru Nanak had emphasized inward meditation rather than exterior ritual, Sikhs now maintained identifiable external trappings, as Guru Gobind Singh rallied the community to a more militant spirit.

Guru Gobind Singh ended the line of human Sikh Gurus by consecrating the Adi Granth itself (which he renamed the Sri Guru Granth Sahib Ji) as a permanent Guru, to be revered as the body and spirit of the ten prior Gurus.

RANJIT SINGH AND THE SIKH KINGDOMS

After Guru Gobind Singh died at the beginning of the eighteenth century, Sikhs, united through the Khalsa, began to gain power, and the Mughal empire (whose emperor Aurangzeb had died the previous year) began to decline. Finally, at the end of the century, Punjab was unified by "The Lion of the Punjab," Ranjit Singh, who reigned for forty years, from 1799 through 1839.

In 1801 Ranjit Singh was proclaimed Maharaja of the Punjab. His extraordinary personality dominated the region until his death in 1839. During his reign the Sikh kingdom expanded as he defeated the Hindu kingdoms of the Punjab Hills, the Muslim strongholds of the Afghans and Mughals, the whole of Kashmir, and large parts of Ladakh. His courtiers, artists, and soldiers were Hindus and Muslims as well as Sikhs, and a cosmopolitan touch was added by the frequent arrival of Europeans, either on official embassies, or as individuals employed by the maharaja.

Following the death of Maharaja Ranjit Singh, the Punjab

throne was affected by a series of unfortunate deaths and brutal murders. Maharaja Sher Singh, second son of Ranjit Singh, was crowned in 1841 and murdered two years later by a rival faction who supported British annexation of Punjab. By 1846 the British were able to attack but met unexpected resistance from the Khalsa army. Through bribery and treachery, however, the British succeeded in their annexation of Punjab in 1847.

AFTER THE FALL OF THE SIKH EMPIRE

Following the British victory, the Sikhs' Punjab empire was broken up into separate princely states, which were initially under the control of the British East India Company and later under direct British colonial rule. Sikh martial traditions made them valuable soldiers, and for the succeeding century they were cultivated by the British to assist in their colonial rule. They continued in this role in the new Indian state, often serving as bodyguards for Indian leaders.

With the partition of India in 1947, heavy conflict again erupted between Sikhs and Muslims, and this was a motivator of Sikh emigration. In the unsettled climate of the time, hostility also developed with Hindus. Sikhs resented the emergency powers claimed by Indira Gandhi, which they viewed as weakening their control in Punjab. A Sikh leader named Sant Jarnail Singh Bhindranwale articulated Sikh complaints. He was rumored to be stockpiling weapons in the Golden Temple in Amritsar. Gandhi ordered a military action, called Operation Blue Star, to remove Bhindranwale and his followers from the temple, and this resulted in hundreds of deaths and significant damage to the temple, considered a sacred place by Sikhs. Four months later, Gandhi was assassinated by two of her Sikh bodyguards. Riots erupted, and at least eight thousand Sikhs were massacred in a backlash against this atrocity.

SIKHS IN AMERICA TODAY

Tradition has it that the Sikh founder, Guru Nanak, wandered far and wide between 1498 and 1520, consulting with religious figures

The Golden Temple at Amritsar, 1840. India. Colors and gold on paper. *The Kapany Collection.* Sikhism's most sacred site of worship is the Golden Temple at Amritsar, in the modern state of Punjab. Accurately depicted in this painting embellished with gold, the actual building is covered with gold leaf and surrounded by water. The temple was built under the leadership of Guru Arjun (Guru 1581–1606), who dug the pool in which the temple was constructed. Guru Gobind Singh gave the Khalsa responsibility for defending the principles of religious freedom and justice, as taught two centuries earlier by Guru Nanak.

Thanks to Kristina Youso, scholar of South Asian art, who contributed captions for the original version of this essay. Revised versions accompany some of the illustrations here.

and teachers from different traditions, including Hindu priests, Muslim sheikhs and Sufi mystics, Jain and Buddhist monks, and Hindu yogis. He concluded that asceticism, or withdrawal from society, is a false path to enlightenment, and he urged Sikhs to be actively involved with family and community (Nanak himself married and had two sons).

Such involvement continues to characterize Sikhs. Most of the more than 150,000 Sikhs in America today have become citizens. A report in *On Common Ground: World Religions in America* (Columbia University Press) characterizes American Sikhs as belonging to an energetic community with a strong sense of public service: "From South Florida to Southern California, gurdwaras commonly sponsor Red Cross Blood Drives on their premises. The Sikhs of Durham, North Carolina, contribute to a soup kitchen for the homeless. Sikhs participate in the Walk for Hunger in Boston. In Los Angeles, Sikhs from some six gurdwaras participated in clean-up efforts after the 1992 riots. In cities where interfaith councils have sprung up, Sikhs are invariably active members." Some gurdwaras make available a pamphlet that argues that "the Sikh heritage of truth, justice, freedom, and respect for other faiths is consistent with the American traditions articulated so well by Franklin Roosevelt as: freedom of expression, freedom of religion, freedom from want, and freedom from fear."

An article in my local paper last week announced the appointment of a new postmaster in the nearby East Bay community of Lafayette: "The soft-spoken, humble man was gracious and made a point to thank everyone involved in his journey: family, friends, co-workers, and mentor Ray Davis, Berkeley's postmaster." According to the article he was a letter carrier for twenty-eight years who rose through the ranks. He is married, with two daughters and six grandchildren. He is also president of the Sikh temple across the valley from where I am sitting as I write this.

Gurdwaras make good neighbors.

Measure of Happiness

IN THE LAND OF THE DRAGON

~~~~~~

You know it as Bhutan (a word that may derive from a phrase meaning "beyond Tibet"). But to speakers of Dzongkha, its official language, it is Drukyul, "the land of the Thunder Dragon." The dragon, which appears in the flag of Bhutan and is referenced in its national anthem, represents the fearsome deities who protect the mountain kingdom. Its roar proclaims the truth of Buddhism, the state religion.

Bhutan is a small country, about the size of Switzerland. Estimates of its population vary, but it is probably a little larger than that of San Francisco (Bhutan's sparse population density is unusual among Asian nations). Historically, it has been exceptionally isolated. While a narrow opening permits access from India to subtropical lowlands in the south, deep gorges make passage from there to the rest of the country more difficult. For cultural as well as geographic reasons, access to the central and northern areas — high plateaus hemmed in by some of the world's tallest mountains — has mainly been through alpine passes from Tibet. More than half the country is covered with forests, another tenth by glaciers. Thick clouds often cover the high peaks in late summer, when monsoon rains from the Bay of Bengal drench the countryside. Then the roar of the Thunder Dragon echoes through the valleys, announcing the rains that the Drukpa — the people of Bhutan — depend on for their agricultural existence.

So thunder is responsible for the name of the country and its people. As the story goes, a monk named Tsangpa Gyarey Yeshey (1161–1211) was consecrating a monastery when he heard a peal of thunder, thought to be the voice of the dragon (*druk*). That is why he named the monastery Druk and his religious school Drukpa.[1] Students of his lineage, it was said, spread as far as an eagle could fly

---

[1]   *Drukpa* refers broadly to the people of Bhutan and more narrowly to its largest religious sect.

◀ Religious pilgrims from the eastern region of Bhutan. *Photo by rajkumar1220, http://bit.ly/RpKMoi.*

in eighteen days. A saying had it that "half the people are Drukpa, half the Drukpa are beggars, and half the beggars are Tantric adepts."

Bhutan is the only Vajrayana ("Tantric" or "Esoteric") Buddhist kingdom in the world. In part because of its remoteness, but also as a result of its population's fierce independence, Bhutan is one of the few countries in Asia never colonized. It is known for its vigorous efforts to preserve its Buddhist heritage and traditional culture, which remain vibrant and active today.

Vajrayana Buddhism came to Bhutan centuries before Tsangpa Gyarey founded the Drukpa school. Its arrival is attributed to Padmasambhava (Guru Rinpoche), who is said to have brought the religion from India in the eighth century. Padmasambhava means "Lotus Born," and according to tradition he was incarnated as an eight-year-old child appearing in a lotus blossom. He is widely revered in both Bhutan and Tibet.

In the tenth and eleventh centuries, during what is called "the later spread of the Dharma," the popularity of Vajrayana Buddhism mushroomed. By around 1200, several schools of Buddhism were thriving. In the centuries thereafter, many monks arrived from abroad to help spread the faith. Figures like Drukpa Kunley (1455–1529), known as the "Divine Madman," engaged the popular imagination,[2] and scholars like Pema Karpo (1527–1592), the "Omniscient White Lotus," helped to systematize Drukpa teachings.

In Himalayan forms of Buddhism, deities often take ferocious and terrifying forms. These are not demons but frightening forms of benevolent deities who protect the faithful and represent the vanquishing of evil. Vajrayana Buddhism encompasses a large and complex range of deities of all sorts. Adepts of this school often employ meditation, mantra recitation, dance, and ritual as aids to invoking a personal deity. Through such techniques practitioners may seek to

---

2 Consistent with the country's thunder theme, he liked to lead young women to enlightenment with the aid of his personal "flaming thunderbolt." Many Bhutanese houses still display large painted phalluses, often wrapped in bows, in his honor, and at a temple in Punakha, childless couples may be blessed by a bamboo effigy of Drukpa Kunley's phallus.

Drukpa Kunley, the "Divine Madman," considered the phallus a potential instrument of enlightenment. Many walls in Bhutan, such as this one in Nobding Village, are decorated with painted phalluses bedecked with bows. *Photo by rajkumar1220, http://bit.ly/1qgpmUL.*

become embodiments of the deities, which can be viewed as symbolic expressions of the mind. In this sense, Vajrayana Buddhism is intensely personal, and it infuses every aspect of Bhutanese society.

All unhappy countries are alike,[3] but each happy country is happy in

---

3   If you believe the WIN-Gallup International Global Index of Happiness (Jan. 1, 2013), the least happy countries are Portugal, Iraq, Romania, Palestinian territories, and Lebanon. Respondents were asked, "As far as you are concerned, do you personally feel happy, unhappy or neither happy nor unhappy about your life?" Bhutan was not surveyed. (Rankings that show countries like Denmark, Norway, Austria, the Netherlands, and Switzerland at the top heavily factor in economic measures. It's an old tradition — "a large income is the best recipe for happiness," Mary Crawford opined in Jane Austen's *Mansfield Park*.)

its own way.[4] Over the course of the twentieth century Bhutanese leaders gradually realized that the country's isolationism was not sustainable in a modern globalized world. Bhutan had among the highest poverty, illiteracy, and infant mortality rates in the world. Until the 1960s it had virtually no roads, electricity, motor vehicles, telephones, or postal service. To address this, it embarked on a program of modernization. In 1953 a national assembly was established. In the 1960s roads were built connecting the country to India (in part as a response to the Chinese takeover of neighboring Tibet). But change came slowly — for example, only in 1999 was a ban on television and Internet lifted.

In 1972, amid this slow process of modernization, young King Jigme Singye Wangchuck established as a measure of progress an alternative to the conventional Gross National Product that he called Gross National Happiness. What a charming notion! But is it just a quaint quirk of a small and impoverished nation of mainly subsistence farmers, or could it actually be useful for something? It is intended to recognize other aspects of development than just economic advancement. King Wangchuck explained that Bhutan, as a small landlocked country without military or economic power, had little choice but to focus on its unique culture. But what is happiness in the context of Buddhism, and in the context of governance? Is happiness quantifiable?

Happiness is a topic often touched on in Buddhist teachings. Sayings attributed to the Buddha are collected in a document called the Dhammapada ("dharma verses"). The first two verses concern suffering and happiness. The second reads, "All that we are is the result of what we have thought: it is founded on our thoughts, it is made up of our thoughts. If a person speaks or acts with a pure thought, happiness follows him, like a shadow that never leaves him." The Dalai Lama echoed this in his book *The Art of Happiness*, when he said, "Happiness is not something ready made. It comes from your own

---

4   By the WIN-Gallup measure, the happiest countries are Colombia, Malaysia, Brazil, Saudi Arabia, and the Philippines.

Bhutanese monks beside an image of the wrathful form of a deity. *Photo by Radio Nederland Wereldomroep.*

actions." Well, great. Is this helpful? How do we total up the purity of a people's thoughts to calculate its gross national happiness?

The Dalai Lama also said, "Choose to be optimistic, it feels better," so let's not give up. There is another way of looking at happiness. Another Buddhist saying goes, "Happiness (*sukka*) is what can be borne with ease, suffering (*dukka*) is what cannot be borne with ease." Here we start to get at a kind of happiness defined not as an emotional state but as a quality of well-being or satisfaction. When we start thinking about happiness as a collective measure of well-being we might begin to see it as something that is quantifiable. This is what Bhutan has attempted to do.

The four pillars of Bhutan's GNH are being economically self-reliant, sustaining a pristine environment, preserving and promoting traditional Bhutanese culture, and participating in good democratic governance.⁵ But these goals sometimes conflict. Being economically self-reliant has led to the development of hydropower, but the creation of a giant reservoir at Amo Chhu will submerge three villages that are home to the oldest groups of inhabitants of the country — hardly the best way to preserve traditional culture. And the imperative to preserve traditional culture took the unfortunate form of strict imposition of Buddhist dress and practices upon the country's Hindu Nepalese minority, which once made up about a sixth of the country's population. This led to the exodus of many long-time residents, a large number of whom ended up in a United Nations refugee camp in eastern Nepal; the camp houses more than 100,000 refugees. Some of them have resided there for decades.

King Jigme Singye Wangchuck was a generally popular ruler who never seemed to waver in his belief in GNH. As part of his vision for raising national happiness, he was convinced that democratic government was an essential aspect of a happy state — ironically, the monarch himself was probably the country's strongest advocate for democratic government. In 2008 he abdicated his crown as part of the establishment of a democratic state. His son, the new king, would be but a constitutional monarch. Elections would be held to choose a prime minister.⁶

The new figurehead king was on board with his father's program. He has said that "GNH has come to mean so many things to so many people but to me it signifies simply — Development with Values.... Our government must be human." But during the 2013 national elections some critics said GNH should really stand for "Government Needs Help." That July, Tshering Tobgay, an opposition leader who argued that Bhutan needed to focus more on solving the problems of unemployment, poverty, and corruption, and on improving the country's relationship with India, was elected

---

5   There are numerous indicators under each of these headings, things like psychological well-being, spirituality, meditation, living standards, education, health, ecological diversity, good governance, artisanal skills, hours of sleep per day, cultural involvement, and community vitality.
6   Only college graduates were eligible to run.

Rice paddies stretch before the Tashichhodzong at Thimphu, the seat of Bhutan's government since 1952. Bhutan's economy remains mostly agricultural. *Photo by Mark Fenn.*

prime minister. "If the government were to spend a disproportionate amount of time talking about GNH rather than delivering basic service," he said, "it would be a distraction."

Nonetheless, Bhutan's GNH remains a prototype for an alternative measure to GNP. It was a topic of discussion at the Rio+20 environmental conference in Rio de Janeiro in 2012. Columbia University's Earth Institute issued a lengthy (and wonky) *World Happiness Report* that included a case study on Bhutan's initiative.[7] So how happy is Bhutan? In 2007, a study from the University of Leicester applied a psychological metric called "Subjective Well-Being" and concluded that Bhutan ranked eighth out of 178

---

7   Karma Ura, Sabina Alkire, and Tshoki Zangmo, "Gross National Happiness and the GNH Index." *World Happiness Report*, ed. John Helliwell, Richard Layard, and Jeffrey Sachs, New York: Earth Institute, Columbia University, 2012.

countries (and it was the only one in the top twenty with a low GDP). But a Bhutanese government-supported GNH survey in 2010 got a different result. It found that 59 percent of Bhutanese polled were "not yet happy."[8]

King Jigme Singye Wangchuck's vision of Gross National Happiness has produced results that would have been hard to foresee in 1972. One of these is the development of a nascent Bhutanese film industry, known as "Drukwood." Bhutanese filmmakers have produced feature-length movies, as well as documentaries, animations, and shorts. Leading the way was a filmmaker who had studied with Bernardo Bertolucci and others, Khyentse Norbu (Dzongsar Jamyang Khyentse Rinpoche), who is regarded as the third incarnation of a lama who founded a lineage of Himalayan Buddhism; he is prominent as a spiritual leader and works actively with nonprofits and charitable organizations. His *The Cup* (1999) follows two adolescent novices in a remote monastery as they attempt to find a way to watch the 1998 World Cup final on television. The arrival of television serves as a way to explore the tensions between tradition and modernization.

Norbu's second film, *Travellers and Magicians* (2003), the first feature film to be produced entirely in Bhutan, follows the journey of a young chain-smoking minor government official who wears an "I Heart New York" T-shirt, listens to Western pop music on a boom box, and dreams of traveling to America. To accomplish this, he hitchhikes west, accompanied at times by an apple seller, a Buddhist monk, and a paper maker and his daughter. Against a backdrop of stunning mountain scenery, the monk coaxes the official into being more mindful of his surroundings. Gradually the restless young man stops smoking and thinking of faraway places and becomes more aware of the beauty of the scenery — and of the paper maker's daughter.

---

8   Lowest scores were in the categories of "time use" and "living standards." Schooling, donations, cultural participation, and knowledge were among the factors found most "insufficient."

Monk with dragon-headed dramyin. Still from *Travellers and Magicians* (2003), directed by Khyentse Norbu.

The monk relates the story of an apprentice magician who, like the official, sought to escape village life. It becomes a strange and haunting account of dangerous misplaced passion, as he describes how the young man enters into a tragic affair with the young wife of an old man. As he unwinds his tale, the monk strums his dramyin, the traditional Bhutanese six-string lute. Like all dramyins, it has a long neck, and it is topped at the head with an ornate carved dragon. The monk strums, the story unfolds. And so, once again, the voice of the dragon cascades down the steep mountain valleys of Bhutan.

Nur Jahan

EARLY MODERN WOMAN OF POWER

～∿≀∿～

In the early modern world, it was difficult for women to compete in struggles of power as independent players. Most built instead upon their roles as wives, mothers, daughters, or consorts (the most notable exception was Elizabeth of England). One of these was a woman whose birth name was Mihrunnisa ("Sun of Women"). In March 1616 she acquired a new name — henceforth she would be known, and become famous, as Nur Jahan ("Light of the World"). The name was given to her by her husband, Jahangir, ruler of the Mughal empire. Jahangir left much of the day-to-day governance of the empire to his favorite wife. A Dutch observer at the Mughal court went so far as to claim that Jahangir was "King in name only" and that "misunderstandings result, for the King's orders or grants of appointments, etc., are not certainties, being of no value until they have been approved by the Queen." Another Dutch observer, no better friend of the queen, claimed that Jahangir "suffered in his mind because he found himself too much in the power of his wife, and the thing had gone so far that there were no means of escaping from the position. She did with him as she liked, his daily reward being pretended love and sweet words, for which he had to pay dearly."

Jahangir was not someone to take lightly, and Nur Jahan had to have possessed considerable resources of courage and cunning to gain such control over him. Normally mild, and often accused of passivity, the Mughal ruler was capable of erupting in flashes of cruelty. He had men killed for breaking a china dish. He killed servants he thought had got in the way of a good hunt. He ordered the thumbs of a man cut off who had taken down some trees he happened to like. He had a woman who had been caught kissing

◀ Idealized portrait of the Mughal empress Nur Jahan (1577–1645), ca. 1725–1750. India; Rajasthan, Kishangarh. Opaque watercolor and gold on paper. *Los Angeles County Museum of Art, Gift of Diandra and Michael Douglas*, M.81.271.7.

a eunuch buried up to her armpits and kept without water in the hot sun (she died in less than a day). When his first-born son, Khusrau, unsuccessfully attempted to overthrow him, Jahangir had the leaders of Khusrau's revolt beheaded or impaled. Then he placed their heads on stakes on either side of a road and personally led his son, strapped to an elephant, between them, "introducing" each head to him in turn.

Nur Jahan was one of the most powerful women of premodern India. She had coins minted in her own name, collected duties and tariffs, and engaged in international trade. She owned a line of ships that carried pilgrims and cargo to Mecca. Her patronage was often sought and often needed. She amassed considerable private wealth and ruled with a firm hand.

She was Persian, born in Kandahar, now the second-largest city in Afghanistan but at that time a trading town on the border between Persia and the Mughal empire. Her parents were on their way to India, fleeing difficult economic circumstances in Persia and hoping to gain favor at the Mughal court, where Persian learning and sophistication were held in high esteem. The family lost most of their possessions to thieves during the journey but were favorably received in Jahangir's court. They prospered, and Nur Jahan's father rose to a position of prominence.

Nur Jahan's story has fascinated many people in South Asia and elsewhere, and as a result a great deal of legend has surrounded her; it is difficult to be certain of the historical truth of many aspects of her life. A story has it that Jahangir and Nur Jahan fell in love as teenagers. Unfortunately, she was to be wedded to another man, and only after his death, when she was in her thirties, would she and Jahangir finally marry. How might the young lovers have met? Jahangir, then merely Prince Saleem, was walking, so the story goes, through a garden. As ruler he would be famous for his fondness for beautiful things, and already he displayed his aesthetic inclinations. He was carrying two pigeons as he walked, when he noticed some beautiful flowers that he wished to pick. As chance would have it, the young Nur Jahan — herself celebrated for her beauty — was passing by just then, and Jahangir asked her to hold the pigeons so that he could pick the flowers. But when he returned to the girl he found her with only one of the birds. "How did that happen?" he demanded. "Like this!" she replied, releasing the second pigeon into the air, and Jahangir was captivated by the young woman's wit and charm.

All such stories probably belong to the realm of legend. In 1594, when she was seventeen, Nur Jahan was married to a young man of the Persian community, and it is doubtful that she had had significant contact with Jahangir before that time. Many of the expatriate Persians, including most of Nur Jahan's family, were then viewed with suspicion as a result of having placed their bets on the wrong horse in the inevitable conflicts that always seemed to rise up over issues of succession among the Mughals. Nur Jahan's husband was given an undesirable post in Bengal. Not long after ascending the throne in 1605, Jahangir became suspicious of him and sent a delegation to check up on him. Somehow a melee resulted in which Nur Jahan's husband killed the leader of Jahangir's party and was himself killed in response.

Some say that Jahangir had arranged Nur Jahan's husband's death because he was already in love with her, but there is no evidence for this. Now a widow with a young child, she returned to the Mughal court (then in Agra) and entered the *zanana,* the community of the harem, as a lady-in-waiting to one of Jahangir's stepmothers. It was the custom of the Mughals to care for the widows of courtiers, and they were often adopted by women of influence.

It is unclear how many women were resident in Jahangir's zanana; the likeliest guess seems to be a thousand or more. Besides his wives and concubines there were the female members of his family and their children, as well as ladies-in-waiting, servants, guards, entertainers, and many other women, from all ethnic groups and levels of society. The community was in effect a largely self-governing city. It was guarded by women armed with daggers and bows and arrows; the guards were changed every twenty-four hours to maintain vigilance and protect against intrigues. (Nur Jahan herself was said to be the most accomplished archer of Jahangir's court; she was equally adept with firearms, once, it is said, bringing down four tigers with just six bullets.) Because of the practice of *parda,* or seclusion of women, very few men were ever allowed inside, although the higher-ranking women could have two or more eunuchs as attendants. The main exceptions to the exclusion of men were visits from husbands, who could also sometimes bring fathers and brothers with them. After his marriage to Nur Jahan, Jahangir granted to her father the extraordinary privilege of access to the zanana without the women being veiled, a clear sign of the powerful position she had attained.

As a woman of the zanana, Nur Jahan met Jahangir at the Nouroz festival of 1611. Nouroz is the traditional Persian (originally Zoroastrian) festival of the new year, which occurs on the first day of spring by the solar calendar. It was also one of the two main festivals observed by the Mughal court (the other being the emperor's birthday). Nouroz was a particularly festive time for the women of the zanana, for a bazaar was then set up in the emperor's palace compound where they were allowed to shop at stalls, almost as if they were out free in the world. The stalls were operated by the wives of merchants. The emperor would also go from stall to stall, chatting and flirting with the women. As he made his rounds during the 1611 Nouroz, he chanced upon Nur Jahan and was startled by the beauty of her unveiled face. The two were married two months later, in May 1611. She was the last of the emperor's wives.

Jahangir's line was susceptible to alcoholism. Two of his brothers died at an early age from the disease. Jahangir compounded the effects of heavy alcohol use through the addition of opium, which he also consumed in large quantities on a daily basis. In this stupefied (and probably constipated) condition, he became disinterested in, and perhaps incapable of, tending to the details of governance. It was Nur Jahan who triumphed in the struggle to fill this vacuum and who became in many respects the de facto ruler of the Mughal empire.

Nur Jahan was thirty-four or thirty-five years old when she married Jahangir (who then called her Nur Mahal, "Light of the Palace"). Women over thirty were considered in the Mughal court to be of advanced years, and the Mughal emperor rarely had sexual relations with them. An English visitor reported that the nobles of the court never "came near their wives or women, after they exceed the age of thirty years" and such women were never "much regarded by those great ones, after the very first and prime of their youth is past." Nur Jahan had no children by Jahangir—nor did any other woman of the zanana after their marriage—maybe his heavy consumption of alcohol and opium rendered him impotent. Although there is little doubt that it was her beauty that first inflamed the emperor's passions, her relation to him seems quickly to have become mostly maternal in character.

The mother-son relationship was particularly valued among the Mughals, according to Nur Jahan biographer Ellison Banks Findly. "Given the structure of Mughal households, where religious custom obligated providing shelter for any older unattached women and where 'multiple mothers' (wet-nurses, barren aunts and foster mothers of all types) were the norm, Jahangir found it easy to feel strongly for the older women around him." Jahangir had said

Emperor Jahangir and Empress Nur Jahan (detail), ca. 1830. Nepal. Opaque watercolor, gold, and silver on paper. *Los Angeles County Museum of Art, Gift of the James and Paula Coburn Foundation,* M.2005.154.9.

of a couple such women that they were as dear to him as his own mother, and he seems easily to have projected a maternal role onto his final wife. His reverence for mothers probably contributed to his collecting of Western Madonna-and-child paintings. Thomas Roe, who established the first official English embassy to the Mughal court in 1616, was constantly writing home for more and better paintings on this theme, and images of the Madonna appear in the Mughal court paintings sponsored by Jahangir.

Jahangir was aware that his drug use was affecting his health, but he could not control it. Only Nur Jahan was able to instill a degree of moderation, reducing his intake by degrees and then rationing his usage at a still high but somewhat less excessive level. By controlling Jahangir she effectively held the reins of power, although, because of the practice of *parda,* she was often forced to govern from behind a screen. Visitors would hear a whispered voice giving directives to Jahangir during their audiences. Her father and brother completed the ruling junta, and after her father died she teamed up effectively for a time with her brother. But as Jahangir's health continued to decline, the empire's attention turned increasingly to the troubling matter of succession.

The Mughals did not subscribe to the practice of royal inheritance by birth order. The eldest son had no automatic priority over other male descendants. Jahangir's father, Akbar, had for a time favored his grandson Khusrau over Jahangir, and Jahangir had led an army against his father's forces before reconciling with him. Jahangir later had Khusrau blinded (some say with an herbal concoction, some with a glass held to the sun, some by sewing patches over his eyes, some by puncture with a wire — the last is unlikely, since physicians later sought to restore his sight). Unrestrained by the mediation of their father, Nur Jahan and her brother began to vie with each other for power, and a complicated tangle of deceptions and treacheries ensued, as each promoted a different candidate to succeed Jahangir.

It was a long struggle well fought, but one that Nur Jahan finally lost, and her brother's candidate, Jahangir's third son, assumed the crown as Shah Jahan. He would be best known in the West for building the Taj Mahal as a sepulchre for his wife, a niece of Nur Jahan. Despite Nur Jahan's years of effective governance, because she was a woman her power was still in some sense by proxy, and without her husband she could not hold on to it. She was forced to retire to Lahore where she lived under guard on a pension provided by her triumphant brother. It was said that she "never went to parties of amusement of her own accord, but lived in private and in sorrow" for the next eighteen years until her death in 1645.

AUSTRALIA,
SOUTHEAST ASIA

Getting Henry

HENRY HANDEL RICHARDSON AND
THE GETTING OF WISDOM

∾∾∾

> Each of her novels is an effort to understand and to make us
> understand the complexities of a human situation, and this
> is in itself an invigorating and sometimes subversive exercise
> in following truth along unexpected paths.
> — Karen McLeod

> Your little rag of a girl is a most adorable little beast.
> — H. G. Wells

Readers who enjoyed Henry Handel Richardson's first novel, *Maurice Guest,* must have been perplexed when *The Getting of Wisdom* appeared two years later, in 1910.

Maurice Guest was the story of an English piano student who falls in love with a young Australian woman; attempting to win her away from a brilliant, dissolute Polish violinist, he begins a tortured descent that ends in suicide. It was "a book set within the closed hothouse atmosphere of a conservatorium"[1] combining "the realistic expansiveness of many characters and many events with a gathering claustrophobic intensity that does not let up until the final page."[2] ("Morbid, depressing, dull, verbose, degraded, coarse, erotic and neurotic were some of the adjectives applied to this book," the author later complained.)[3]

---

1   Ken Goodwin, *A History of Australian Literature* (London: Macmillan, 1986), 62.
2   Karen McLeod, *Henry Handel Richardson: A Critical Study* (Cambridge: Cambridge University Press, 1985), 36.
3   Nettie Palmer, *Henry Handel Richardson: A Study* (Sydney: Angus and Robertson, 1950), 43.

◀ Henry Handel Richardson at age thirty-four in 1904.

Now, in his second book, Mr. Richardson had turned to the trivial concerns of an Australian schoolgirl.

Ethel Florence Lindesay Richardson was born in Melbourne on January 3, 1870. Her family and friends called her Ettie or Etta. She hated the name her parents had given her, but this was just one reason for her adopted pen name. Those who knew her agreed that she was reclusive and retiring, and her pen name kept her from the public eye. (Most of her central characters are also solitaries.) Her longtime secretary-companion, Olga Roncoroni, said that Richardson's "chief characteristic . . . was her shyness. She found it very difficult to make personal contact with people."[4] Once, when the press sought to interview her on a holiday voyage, she locked herself in the ocean liner's lavatory until the reporters got tired and went away. According to Nettie Palmer, her biographer and tireless advocate (and a fellow graduate of the Presbyterian Ladies' College in Melbourne, as well as a fine writer in her own right):

> For Henry Handel Richardson, solitude was as necessary as food and music. She had few friends; she did not enjoy social gatherings; she was not spiritually at home in London [where she spent her later years] and looked out at it from her high windows with alien and incurious eyes. English life could never be a background for her work. All the experiences that mattered to her, and from which she was to select her themes, had been accumulated long before, when she was a child in Australia or a student in Germany; and it was her firm belief that any novelist should have seen and felt enough in his early years to set him pondering for a lifetime.[5]

Richardson must also have cherished the resonance of "Handel,"

---

4 Edna Purdie and Olga M. Roncoroni, eds., *Henry Handel Richardson: Some Personal Impressions* (London: Angus and Robertson, 1957), 78.

5 Palmer, 2.

since her life was strongly associated with music. But, she explained, there was a more important reason to hide behind her male mask, for "there had been much talk in the press about the ease with which a woman's work could be distinguished from a man's; and I wanted to try out the truth of the assertion" in *Maurice Guest*.[6] Germaine Greer elaborates:

> Henry Handel Richardson meant not only to write in a manner which displayed the masculine virtues of power and authority, she wished also to write the story of a degrading sexual obsession from the point of view of its masculine victim. There was to be no hypocrisy in the telling, for the object of his passion was both in love with and had been abandoned by another man. She would accept him as a substitute and lead him into a maze of depravity while Henry Handel Richardson would keep pace with him all the way, to morgues where female suicides lay destroyed by homosexual lovers, to drunken debauches and the seamy bed of a prostitute, until his suicide, when she would look through his eyes at his last glimpse of this world. To attempt all this as Mrs Robertson would be even now to court disaster in the shape of ridicule. . . .[7]

Whatever her reasons, Richardson was adamant about her pen name and resented the use of her married name, Mrs. Robertson (from 1895 until his death in 1933, she was married to scholar J. G. Robertson, who wrote the first English history of Germanic literature). After all, Richardson was her name, and her career, she took pains to point out, was distinct from her husband's. And "Henry Handel" had been in her family. "I've worked more than twenty years to establish my

---

6   Cited in Germaine Greer, "Introduction," in the Virago/Dell edition of *The Getting of Wisdom* (New York, 1981; the introduction is unpaginated).

7   Greer.

own name," she once said. "Why shouldn't I have it?"[8] Olga Roncoroni recalled an incident that demonstrated the strength of Richardson's feelings about her adopted name:

> In 1935 H. H. was awarded the King George V Silver Jubilee Medal. The medal reached her through Australia House, and the accompanying document, headed "Buckingham Palace", announced that the award was made to "Mrs. J. G. Robertson — for her work as an author". H. H. immediately returned the document to Australia House, saying that since her work had not been written under her married name she could not accept the medal under that name. Within a short time a new document arrived — made out to Henry Handel Richardson. On this point she was adamant; nothing infuriated her more than a refusal to accept the name under which she had always written.[9]

Many of the outlines of Richardson's life are reflected in her novels. Like Laura Rambotham in *The Getting of Wisdom*, she moved from a rural suburb of Melbourne to attend the Presbyterian Ladies' College there. Like Maurice Guest, she was a music student in Leipzig, following her graduation from the PLC. Her father, like Richard Mahony in her postwar trilogy, became mentally ill at the end of his life, causing him to be institutionalized. (Richardson, like Laura, was left in the care of her mother.)

Yet in many ways Laura is unlike Ethel. Laura is careless, bad at mathematics, not athletic; Ethel Richardson was first in Latin, English, History, and Music, and the school tennis champion besides. Nonetheless, she said that she could not "remember ever being really happy at school," though at the end of her life she wrote approvingly of the discipline. "I came in for a very bad time," she writes. "Some of my faculties may have been blunted during the process, but it was certainly

---

8 Purdie and Roncoroni, 48.
9 Purdie and Roncoroni, 112.

to the good in the long run. For the boy or girl who goes out into the world without knowing how to conform to its rules is surely to be pitied. The inevitable trimming and shaping are best got over early."[10]

Richardson, who always undervalued *The Getting of Wisdom* (she described it as "just a merry and saucy bit of irony" that she wrote as a diversion while working on *Maurice Guest*), was no better a critic of it than others who have written about it. In fact, the novel so perfectly reflects the attitudes of a child — the ephemeral crises and disasters that are so foreign to the adult perspective — that it is difficult for adults to discuss, and it is unique among Richardson's works. She "does not estimate children's behavior with the 'teacherly' preoccupations and standards of the adult world, but estimates both the childhood world and the adult world with the preoccupations and standards of a child actually experiencing them."[11]

"It is almost as if the clear-eyed, passionate child who was almost suffocated by educational authoritarianism sneaked out of her while her back was turned and wrote a perfect novel that the self-conscious adult had no power to understand," notes Greer in the most perceptive of her many perceptive comments on the novel.[12]

So "the getting of wisdom" is distinctly ironic, as Laura learns lessons of accommodation, submission, and suppression of spontaneity.

The novel's childlike spontaneity and honesty are among its most innovative qualities. Nettie Palmer observed:

> H.H.R. had framed her work, not on conventional lines, but according to her own vision of the truth. In this it was an utterly unusual, an original book. For stories of school-life, like those of youth in general, had scarcely ever been written, at least in English-speaking countries, with even an approach to honesty. In them the emotion was misdirected to docility.

---

10 Henry Handel Richardson, *Myself When Young* (London: Heinemann, 1948), 64.

11 Vincent Buckley, *Henry Handel Richardson* (Melbourne: Lansdowne Press, 1961), 64.

12 Greer.

They seemed to have been designed by teacherly persons, their object the concealment of the truth about the relations between young people themselves or between young people and the grown-ups who expected their obedience and took for granted their delighted co-operation in adult schemes."[13]

Richardson's approach to the school experience, the coming of age, anticipates Joyce's *A Portrait of the Artist as a Young Man,* published six years later. (Joyce's associate Stuart Gilbert was a Richardson enthusiast. "There is no book previous to *Ulysses* that I have read so often and so often recommended as *Maurice Guest,*" he wrote. "To my mind it is the best novel written in the twenty years preceding the war.")[14] For most readers today, *Maurice Guest* shows its age, whereas in *The Getting of Wisdom,* more than any of her other books, Richardson writes with a directness, simplicity, ease, and economy of means that ushered in the twentieth century. "Every stroke is subordinated to the main design, the enactment (rather than description) of the implacable destruction of a child's innocence," Germaine Greer observes. "*Maurice Guest,* for all its outspokenness about sex and perversion, is a nineteenth-century novel; in *The Getting of Wisdom* we are suddenly aware that a tenth of the twentieth is almost over."[15]

Sexuality and roles of dominance and submission pervade the novel. Laura's transition from her country home, where she dominates her sister, to the Presbyterian Ladies' College, where she must submit to domination, is the fundamental shift that sets the story in motion. Dorothy Green has written:

> The book is permeated with curiosity about sex, much of it unwholesome; the goal of most of the girls and women is matrimony, which sums up all they can conceive about relations between the sexes. Laura's tentative suggestions that friendship

---

13   Palmer, 30.
14   Quoted in McLeod, 230.
15   Greer.

might be a possible one is contemptuously dismissed, half-understood, by the school flirt, and only Laura casts doubt, privately, on marriage as a goal, "an event, which though it saved you from derision, would put an end for ever, to all possible, exciting contingencies". Laura gets on best with women teachers, "to whom red lips and a full bust meant nothing"; does not want Bob to be "gone on her" nor to have to "fish for him", if he is; has less talent for capturing a boy's attention than an eight-year-old child; and her most intense emotional experience is her obsessional passion for an older fellow-student. Both Laura's admirer, Chinky, for whom boys are "dirty, horrid, conceited creatures" and the flirt Maria are well aware of male egotism, but Maria has already decided to exploit it for her own ends, Chinky to reject the sex.

As for the intellectual side, Laura accepts the geography mistress's definition of a "real woman's brain" as one without any intelligent curiosity, but in the effort to live up to Miss Hick's requirements, she exposes their weakness: too much masculine reverence for inert facts is no better than too much "feminine" concentration on the sense of the facts. History is at present vindicating Laura.[16]

Richardson was attacked by some critics for her dependence on her husband, her reliance on his income and patronage, as well as, some charged, her emotional dependence. Yet she supported her sister, who was considered a "militant suffragette," and she participated in rallies and protests (over her husband's objections), even on one occasion dropping an ink bomb in a letter box. She urged Nettie Palmer, "Do write on George Eliot. She needs to be lit up by a woman. We have taken men's opinions on persons and things for so long—far too long."[17] Richardson's marriage was childless, and she

---

16   Dorothy Green, "Power-Games in the Novels of Henry Handel Richardson" in Shirley Walker, ed., *Who Is She?* (New York: St. Martin's Press, 1983), 94–95.
17   Palmer, 193.

Portrait of Henry Handel Richardson with Yellow Scarf, 1920s, by Rupert Bunny (Australian, 1864–1947). Oil on canvas, 46 x 38.5 cm. *National Library of Australia.*

often remarked that gifted women had better things to do than make babies. Her married life was marked by frequent depressions, and she commented disparagingly on the institution of marriage. The suggestion has been made that her marriage was never consummated.[18] Still, Karen McLeod, whose *Henry Handel Richardson: A Critical Study* is remarkable for its discrimination, balance, and good sense, maintains that Richardson was "devastated" by the death of her husband: "She had been married for 38 years to a man who cherished her emotionally and intellectually, and for whom, as she wrote in her diary, all her books were written."[19] Richardson herself wrote that "in him I lost husband, father, brother rolled in one. He was everything to me."[20]

But, like Laura, Richardson was attracted to women. Her friend Morchard Bishop once hinted that *The Getting of Wisdom* was "a more personal book than the others, and tells us a good deal about its author if we care to take the trouble to read between the lines."[21] McLeod notes that Richardson "did share with Laura an intense passion for an older girl, which left her feeling bleak and deserted when the girl left school, although she admits that she was the one who turned away: 'I wanted her to myself, by herself, and if I couldn't, then I didn't

---

18   Green, "Power-Games," 96.
19   McLeod, 13.
20   Purdie and Roncoroni, 103.
21   Purdie and Roncoroni, 56.

want her at all.'"[22] But she did not "turn away" completely. As Nettie Palmer relates, the relationship "filled her later school-years with an underground excitement. It seems that this infatuation with 'Evelyn' was something more than one of the ordinary affairs of adolescence; she confesses that the attraction the girl had for her was so strong that few others surpassed it. The two were to keep in touch for many years, in fact until the death of 'Evelyn.'"[23] Throughout her life Richardson had female secretaries and companions, and would travel with them on her frequent holidays and voyages, rather than with her husband. Her final companion, Olga Roncoroni, was a young agoraphobe for whom Richardson arranged psychiatric help. They were friends for nearly thirty years; Roncoroni was her secretary for more than a decade before Richardson's death, and a consolation to her after the death of Professor Robertson.

Richardson experienced waves of popularity and neglect. The publication of *Maurice Guest* in 1908, followed by *The Getting of Wisdom* in 1910, earned her moderate acclaim. Her massive trilogy, *The Fortunes of Richard Mahony,* the first volume of which was published during the World War I in 1917, was initially so neglected that her publisher, Heinemann, sought to be released from the publication of the final volume, which had to be underwritten by Richardson's husband's personal funds. Surprisingly, that book (*Ultima Thule*) went into a number of printings and ushered in a second wave of popularity for the happy author (Heinemann quickly bought back the rights, despite having let the previous volumes go out of print). Thereafter, Richardson's reputation again slowly waned, though her books continued to be reissued.

In 1960, Heinemann republished *The Getting of Wisdom* in its New Windmill Series. For this edition the publisher deleted the German-language epigraphs, taken from Nietzsche, and made numerous editorial changes in the language, vocabulary, and punctuation of the text, apparently in an effort to "modernize" it. Following Bruce Beres-

---

22 McLeod, 6.
23 Palmer, 22.

ford's 1977 film adaptation of *The Getting of Wisdom,* Virago/Dial issued a paperback version of the book (with a still from the movie on the cover). For years this was the edition most readily available,[24] and we were fortunate to have it, since otherwise the book would have been almost completely inaccessible; it also included the valuable introduction by Germaine Greer. Unfortunately, it reproduced the 1960 edited text. (To imagine the author's reponse to this edition, consider that in 1939, when Richardson discovered unauthorized changes made by the publisher in the second proofs of her last novel, *The Young Cosima,* she insisted quite forcefully on removing all of them, and succeeded in doing so.)

The most immediately visible of the editorial alterations of the 1960 edition was the omission of the epigraphs placed by Richardson at the heads of eight of the chapters. The epigraphs help to illuminate the events of the chapters and to develop the theme of the getting of wisdom. The epigraph to chapter XVII, which offers the comment that "he who cannot lie does not know what truth is," intended by Nietzsche as a criticism of small-minded pedants, is especially pertinent to Laura's experience. Karen McLeod adds that "the act of lying itself demands an imaginative vigour that is valuable, although neither Laura nor her schoolfellows realise it at this stage."[25] And McLeod observes that "the injunction that prefaces the final chapter, that Laura should learn to 'dance beyond herself' is vivid, full of possibilities and an enriching of the final paragraphs," a valuable appreciation of the significance of the epigraph to the work. The epigraphs also contribute, I feel, to the book's comic or ironic quality, casting a mock epic importance on a schoolgirl's petty trials and preoccupations.

In an appendix to her work, McLeod provided these translations of the epigraphs (keyed to the chapters where they occur).[26]

---

24 That is, until the publication in 1993 of a Mercury House edition that restored the original 1910 text and combined it with reproductions of paintings by Frederick McCubbin (1855–1917).
25 McLeod, 85–86.
26 McLeod, 244–245. According to McLeod, the first translation

CHAPTER XII: The neighbor reigns, one becomes a mere neighbor. (Da regiert der Nachbar da wird man Nachbar.) From *Nietzsche contra Wagner*, section 2.

CHAPTER XVII: Inability to lie is far from being love of the truth. . . . He who cannot lie does not know what truth is. (Ohnmacht zur Luge ist lange noch nicht Liebe zur Wahrheit. . . . Wer nicht lugen kann, weiss nicht, was Wahrheit ist.) From *Thus Spoke Zarathustra*, part 4.

CHAPTER XVIII: The criminal is often enough not equal to his deed. (Der Verrecher is haufig genug seiner Tat nicht gewachsen.) From *Beyond Good and Evil,* section 109.

CHAPTER XX: How should a stream not find its way to the sea at last! (Wie sollte ein Strom nicht endlich den Weg zum Meere finden!) From *Thus Spoke Zarathustra,* part 2.

CHAPTER XXII: And do not forget to laugh well! (Und vergesst mir auch das gute Lachen nicht!) From *Thus Spoke Zarathustra,* part 4.

CHAPTER XXIII: Good and evil and joy and sorrow and I and you. (Gut und bose und Lust und Leid und Ich und Du.) From *Thus Spoke Zarathustra,* part 1.

CHAPTER XXIV: What does not kill me makes me stronger. (Was mich nicht umbringt, macht mir starker.) From *Twilight of the Idols.*

CHAPTER XXV: None of you has learned to dance as a man ought to dance — beyond yourselves! (Ihr lerntet alle

---

is by W. J. Kaufmann from *The Portable Nietzsche* and the others are from R. J. Hollingdale's Penguin translations.

nicht tanzen, wie man tanzen muss — uber euch hinweg tanzen!) From *Thus Spoke Zarathustra,* part 4.

Richardson was, like many of the great writers of the early decades of the twentieth century (Joyce, Pound, Conrad, Stein), an expatriate. In Australia she is held in the mixture of respect and — resentment is too strong a word — regret with which expatriates are viewed in countries that have been outside the centers of power and must struggle for attention (one thinks, for example, of the mixture of pride and criticism with which some Argentines have viewed their great expatriate writer Julio Cortázar). She returned to her homeland only once after age eighteen, to do research for her writing. Dale Spender, in *Writing a New World: Two Centuries of Australian Women Writers,* says that "Henry Handel Richardson is a writer with an international reputation although whether . . . this is primarily because she chose to lead her literary life outside Australia, or whether it is a testimony to the quality of her work, I cannot tell."[27] Australian critic Vincent Buckley reported an acquaintance arguing that "Richardson does not see things as an Australian would,"[28] and nationalistic writer Miles Franklin said of the postwar trilogy *The Fortunes of Richard Mahony,* "here at last was a work by an Australian in which the English-thinking Australians could take pride."[29]

Yet Spender agrees with Nettie Palmer that "the way in which Henry Handel Richardson linked personality and setting had changed the direction of the novel."[30] It is often a characteristic of expatriates to write with particular vividness of their homelands, and this Richardson does by intertwining setting and pyschology with consummate subtlety. As a result, says Dorothy Green, "there are few Australian novels which create an autonomous world and

---

27 Dale Spender, *Writing a New World: Two Centuries of Australian Women Writers* (London: Pandora, 1988), 245.
28 Buckley, 5.
29 Cited in Leonie Kramer, *The Oxford History of Australian Literature* (Oxford: Oxford University Press, 1973), 22.
30 Spender, 245.

Henry Handel Richardson in 1945. *Detail of photo by Howard and Joan Coster.*

which at the same time convey a vision of metaphysical life, but Richardson's are among them, and . . . still supreme among them."[31] For Richardson was, as Leonie Kramer states in her *Oxford History of Australian Literature*, "the first substantial Australian novelist to convey a large consistent vision of life."[32]

---

31 Dorothy Green, *Ulysses Bound: Henry Handel Richardson and Her Fiction* (Canberra: Australian National University Press, 1973), 22.
32 Kramer, 96.

House of Hope

MONTIEN BOONMA'S TEMPLE OF THE MIND

≈∾≈∾

"Life," said the Buddha, "is suffering." "Life," said Chief Joseph of the Nez Percé, "is good."[1] How can these sages' remarks be reconciled? The obvious answer would be to conclude that suffering is good.

But that doesn't seem right. Maybe it's a false syllogism. Try this: "The ocean is blue. The ocean is salty. Therefore, blue is salty." But not all blue is salty. Clearly not all equivalences, paradoxically, are equal.[2] The trick, then, is to transform suffering, to find a different equivalent. An equivalent difference. Easier said than done.

Montien Boonma's life was full of suffering. In 1985, after a stint living at Cholaprathanrangsit, a strict Buddhist temple at Nonthaburi in his native Thailand, the young artist, who had studied at Silpakorn University in Bangkok, got married. But he left his wife, Chancham, behind for a two-year residence to continue his art studies in Europe. There he became exposed to the work of the Fluxus group (which sought to break established boundaries between art and life) and the Arte Povera movement (which advocated a return to simple objects and messages); the German artist Joseph Beuys, who viewed art as social performance and spiritual exercise, was an important influence.

On his return to Thailand he was advised by a trusted monk to continue living apart from Chancham until they had been separated for ten years. He took a job teaching in Chiang Mai, in northern Thailand, where his connection to traditional Buddhist culture

---

1   I can't locate this quote, but Dale Pendell reports it in his *Pharmako/poeia*.

2   "'You might just as well say,' added the March Hare, 'that "I like what I get" is the same thing as "I get what I like"!'"

◀ *House of Hope*, 1996–1997, by Montien Boonma. Steel, herbs and medicines, wood. *Collection of the Estate of Montien Boonma. Photo by Kaz Tsuruta.*

deepened. At this time Chancham developed breast cancer. "In 1991, in September, when I went to stage my exhibition in Japan, we found out she had cancer. So the ten years were up," Boonma said. "All this made me believe more in the spiritual, because it seemed as if it were all fated."

Then Boonma developed lung cancer. After a fall, he was also diagnosed with a brain tumor. The couple sought to supplement traditional medical treatment with spiritual healing. They visited monasteries and pagodas, and they experimented with medicinal herbs.

Chancham died in 1994. The following year, her father died of lung cancer. Six years later, Boonma died. He was forty-seven. He left behind an eleven-year-old son.

Somehow Boonma transformed his suffering into poignant art-works of surpassing originality and beauty. Each of his art objects composes a defined space that seems filled with his hopeful spirit. "Whatever we believe in," he said, "we create a space there." His works incorporate a variety of nontraditional materials, such as herbs, ash, soil, wax, cement, discarded objects, and perishable items, but they often manifest traditional Buddhist themes.

Among the remedies he sought for his family's illnesses was the giving of alms at temples, and he found an example of a defined space in the alms bowls employed by monks. "I gazed into the bowl," he said, and "after a while the bowl gazed back at me.... When I think about the space in the bowl, I prefer to be inside this space, which is separated from the outside world. I would like to place my mind inside the bowl."

The bowls seemed to meld body and mind, emptiness and ful-fillment. He began to draw alms bowls each morning as a meditative practice. Many of his works incorporate bowls. Some are hollow, others are solid. Some are three-dimensional, others are flat repre-sentations. One of the last pieces he made (*Untitled,* 2000) juxta-posed large charcoal drawings of empty bowls with bowl-shaped (but solid) objects of polished brass.

Herbs and spices often appeared in his work. The herbs symbolize not only healing but also devotion and a sacred space. For Boonma,

"Medicinal herbs represent one's hope to reach somewhere or something that exists. . . . It is all about possibilities and acceptance."

Herbalism is traditionally employed by monks as a healing art, and the path to enlightenment can itself be seen as a process of healing. The Buddha is sometimes characterized as the King of Medicines or the Supreme Physician. Boonma's *Perfume Painting* (1997) is a circular wooden object completely covered with herbs. Entering a Montien Boonma installation is an experience that engages all of the senses. For his *Lotus Sound* (1992) he created a permeable semicircular wall made up of hundreds of bells.

In the early 1990s Boonma became influenced by the teachings of a monk based in northeastern Thailand, whose message inspired him to use art to cre-

▲ Self-Portrait: *A Man Who Admires Thai Art*, 1982, by Montien Boonma. Colored pens on photographic print, 18 x 20 in. *Collection of Chongrux Chanthaworrasut, Bangkok.*

ate contemplative environments that would serve as spaces for meditation. A kitchen filled with herbs and spices might be a kind of refuge within the home, and the home itself a sanctuary within the wider world.

For Boonma "the house is a metaphor of hope." In his installation *House of Hope* (1996–1997), which he conceived as a memorial to his wife, he hung thousands of strings of medicinal herbal balls from a steel grid to shape the outline of a house. The visitor is invited to climb a stepped platform to be within the space. The strands of herbs are like prayer beads — they could be viewed as ascending prayers or descending blessings. Surrounding walls, painted with herbal powders, evoke temple walls stained from candle smoke and incense. The room is both open and closed. It shimmers, but it is still.

I want to inhabit Montien Boonma's house of hope.

AFRICA

Malik Ambar

UP FROM SLAVERY

❦

In Africa, well into the modern era, there were many varieties of trade in slaves. By far the harshest was the West African trade that produced plantation slaves for the Americas. In North Africa, slaves confined to Mediterranean galleys had essentially received death sentences, but other slaves — like Miguel de Cervantes — could usually obtain their freedom through the payment of ransom or by converting to Islam. There was also an East African trade that took slaves to India and elsewhere. One of those slaves managed, remarkably, to rise to a position of prominence. He was known as Malik Ambar, and he was born in the mid-sixteenth century in the remote highlands of Ethiopia, or Abyssinia as it was then known.

Ethiopia at that time was under the control of the Solomonic dynasty, so called because it claimed descent from Solomon; but Malik Ambar was probably from a non-Christian region, like the majority of Ethiopian slaves (called Habshis) at this time. His name then was Chapu. Only later did he acquire the name by which he is remembered today — "Malik" means "king" and "Ambar" means "ambergris," which is probably an allusion to his dark skin, since aged ambergris turns a dark gray to black color.

He was sold in a slave market on the Red Sea and taken to Baghdad, where he was purchased by a merchant who educated him and converted him to Islam. Most slaves were sold by the Solomonic Christians in exchange for Indian cottons, which were extremely popular at this time. Ambar was resold several times, eventually coming into the possession of a man named Chengiz Khan, who was chief minister of the sultanate of Ahmadnagar in the northwest of India's Deccan plateau. This region, together with Bijapur to its south, had the highest number of Habshi slaves in India. In fact, Chengiz Khan himself was a former slave.

◀ The Mughal emperor Jahangir Shoots an Arrow through the Mouth of the Decapitated Head of Malik Ambar, 1616, by Abul Hasan. India. Opaque watercolors on paper. *Chester Beatty Library, Dublin*, cbl In 07A.15.

Malik Ambar, 1620s, by Hashim. India. From the Nasir al-Din Shah Album. *Musée des Arts Asiatiques-Guimet, Paris*, 7172 Ravaux (App. 6.4). The album to which this image of Malik Ambar was attached came into the possession of the ruler of the Qajar region in present-day Azerbaijan in the nineteenth century. Most of the folios in the album are now in the Gulistan Palace Library in Tehran, where they have only occasionally been made accessible to scholars.

Malik Ambar, like many Habshi slaves in Ahmadnagar, was purchased to augment the sultanate's military forces. Military slavery was an entirely different institution from the plantation slavery of the Americas. Because the loyalty of military slaves was critical, they were better cared for. The idea behind the institution of the military slave was that by removing warriors from their family ties, factionalism based on kinship could be held in check. The same idea was behind the janissary troops of the Ottomans, who were mainly preadolescent Christians from the Balkans, given up to the empire as a kind of tax called the *devshirme*; they were given military and Islamic training, and were supposed to remain celibate. It was also behind the extensive employment of eunuchs in the Chinese imperial court. In all of these contexts the childless men were also relied on as bodyguards and guards of the harem or the emperor's concubines.

Around 1575 Malik Ambar's master died, and his widow freed him. He took a wife and rose to be a cavalry commander in charge of about 150 men. The Mughal emperor Akbar, who pursued an aggressively expansionist policy, sought to conquer the sultanate of Ahmadnagar. In 1595 Mughal troops besieged the fortress in the city of Ahmadnagar, being turned back only by a spirited defense led by the sister of the recently deceased sultan. Five years later, however, the fortress fell to the Mughals. Malik Ambar took advantage of the ensuing chaos. The Mughals had imprisoned the Ahmadnagar sultan, but Malik Ambar found a young member of the royal family to install on the throne as figurehead ruler. He also arranged for the young sultan to marry his daughter. Ambar would be the power behind the throne.

He was not without rivals. For several years Malik Ambar and his main rival, a man named Raju Dakhni, led separate armies against the Mughals. Finally in 1606 Ambar confronted and defeated his rival in battle, and imprisoned him in the fortress in his new capital. Now the uncontested supreme military commander, he won victories against a rival state to the south; he held the coast against European powers; and, though he did not regain the city and fortress of Ahmadnagar, he defeated the Mughals in a series of clashes and won control of the countryside. With each victory more soldiers joined his side.

But by 1610 the puppet sultan had begun to resist some of Ambar's directives. One of his senior wives, a woman of Persian descent, goaded him to assert his independence. A Dutch observer reports that she called Ambar's daughter, a younger wife of the sultan, "a mere slave girl," and slandered Ambar besides. Ambar was swift to respond: he had both the sultan and his Persian wife poisoned, and installed their five-year-old son as the new sultan.

Thanks to his military successes and his adroitness at palace intrigue, Malik Ambar enjoyed a long reign as the prime minister and was effectively the ruler of the Ahmadnagar sultanate. Observers agree that he was a skillful and evenhanded administrator. One of his main accomplishments was the rationalization of the tax system. He assessed the fertility of land holdings and imposed taxes based on a percentage of the actual produce, allowing the substitution of cash payments in place of a percentage of the yield. A Dutch visitor in 1617 reported that Ambar was "very much loved and respected by everyone and keeps good government."

The tomb of Malik Ambar, near Rozah (Khuldabad), Aurangabad. India. *Photo by Terv-lugt, http://bit.ly/1roS9wM.*

The Mughal emperors Akbar and Jahangir both dispatched armies against him, winning only fleeting victories, as Ambar proved a master of guerrilla tactics. He developed brigades of light cavalry that made quick harassing raids on enemy supply lines while avoiding direct engagement with the main Mughal military force. Jahangir grew obsessed with Malik Ambar. He called him "Ambar the black faced" and "Ambar of dark fate," and referred to his followers as "rebels of black fortune."

In the fall of 1616 Jahangir dispatched his son Khurram to lead a large force in an assault on the Ahmadnagar sultanate. Shortly before Khurram departed, Jahangir was sitting in his palace when he saw an owl fly onto a nearby roof. Because owls are associated with the night, like the blackness that so impressed Jahangir about his enemy, he associated Malik Ambar with owls. Calling for a gun, he shot at the bird and killed it, or so he wrote in his reign journal, the *Jahangirnama*.

He subsequently commissioned a painting called *The Defeat of Malik Ambar*, in which the association with owls is emphasized — a caption reads, "The head of the night-coloured usurper is become the house of the owl" — and his fantasy of defeating his nemesis was fulfilled, if only within the margins of the painting.

Khurram did defeat Malik Ambar, forcing him to pay tribute to the Mughals. Jahangir was so pleased with this result that on his son's return he rewarded him with the name by which he would later be known as emperor, Shah Jahan, "Ruler of the World." But the victory proved temporary. Malik Ambar returned to battle and won back the lost territory. He continued to be a thorn in Jahangir's side until the two rival leaders died within a year of each other.

Malik Ambar died in 1626, when he was probably in his late seventies. Jahangir died in 1627; he was fifty-eight. Upon news of Ambar's death a Mughal chronicler graciously conceded that "this Ambar was a slave, but he was an able man." Seven years later his kingdom finally fell to the Mughals.

Because military slavery, unlike plantation slavery, did not make much use of women, the Habshis married Indian women and were gradually assimilated into society. By the eighteenth century the institution of Ethiopian slavery had ceased to exist in India, and the Habshis had virtually disappeared as a distinct group.

Journeys of the Iron Man

The big-footed warrior advances. He raises a spindly metal arm to brandish an enormous scimitar-shaped sword decorated with geometric cutouts. In his other hand he swings a bell. His expression is deadpan, perhaps grim, but his fearsomeness is undercut by what appears to be a goofy hat that he wears at a jaunty angle. The hat is round and flat like a saucer, embellished around the brim with an assortment of curious iron implements. To me he looks about as fierce as another warrior with a frou-frou hat, Donatello's David. Donatello's warrior resides in the Museo Nazionale del Bargello, Florence; this one is in an annex of the Louvre called the Pavillon des Sessions.

Officially it counts among the collections of the Musée du Quai Branly. The brainchild of former French president Jacques Chirac, the Branly is devoted to what once was called "primitive art" (a term now taboo), collected from cultures of Africa, Asia, Oceania, and the Americas. Most of its objects are housed in the museum's main building near the Seine, midway between the D'Orsay Museum and the Eiffel Tower, but a few, like this one, are exhibited in the Louvre, a couple of miles away. How did the iron warrior end up there?

Pieced together from metal scraps, the warrior — who represents Gu, the god

▲ David, 1430–1432, by Donatello. Bronze. *Bargello Museum, Florence. Photo by Patrick A. Rogers.*

◀ Sculpture dedicated to Gu, the god of ironworking and warfare, ca. 1850–1858, by Akati Akpele Kendo. Fon culture, Republic of Benin. Iron. *Musée du Quai Branly*, Inv. 71.1894.32.1. This photograph was taken in the Musée d'Ethnographie du Trocadéro, Paris, at the end of the nineteenth century, not long after the death of King Glele, who had commissioned the sculpture.

Seated figure, ca. 600 BCE–300 CE. Nok culture, Nigeria. Terra-cotta. *Louvre Museum, Deposit of the Federal Republic of Nigeria, 70.1998.11.1. Photo by Jastrow.*

of ironwork and warfare — looks like what we might consider "outsider art," but he was actually commissioned directly by a powerful king, the Fon monarch King Glele of Dahomey (now Benin). It's worth remembering that West Africa has an ancient artistic tradition that includes many objects of a high degree of naturalism. (By terming these works "art," we are, some would say, already casting a tinge of colonialism over them. Yet from our present vantage point they look like what we think of as art.) West Africa was one of seven locations in the world where civilization — in the anthropological and historical sense of large, complex social structures — seemingly arose independently. (The others are Mesoamerica, the Andean highlands, China, South Asia, Iraq, and Egypt.) In West Africa, the Nok culture created refined objects of terra-cotta hundreds of years before the beginning of the common era. So this was actually insider art, positioned toward traditional West African art in not such a different fashion from the way artists like Picasso were positioned with respect to traditional Western art. (That artist and the warrior would, as we shall see, encounter each other.)

King Glele commissioned the iron man around the middle of the nineteenth century from an artist (let's call him that) named Akati Akpele Kendo. The Fon people inhabit the West African country of Benin and the southwestern portion of Nigeria. They share some cultural elements with the Yoruba to their east, although their languages are not closely related. This is the part of Africa that Europeans called "The Slave Coast," and the Fon were highly active in the slave trade. Though formerly a vassal state of the Yoruba, by the height of the slaving era they had won their independence and indeed regularly captured Yoruba people and sold them to the Portuguese for export into slavery in America. It is estimated that ninety percent of Africans brought to America for slavery came from the West African region stretching from the Senegal River in the north to Angola in the south. Humans were the Fons' only cash crop during the reign of Glele's father, Ghezo (r. 1818–1858). But over the course of Glele's reign (1858–1889), the slave trade dried up, and he was forced to try to convert the economy to a less valuable commodity, palm oil. Perhaps ceremonial objects became more elaborate at this time because the king's role as purveyor of wealth was threatened and so he felt the need for more symbols asserting his authority.

"An Amazon in the Dahoman Army," from F. Forbes, *Dahomey and the Dahomans* (London, 1851).

A slave economy depends on military force, and the iron warrior was created for a military purpose. The king had large numbers of troops at his command. Among them was a regiment of all-female troops that the kingdom's European partners called, inevitably, the Dahomey Amazons. They seized the imagination of Europe, reflecting its exoticizing impulse.

Assisting King Ghezo had been a Portuguese man from Brazil

named Francisco Félix de Sousa, probably the most notorious of all slave traders. Ghezo appointed de Sousa viceroy of the slave port of Ouidah, where he lived in opulence with a harem of around a thousand women. Edna Bay, an authority on this period, characterizes de Sousa as "deeply influential as an intermediary between European and African cultures."[1] His story was partially fictionalized in Bruce Chatwin's *The Viceroy of Ouidah,* which recounts how, a hundred years later, many of his countless descendants would gather to celebrate what they regard as a time of glory. "They mourned the Slave Trade as a lost Golden Age," Chatwin wrote, "when their family was rich, famous, and white."

Chatwin's book served as a basis for a film by Werner Herzog called *Cobra Verde.* A. O. Scott, reviewing the film in the *New York Times,* wrote that Herzog "sets out to show that he, and by extension the part of the world that fancies itself civilized, is far more savage than any Amazonian or African tribe." As Walter Benjamin said, "There is no document of civilization that is not at the same time a document of barbarism."

The Fon (and de Sousa, it is said) practiced a religion called Vodun, from which the English word *voodoo* derives. Vodun is a religion featuring spirits ranging from a prime creator god to an array of major and minor deities to a host of lesser spirits animating creatures and objects. Access to the spiritual world is mediated by priests. The religion is still practiced by some thirty million people in West Africa. "Voodoo is older than the world," Janvier Houlonon, a Benin Vodun practitioner, was recorded saying in a "Radio Expeditions" NPR report. "They say that voodoo is like the marks or the lines which are in our hands — we born with them. Voodoo are in the leaves, in the earth. Voodoo is everywhere."

Prophetic imagistic phrases played a large role in Fon religious practice and culture. Suzanne Preston Blier has shown how they

---

[1] Edna Bay, *Asen, Ancestors, and Vodun* (Urbana: University of Illinois Press, 2008).

Scene from *Cobra Verde* (1987), a film directed by Werner Herzog, starring Klaus Kinski as the slave trader Francisco Félix de Sousa.

helped to determine King Glele's governance.[2] As a youth, Glele participated in a divination ceremony to determine the particular symbols and phrases that would influence his fate. From one of these phrases, *Glele [gele lile] ma yon ze,* "The cultivated field is difficult to move," he took his throne name. The phrase suggests he will be steadfast in battle, impossible to budge.

Another phrase that was important to Glele was *Basa gla jig u honlon ma don,* "The audacious knife gave birth to Gu, and the vengeance continues." This phrase encouraged him to continue his father's assault on the Yoruba. When Ghezo died in 1858 and Glele came to power, he commissioned the iron warrior from a Yoruba

---

2   Suzanne Preston Blier, "Divination Portraits of a Lion King and Man of Iron," *African Arts,* vol. 23, no. 4 (Oct. 1990).

ironsmith who was a slave in his workshop. This was Akati Akpele Kendo. Kendo apparently forged the warrior out of scraps of European ironwork. He also produced a set of extremely large swords, each nearly five feet high, which were to be ritualistically arranged in a circle around the iron warrior. The objects on the brim of the figure's hat — including such things as a hoe, a hook, an ax, a spear — echo on a smaller scale the encircling monumental knives. The headpiece resembles the altarpieces called *asen* in which symbolic objects are enshrined as devotions to ancestors, reinforcing the king's connection to his powerful parent.

According to Basharu Nondichao, a descendant of a late-eighteenth-century Dahomean king, Glele instructed Kendo to model his work after an existing sculpture of Gu (probably in a different medium). The warrior was a highly symbolic work — every lug and bolt had a role to play in the narratives it was meant to convey. Nondichao says that the warrior is "an assemblage of all the objects in metal that are associated with Gu. . . . It completes the power of Gu that was here already."[3]

The warrior would accompany Fon soldiers into battle. Presented to the enemy, he would ensure their victory. The iron warrior, in this phase of his existence, was a *bo* (Vodun power object). But he would have other roles to play over the course of his journeys.

The problem was the French. By the late nineteenth century the once-powerful Portuguese empire, which had bedeviled West Africa for centuries, did not amount to a lot. Like the descendants of Francisco Félix de Sousa, it had fallen on hard times, partly as a result of the declining trade in slaves. In 1807 Britain began patrolling the African coast and arresting slaving vessels. In 1808 Jefferson prohibited the importation of additional slaves into the United State. By King Glele's time few markets remained.

The French were the current power in the region. France's colonialist interest in Africa went back to the late eighteenth century, when Napoleon had shocked the Ottomans by occupying Egypt in

---

3   Blier, 50.

1798. Already at that time rivalry with the English played a large role in French ambitions, as by controlling Egypt Napoleon hoped to limit British access to the east. But distractions at home kept the French from holding on to most of their gains. In 1840 they took Algeria. But they didn't really get serious about being a power in Africa until the 1870s, when the Scramble for Africa began.

Until that time direct European control of the continent was patchy and mostly limited to coastal regions. Portugal had led the way. Britain had been active. Now Germany, France, Belgium, Italy, and Spain coveted their own parcels. And France. French strategists looked at a map of Africa and decided they wanted to cut a continuous swath east to west. England had the same aspirations north to south. Conflict between the powers was inevitable.[4]

But first there was the small matter of the Africans themselves. France contrived a pretext for war out of local rivalries and disputes. The ensuing Franco-Dahomean wars lasted from 1890 through 1894. The Dahomeans proved a stubborn opponent, but in the end they were no match for French war technology. In 1894 the European conquerors placed a puppet ruler on the Dahomean throne. He proved noncompliant, so they dissolved the kingdom. In 1895 the French combined their territories of Mauritania, Senegal, French Sudan (Mali), French Guinea, Ivory Coast, Upper Volta (Burkina Faso), Dahomey (Benin), and Niger into an entity known as French West Africa. It would endure until 1960.

What of King Glele and the iron warrior? Despite his prophetic saying that "the cultivated field is difficult to move," and his "strong name" that threatened "no animal displays its anger like the lion," Glele had been forced to flee. Within a few years he would be dead. The iron warrior lay abandoned at Ouidah. His spiritual powers had failed the Fon. They had retreated inland in a last-ditch defense. The warrior was seized and exhibited by French troops as a symbol of their victory. The iron man, in this phase of his existence, was no longer a *bo*. He had become nothing more than a trophy of war.

---

4   The continent would be a key theater of action in World War I.

Maureen Murphy has traced the warrior's subsequent travels.[5] From Ouidah it was taken to Paris by the victorious French general, Alfred-Amédée Dodds, where it was accessioned into the collections of the Ethnographic Museum of the Trocadero. Founded a few years before, in 1878, the Trocadero was the first anthropological museum in Paris. It was housed in a structure intended for the 1878 World's Fair; the building would be demolished in 1935. The museum was seriously underfunded. Entire sections were forced to shut down for decades. Display cases were made out of the crates the objects were shipped in. The museum was not allowed to house objects from Italy, Greece, Egypt, or Asia, which (in a preview of more recent turf wars described below) were considered the purview of the Louvre. Its overarching conceit was the progress of humanity from the primitive to the civilized. In this context, the iron man was no longer a symbol of power. He had become an ethnographic specimen.

In the early twentieth century, with the French colonial adventures in Africa fresh in their minds, some French intellectuals began to argue against colonialism. For example, Alfred Jarry, in *Ubu Colonial* (1901), satirizes the colonialist attitude. Ubu returns from a "disastrous voyage . . . undertaken by us at the expense of the French government" and describes his colonial practice:

> Our first difficulty in those distant parts consisted in the impossibility of procuring slaves for ourselves, slavery having unfortunately been abolished; we were reduced to entering into diplomatic relations with armed Negroes who were on bad terms with other Negroes lacking the means of defense; and when the former had captured the latter, we marched the whole lot off as free workers. We did it, of course, out of pure philanthropy, to prevent the victors from eating the

5   Maureen Murphy, "Du champ de bataille au musée: les tribulations d'une sculpture fon," *Histoire de l'art et anthropologie* (Paris: INHA / Musée du Quai Branly, 2009). Murphy's essay is excellent, and I generally follow her argument in succeeding pages.

Les Demoiselles d'Avignon, 1907, by Pablo Picasso. Oil on canvas. *Museum of Modern Art, New York, acquired through the Lillie P. Bliss Bequest,* 333.1939.

defeated, and also in imitation of the methods practiced in the factories of Paris.[6]

A friend of Jarry, Pablo Picasso became interested in the artistic and spiritual qualities of African artworks. He visited the iron warrior at the Trocadero museum. He described the

---

6   For more in this vein, see Patricia Leighten, "The White Peril and L'Art Nègre: Picasso, Primitivism, and Anticolonialism," *The Art Bulletin,* vol. LXXII, no. 4 (Dec. 1990).

experience, which had an enormous impact on his personal artistic development:

> A smell of mold and neglect caught me by the throat. I was so depressed that I would have chosen to leave immediately, but I forced myself to stay, to examine these masks, all these objects that people had created with a sacred, magical purpose, to serve as intermediaries between them and the unknown, hostile forces surrounding them, attempting in that way to overcome their fears by giving them color and form. And then I understood what painting really meant. It's not an aesthetic process; it's a form of magic that interposes itself between us and the hostile universe, a means of seizing power by imposing a form on our terrors as well as on our desires. The day I understood that, I had found my path.

In 1908 and 1909, according to art critic Julian Bell, Picasso painted "what seem variants" on the iron warrior.[7] The profound effect of his encounter with African art on his painting was already evident in his *Les Demoiselles d'Avignon* (1907), in which the faces of two of the figures seem to reflect styles of African masks. Picasso had sensed the Vodun underpinning of the objects:

> They were magic things. . . . Spirits, the unconscious (people still weren't talking about that very much), emotion — they're all the same thing. I understood why I was a painter. All alone in that awful museum, with masks, dolls made by the redskins, dusty manikins. *Les Demoiselles d'Avignon* must have come to

---

7 Julian Bell, *Mirror of the World: A New History of Art* (London: Thames and Hudson, 2007). Bell goes on to say, "Another possibility is that Akati himself was influenced by sculpture from Paris: French Catholic missions were operating on the African coast before the French invasion of 1894, and the war-god's stance and the base for his feet seem to echo the look of the plaster saints that adorned their chapels."

me that very day, but not at all because of the forms; because it was my first exorcism-painting—yes, absolutely.[8]

So now the iron warrior had become an artwork. He was exhibited in 1930 in a salon of the Pigalle Theater. The show was controversial. Baron de Rothschild threatened to withdraw support, calling some of the works "obscene." But the organizers, among them Tristan Tzara, prevailed.

In 1935, the warrior crossed the Atlantic as part of a larger show, entitled *African Negro Art,* held at the Museum of Modern Art in New York in 1935. The exhibition would also travel to several other cities. The show was intended to

Head of the Warrior *Gu,* 1935, photograph by Walker Evans.

"increase awareness of African art and to demonstrate its influence on contemporary European and American artists."[9] No attempt was made to group the objects by culture, origin, or function. Walker Evans photographed the objects. He chose to concentrate on details, cropping tightly to the objects' faces. He emphasized the iron warrior's flaws, where the metal of the face had become separated, like the lines on the weathered face of an old person. The warrior had become a subject for portraiture.

---

8 Quoted in André Malraux, *Picasso's Mask,* tr. J. Guicharnaud (New York: Holt, Rinehart, and Winston, 1976).

9 Walker Evans, "The African Negro Art Exhibition, Museum of Modern Art, 1935," *Grand Street* no. 53, "Fetishes" (Summer, 1995). (The quoted text is presumably an editor's comment.)

Installation shot of the iron warrior in the Pavillon des Sessions, Louvre. *Photo by Ellen Christensen.*

The iron figure returned to the Musée de l'Homme, the natural history museum that was the successor to the Ethnographic Museum of the Trocadero. Its curators tried to resist the "aesthetification" of its cultural objects. Nonetheless, the warrior appeared in a show there called *Masterpieces from the Musée de l'Homme.* In an introduction to the catalogue of the exhibition Michel Leiris wrote, "The exhibition shows that this ethnological museum now recognizes the need to call the attention of the public to the pieces they have chosen using aesthetic criteria, criteria that are not ethnological since they respond to our taste as Europeans and not much to that of the makers and users of the objects. Is such an approach appropriate?"[10]

But masterpiece the iron man was now to be. In 2000, French president Jacques Chirac ordered a selection of highlight objects from the Musée de l'Homme and the

10 "L'exposition montre que ce musée d'ethnologie reconnaît aujourd'hui la nécessité d'attirer l'attention du public sur des pièces choisies essentiellement selon des critères esthétiques, critères qui ne sont pas ethnologiques puisqu'ils répondent à notre goût d'Européens et pas forcément à celui des auteurs et usagers de ces objets. Une telle initiative est-elle opportune?" Quoted in Murphy.

Musée National des Arts d'Afrique et d'Océanie to be transferred to the Louvre's Pavillon des Sessions. It was the first step in his vision of creating in Paris a great museum dedicated to, as he said, "the other." It was a vision that "put the social scientists at the École des Hautes Études and the keepers of the Musée de l'Homme into a state of battle-readiness," wrote Jeremy Harding in the *London Review of Books.* "The museum's wonderful collection of artefacts was a storehouse of meanings that could not be indulged by aesthetics alone."[11] As a result, the aesthetes at the Louvre got a limited number of works that were considered artistic masterpieces. The iron warrior was among them.

The rest of the objects would go into a new museum. It would be Chirac's visible legacy, like the Centre in the Beaubourg that is the legacy of Georges Pompidou, like so many other grand projects scattered around Paris that commemorate French leaders. The new museum would be called the Musée du Quai Branly (a safe name, taken from the street on which it is located, in turn named for an inventor of a kind of wireless telegraph). It cost $300 million to create, and it emphasized spectacle. It opened with great fanfare in 2006. But objects were presented without context, arranged along spooky paths meant to evoke a downriver journey to the deepest darkest heart of the jungle, "where suddenly scary masks or totem poles loom out of the darkness and everything is meant to be foreign and exotic," wrote Michael Kimmelman, reviewing the museum in the *New York Times.* "Colonialism of a bygone era," he concluded, "is replaced by a whole new French brand of condescension. . . . The legacy of Duchamp has turned everything in a museum into a readymade."[12]

Meanwhile the iron warrior resides in a less fraught space at the Louvre. He has been officially branded a masterpiece of world art. Made for one king, he now resides in what was once a palace of others.

---

11 Jeremy Harding, "At Quai Branly," *London Review of Books,* January 4, 2007.

12 Michael Kimmelman, "A Heart of Darkness in the City of Light," *New York Times,* July 2, 2006.

EUROPE

The Nightingale and You

Three times he tried to dissolve himself
and by the fourth he was alone staring at the answer
no one could give

In October 2013 I woke up in a vacation rental in Washington, DC, to discover I had lost my voice. This was alarming, since I was scheduled to read the following day at the Library of Congress. I was on a book tour for the unlikeliest of things, a collection of poetry in translation. Then I remembered that some Spanish critics characterize the poet I had translated, José Ángel Valente, as the leader of a movement called the "poetry of silence." Over the course of his career Valente had increasingly focused on the spaces between words and images as much as on the words and images themselves. So I would translate his Spanish silences into English ones.

Modern and contemporary Spanish poetry is not well known in North America. The most familiar names to American readers — Miguel de Unamuno (1864–1936), Federico García Lorca (1898–1936), Antonio Machado (1875–1939), Juan Ramón Jiménez (1881–1958), Luis Cernuda (1902–1963) — remain the modernist poets of the first half of the twentieth century. In general, these poets were influenced by Symbolist currents in European literature (often reimported to Spain through American writers such as Rubén Darío), and later by Surrealism and related movements (often, again, through American poets such as Vicente Huidobro). (There is a great deal of debate in Spanish literary criticism about when and how, or if, the term *modernist* should be applied to these writers, but it is as good a term as any when using a broad brush.) These visionary poets sought to capture, through disciplined imagistic language, heightened moments of reality that were abstracted from historical contexts as a kind of hyperreality, as epiphanic moments preserved in finely wrought verse. Increasingly as the century progressed many

◀ José Ángel Valente in his library. After returning from exile to Spain, Valente settled in Almería, Granada, where he restored a historic house. In 2003, three years after the poet's death, his widow sold the house to the city to honor his wish that it be converted into a "Casa del Poeta." The street in which it is located was renamed Calle José Ángel Valente. *Photo by Luis Matilla, http://bit.ly/1mhbBFq.*

of the poets turned inward, and their poems became more subjective and internalized, though in the 1930s, as civil war approached, some turned to political engagement. (Again an American, César Vallejo, was an important influence.)

In the timeline of Spanish poetry, the war years constitute a huge caesura in the middle of the century. Many poets were killed or exiled — the poet León Felipe, from exile in Mexico, declared that "poetry has abandoned Spain" — while others simply could not give attention to their art, and moreover the apparatus of publication had been dismantled. Spain emerged from the war exhausted, and writers now faced the censorship and repression of the Franco regime. In this context the old modernist concerns seemed archaic and remote. An influential journal was entitled *Postism* — "afterism" — reflecting the desire to move beyond previous literary modes. Poetry became fragmented, as poets tried a variety of approaches to rebuild their literature. Underground writers developed a poetry of protest. Others took refuge in surrealism or existentialism or other isms of the moment. Many sought a direct style that replaced what had come to seem artificial with an unaffected quality of ordinary speech. Eventually a fragile consensus emerged that poetry was about communication, often addressing social and political concerns.

It was amid this fragmented literary scene that a recent college graduate, José Ángel Valente, published his first books of poetry, *A Modo de Esperanza* (In a hopeful mode, 1953–1954, which won the Adonis Prize for Poetry) and *Poemas a Lázaro* (Poems for Lazarus, 1955–1960, which won the Critics' Prize). Born in Galicia in northwestern Spain, Valente had studied romance languages and law, graduating from the University of Madrid in 1953, when he was twenty-four years old. Though initially a supporter of Franco, Valente's father had fallen out of favor with the regime, and Valente would spend many years in voluntary exile, first in Oxford, where he taught Spanish letters and received an M A degree, and later in Geneva and Paris, where he worked as a translator for the World Health Organization and UNESCO.

Valente was court-martialed in absentia in 1972 for remarks critical of the military. (In 1986, a decade after the passing of Franco, he returned to Spain, living in Andalusia.) Nonetheless, his poetry is not often overtly political. He cited with approval the example of Kafka, in whose diary, he noted, "there are fewer than fifty lines devoted to the first world war. . . . The time of the writer," he said, "is not the time of history. Although the writer, like anyone else, can be crushed by it." In writing about Guernica, for example, he was more interested in Picasso's art than in the bombing that inspired it.

> Not the sun but the pale electric bulb full of cold
> horror that gives birth
> to the congealed gray of Guernica.

Though it is not fashionable to say so, Valente's work can be thought of as reviving some of the concerns of the earlier modernist writers, breathing new life into a tradition that had come to seem moribund. Stripping away the baroque and rhetorical flourishes of his predecessors, he took up some of their themes in language that is sharp, clear, and intensely present. (Besides Kafka, among the authors he referenced in his writings were Friedrich Hölderlin, James Joyce, José Lezama Lima, Paul Celan, and Edmond Jabès.) Though he did not reject social commentary, he viewed it as secondary in importance to metaphysical and philosophical exploration. Already in *A Modo de Esperanza* essentialist, transcendental, and mystical impulses appeared. In "First night," for example, he wrote:

> Extend your heart,
> bankrupt it, blind it,
> until in it is born
> the powerful void
> of what can never be named.

So from the outset Valente announced himself as a mystic poet in a modern mode. Just as he sought to move beyond the historical, so throughout his work Valente aspired to the essential and timeless — consequently, beginning in his earliest poetry, he often meditated on death. He wrote in *A Modo de Esperanza*:

I must die. And yet, nothing
dies, because nothing
has enough faith
to be able to die.

The day does not die it passes;
nor a rose, it fades;
the sun sets,
it does not die.
Only I, who have felt
the sun, the rose, the day. and thought,
I can die.

This preoccupation would take a tragic turn with the death of
Valente's son, an event that colored his mature work in the brilliant,
highly distilled prose poems of *No Amanece El Cantor* (The singer
does not awaken, 1992).

From your inundated heart I make out your voice, the dark
fog of death. It inhabits me. Not even death can tear it from
me.

. . .

Sometimes I feel very close to death. I wonder to whom
such an observation can be useful. In the end we do not
write about what is useful I think. So why not articulate a
trivial truism? The proximity of death is the meeting of two
flat empty surfaces that melt away from mutual repulsion. Is
that all? I don't know. To pass to the other side is insufficient
without the true testimony of the witness that I have failed
to accurately transcribe.

Valente often considered his own mortality in his later poems.
(He died in July 2000 after a long battle with cancer.)

as I compose
my biohighlightsnotebibliography I scrutinize the date of
my death and gently, sadly, I can make out the faded glory
of the deceased.

. . .

If after death we rise,
if after death
I come to you as I had come before
and there is something in me that you do not recognize
because I am not the same,
what sadness to die, knowing never
will I attain the shape
of the being you were to me, deep within myself,
as if you were me, had filled me completely,
for now so blind is this separation,
so doomed this wall of words,
suddenly frozen
at the time I need you most,
when I call you, and at times
you look at me still with tenderness
born only from memory.

What sadness to die, reach out to you,
kiss you desperately
and sense the mirror
does not reflect my face,
unfelt by you
whom I loved so much, my
longing without presence.

Throughout the poems there is an expectation, or at least a yearn-
ing, for escape from the passage of time. In modernist fashion, Valente

seemed to suggest that through art the advance of time could be transcended. In "The Sign" he wrote of a "slight object shaped by man,"

> a bowl of sun-baked mud,
> where the endurance of anonymous material
> forms a signal or a sign,
> its fragile form compacted across generations,
> surviving against time,
> the gaze slowly reaches
> around the thin invention
> formed by hand with a fragment of earth,
> rough and alive.
>
> Here, in this object
> on which the pupil pauses and returns
> and seeks the axis of proportion, resides
> for a moment our being,
> and from it another life unfolds its truth
> and another pupil and another dream find
> their most direct response.

Such transcendence, however, could only be achieved by immersion in and passage through the material world.

> The vase that contains supreme
> reality of form,
> created of earth
> so that the eye can
> contemplate freshness.
>
> The vase that exists by containing,
> failing to contain it breaks apart,
> lifeless. Its form
> exists only in this way,
> sonorous, inhaled.
>   The deep vase

with clean curves,
beautiful and servile:
vase and verse.

For Valente poetry itself was a material thing (or a "material memory," the title of his 1977–1978 collection of poems), and writing was, like ceramics, a shaping process.

Poetry was not, as it was for earlier postwar Spanish poets, so much an act of communication as it was a process of discovery. A discovery that was, necessarily, self-discovery.

I await only the signal of the song.
Now I do not know, now I just wait
to know later what I've been.

Valente wrote that poetry was the "revelation of an aspect of reality to which there is no means of access other than through poetic knowledge. That knowledge is produced through poetic language and has its realization in the poem." Every poem, he said, "is an exploration of the material of previously unknown experience, which constitutes its object. . . . The process of poetic creation is a movement of inquiry in which the identification of each new element modifies the rest or erases them, because every poem is a process of self-discovery."

To convert word to substance
where what we want to say can
penetrate no farther
than what the material would tell us
if to it, as to a belly,
we attuned ourselves,
a naked, white belly,
our ears tuned to hear
the sea, the indistinct
rush of the sea, which beyond you,
unnamable love, you engender.

Because for Valente poetry was a process, it was, despite its timeless aspirations, essentially temporal and consequently musical. "When, in the process of writing, we identify a rhythm, an intonation, a note," Valente said, "something radically musical in essence, something that reverts to numbers and harmony, the writing begins to shape itself. Writing requires, above all, great acuity of the ear." Valente's reference to a transcendental perfection of "numbers and harmony" places him in the long Pythagorean tradition that sought to uncover divine harmonies. The rhythms of Valente's lines and the pauses of the breaks between them are essential aspects of his poetic achievement. So a poem like "Be My Limit" could be made into a popular song by Vicente Monera (http://bit.ly/19W72Ia).

Your body can fill my life,
just as your laughter
can drive away the dark wall
of sadness.

A single word from you breaks
blind solitude to bits.

If you bring your inexhaustible mouth
to mine, I endlessly drink
the roots of my own existence.

But you do not know how much
I draw life from the
nearness of your body, or how much
its distance keeps me from myself,
reducing me to shadow.

Light and power, you are
like a burning torch
in the center of the world.

Never go away:
          The deep movements

of your being are
my only law.
               Retain me.
Be my limit.
And I will be the image
of my happiness,
which you have given me.

If Valente's process of poetic discovery was a journey of self-discovery, it was also, ultimately, a mystical journey of self-efface-ment, of immersion through the process of the word into the time-less infinity of love.

When there is nothing left for us,
the emptiness of what does not remain
could finally be useless and perfect.

. . .

And all the poems I have written
return to me at night.
               They reveal
their darkest secrets.
               They lead me
through slow corridors filled
with slow shadows extending to a dark realm
no one knows
and when I can no longer
return they hand me the key to the riddle
in the very question without an answer
that ignites light in my blind eyes.

. . .

The summit of song.
The nightingale and you
are finally the same

Dodgson's Dodges

~~~~~

All old Dadgerson's dodges one conning one's copying and that's what wonderland's wanderlad'll flaunt
to the fair.
— James Joyce, *Finnegans Wake*

Success in book publishing is often said to depend on "word of mouth." On this nebulous concept publishers and authors place any lingering hopes for an ailing title. So it was for Lewis Carroll, disappointed by sales of 13,000 copies of his magnum opus, *Sylvie and Bruno*: "I am quite satisfied that its small sale is not at all due to insufficient advertising," he wrote his publisher, Macmillan, adding hopefully that perhaps "it will get known by people recommending it to their friends."[1]

Rarely has word of mouth taken so long to work its magic. Like others cursed by extraordinary success (his younger contemporary Arthur Conan Doyle, for example, whose public simply would not allow him to kill off Sherlock Holmes), Carroll could never satisfy an audience that wanted only another *Alice*. As a result, little Alice had become a centenarian by the time respect for Carroll's remarkable accomplishment in the two *Sylvie and Bruno* novels really began to spread. Long overdue translations into French (1972), Spanish (1975), and Japanese (1976) signaled a new interest in the work. And with the new interest came a new evaluation: the distinguished French critic Gilles Deleuze termed the work "a masterpiece which shows entirely new techniques compared to *Alice* and *Through the Looking-Glass*."[2]

---

1   Quoted in Derek Hudson, *Lewis Carroll: An Illustrated Biography* (New York: New American Library/Meridian, 1977), 231.
2   Gilles Deleuze, *Sylvie et Bruno L'Envers et L'Endroit* (Paris: Editions du Seuil, 1972), quoted in Jean Gattegno, "Sylvie and Bruno, or the Inside and the Outside," in Edward Guiliano, ed., *Lewis Carroll: A Celebration* (New York: Clarkson N. Potter, 1982), 167.

◀ Lewis Carroll at age twenty-three. Photograph, presumed self-portrait, published in Stuart Dodgson Collingwood (Carroll's nephew), *The Life and Letters of Lewis Carroll (Rev. C. L. Dodgson)*. (London: Unwin, 1898).

The problem was that *Sylvie and Bruno* was very little like the *Alices*. "On one issue," noted one of Carroll's biographers, "he was firmly resolved: that the project should be completely different from the Alice books."[3] Another biographer adds, "*Sylvie and Bruno* bears the same relation to Lewis Carroll's earlier works, *mutatis mutandis*, as *Finnegan's Wake* [sic] to the more intelligible earlier productions of James Joyce"[4] — an assessment echoed by James Atherton, a leading authority on the *Wake*:

> In the Preface to *Sylvie and Bruno* Lewis Carroll remarks that "Perhaps the hardest thing in all literature . . . is to write anything original." But Carroll was so determined to be original that he spent twenty years making sure that the book which he intended to be his masterpiece was unlike anything else ever written. James Joyce worked for seventeen years on *Finnegans Wake*, a book quite as original as *Sylvie and Bruno*; indeed one which will probably remain for ever the standard example of the danger of being too original. Yet many of the wildest and most startling features of *Finnegans Wake* are merely the logical development, or the working out on a larger scale, of ideas that first occurred to Lewis Carroll.[5]

That Carroll attempted something completely new in *Sylvie and Bruno* is not surprising, for he was by nature an inventor. This, of course, is the quality that Joyce, another determined literary inventor, perceived in *Sylvie and Bruno* (significantly, it was the work of Carroll's that Joyce read most attentively),[6] at a time when most oth-

---

3 Anne Clark, *Lewis Carroll: A Biography* (New York: Schocken, 1979), 246.
4 Hudson, 231.
5 James S. Atherton, "Lewis Carroll: The Unforeseen Precursor," in his *The Books at the Wake: A Study of Literary Allusions in James Joyce's* Finnegans Wake (Carbondale: Southern Illinois University Press, 1959, 1974), 124.
6 Atherton, 135.

ers could see only that it was, disappointingly, not another *Alice*. (Another writer intrigued by the books was Evelyn Waugh; in a discussion of them, he called Carroll "one of the great imaginative writers of the language."[7]) As Jean Gattégno remarked, Carroll was "first and foremost, a real inventor, for whom the joy of discovery is one of the greatest delights life has to offer. . . . A joy of discovery, of invention; this is an element we must be very careful never to forget in any effort to capture the personality of Lewis Carroll."[8]

In *Sylvie and Bruno*, Carroll's love of invention is expressed in many ways. "He really thought that absolutely everything could be improved upon, and was prepared to consider any solution that was not a physical impossibility: thus the fantasies devised in the Sylvie and Bruno books are not to be dismissed as sheer nonsense — nor have they always been, as witness the 'black light' described in the Professor's lecture."[9]

But it is in the literary art of the novel that Carroll is most profoundly innovative in *Sylvie and Bruno*.

A VICTORIAN NOVEL

In 1865, Carroll turned Victorian children's literature on its head in *Alice's Adventures in Wonderland*. There had been nothing like the *Alice*s in English children's literature — popular books of the time were didactic stories such as the Newberry Press's *Goody Two-Shoes* and Maria Edgeworth's *Frank* and *Rosamond*. "English books written for children were supposed to be realistic in order to provide essential instruction in religion and/or morality, that the child might become a virtuous, reasonable adult."[10] But in the *Alice*s,

---

7   Kathleen Blake, *Play, Games, and Sport: The Literary Works of Lewis Carroll* (Ithaca, NY: Cornell University Press, 1974), 150.
8   Quoted in Clark, 255.
9   Jean Gattégno, *Fragments of a Looking-Glass,* tr. Rosemary Sheed (New York: Thomas Y. Crowell, 1976), 106.
10 Elsie Leach, "Alice in Wonderland in Perspective," in Robert Phillips, ed., *Aspects of Alice: Lewis Carroll's Dreamchild as Seen through the Critics' Looking-Glasses, 1865–1971* (New York:

Carroll lays bare the lack of reason in the adult world. In "You Are Old, Father William" (recited by Alice to the caterpillar, who pronounces it "wrong from beginning to end"), Carroll parodied Robert Southey's didactic poem, "The Old Man's Comforts and How He Gained Them." Carroll's version begins:

> "You are old, father William," the young man said,
> "And your hair has become very white;
> And yet you incessantly stand on your head —
> Do you think, at your age, it is right?"

So Carroll somersaulted his way into literature, turning literary convention upside down.

The moralizing authority figure is mocked in his portrayal of the Duchess, who argues that "everything's got a moral, if you can only find it" and to illustrate her point offers Alice this bewildering homily:

> And the moral of that is—"Be what you would seem to be"—or, if you'd like it put more simply—"Never imagine yourself not to be otherwise than what it might appear to others that what you were or might have been was not otherwise than what you had been would have appeared to them to be otherwise."

Alice, unlike earlier Victorian child protagonists, is critical, defiant, and self-assertive. She is the only one to stand up to the arbitrary and domineering Queen. "The underlying message of Alice, then, is a rejection of adult authority, a vindication of the rights of the child."[11] This, not its nonsense, is the truly subversive element in the *Alices*.

Nearly a quarter century later, in the two volumes of *Sylvie and Bruno* (*Sylvie and Bruno* was first published in 1889, *Sylvie and Bruno Concluded* in 1893), Carroll launched an attack on

---

Vintage, 1977), 89.
11 Ibid., 92.

the Victorian novel that was perhaps even more subversive. Gathering together diverse materials to include in them, Carroll called the result "litterature," and he challenged the reader to identify the "padding" in the stories. "Victorian novels," as Gattégno observes, "would never dream of describing themselves in this ironic and even sacrilegious way."[12] Nor would most Victorian writers dare to begin as Carroll does, in midsentence: " — and then all the people cheered again" (a device Joyce picked up for the opening of *Finnegans Wake*). Carroll introduces self-reflexive mannerisms that anticipate Joyce, Queneau, Beckett, and the whole line of artifice-oriented modern writing. For example, when the narrator first encounters Lady Muriel, he reflects: "And this, of course, is the opening scene of Vol. I. She is the Heroine. And I am one of those subordinate characters that only turn up when needed for the development of her destiny."

But the most radical element of the novel is its simultaneous, separate, yet mysteriously corresponding plots, which take place in separate planes of reality that shift with dizzying abruptness, as Anne Clark explains:

> Dodgson hinges his story on an intricately worked-out series of hypotheses. First, that besides the world in which we live there exist two others: its counterpart, called Outland, whose society is a kind of burlesque of the real world, and Fairyland as we all understand it. Second, that human beings, unseen and in a state of trance, may observe people and events in Outland, and that in another state, which Dodgson describes as "eerie," they may participate in adventures in Fairyland, without losing consciousness of events in the real world. Thirdly, time may reverse or stand still, and fairies may assume human form. The links between Outland and the real world are the narrator, who passes back and forth between the two, and Sylvie and Bruno, alternately appearing in fairy form or as human children.[13]

---

12   Jean Gattégno, "Sylvie and Bruno," 168.
13   Clark, 246.

The main story lines of the novels concern an attempt by the warden of Outland to usurp the birthright of the fairy children Sylvie and Bruno, and the rivalry of Captain Eric Linden and Dr. Arthur Forester for Lady Muriel Orme, in the English town of Elveston. The first plot has the form of a folktale, the second the form of a romance, but Carroll quickly undermines ordinary expectations of these genres. Characters on one level suddenly transform into equivalent, yet distinct, characters on another level: indeed, the very nature of character is challenged, as Carroll explores the borderline between dreaming and waking, probing the limits of language and logic.

TOWARD MODERNISM

By challenging conventional concepts of reality and character, *Sylvie and Bruno* played an important role in releasing the novel from Victorian notions of realism and preparing the way for the groundbreaking work of early twentieth-century writers such as Joyce, Kafka, Bulgakov, Pirandello, and Breton.

"Is all our Life, then, but a dream . . . ?" asks the first line of Carroll's dedicatory poem, and he continually undermines our expectations of novelistic reality. It was easy enough, in *Alice's Adventures in Wonderland,* to explain that it was all a dream, that the Queen was only a playing card after all, as Alice wakes to find her sister and Dinah just as she had left them. "But *Sylvie and Bruno* is contrived to make it much more difficult for the reader to maintain this sort of psychical distance from the material. He drifts in and out of Fairyland with the Narrator. Thus he is gradually taught to understand that the limits of reality are blurred, that it is not so easy to say that this is the world of reality while that is the world of nonsense and fantasy."[14] In *Sylvie and Bruno* dreams are merely the "other side" of reality, and the two are inextricably joined, leading in and out of

---

14 Edmund Miller, "The Sylvie and Bruno Books as Victorian Novel," in Edward Guiliano, ed., *Lewis Carroll Observed: A Collection of Unpublished Photographs, Drawings, Poetry, and New Essays* (New York: Clarkson N. Potter, 1976), 135–136.

each other like a Mobius strip. "Carroll's aim," as Gattégno puts it, "is to bring dreaming to the very heart of reality seen as an object of study and experimentation."[15]

Carroll's view of character had always run counter to conventional Victorian notions. In the *Alice* books, character had been reduced to two-dimensions: playing cards, disembodied smiles (though Alice herself is elastic, to say the least). Here character becomes fluid, as one person dissolves into another in a series of kaleidoscopic correspondences. Like a modernist novelist, Carroll shows us "the seams in his piece of work, ignoring the so-called motivation of the realistic novel, choosing instead to transform what others call psychological depths into a contact between two surfaces."[16]

NONSENSE AND MORALISM

Lewis Carroll is synonymous with nonsense, and the *Sylvie and Bruno* books contain some fine examples of this most demanding literary form: the Outlandish watch that makes time run backward; Mein Herr's two-party system of life, in which people are divided into teams, one of which tries to do work and the other to prevent it; the mad professor's manic inventions.

Carroll's play with language is similar to his play with story, in that it also often depends on various kinds of doubling. For example, he often uses punning to "move the discourse to another place, interrupting the purpose at hand by introducing a universe that 'does not count,' that does not go or get anywhere. This is the universe of the *Alice* conversations and of most of *Sylvie and Bruno*. Conversations are continually halted by puns, by a splitting of the discourse into two simultaneous and disparate paths, each followed by a respective member of the conversation."[17]

---

15 Gattégno, "Sylvie and Bruno," 169.
16 Gattégno, "Sylvie and Bruno, or the Inside and the Outside," 172.
17 Susan Stewart, *Nonsense: Aspects of Intertextuality in Folklore and Literature* (Baltimore: Johns Hopkins, 1979), 161.

The novels contain some of the best examples of Carroll's non-sense poetry, including "The Mad Gardener's Song," which operates as a refrain throughout the work and announces Carroll's themes of reality and perception:

> He thought he saw an Elephant
> That practiced on a fife:
> He looked again, and found it was
> A letter from his wife.
> "At length I realize," he said,
> "The bitterness of life!"

Or "The Pig-Tale," which offers this caution to the reader (and recalls one of Carroll's lectures in his alter ego of Charles Dodgson, entitled "Feeding the Mind," which asked the question, "I wonder if there is such a thing in nature as a FAT MIND? I really think I have met with one or two: minds which could not keep up with the slowest trot in conversation; could not jump over a logical fence to save their lives; always got stuck fast in a narrow argument; and, in short, were fit for nothing but to waddle helplessly through the world"[18]):

> Little birds are writing
>   Interesting books,
>   To be read by cooks:
> Read, I say, not roasted —
>   Letterpress, when toasted,
>   Loses its good looks.

Carroll's intention, as he saw the end of his life approaching, was to mix nonsense with "some of the graver thoughts of human life." Consequently, the novels contain more philosophizing than other of Carroll's work, and this, together with its sentimentality, especially Bruno's almost unbearably cloying baby-talk, is the most off-putting

---

18   See Blake, 22ff.

element of the books. Many critics, such as John Francis McDermott, subscribe to the notion that Carroll was a split personality. They attribute "the good parts" of *Sylvie and Bruno* to Carroll and "the bad parts" to the dull don, Dodgson. But it is worth recalling that other Victorian classics such as *The Secret Garden* and *At the Back of the North Wind,* and even much of Dickens, are, to various degrees, also marred by a penchant for sentimentalizing. "One has only to compare *Sylvie and Bruno* with any one of the novels of George Eliot (who did not consider herself a Christian at all) to see how pervasive was the religious sense of the time."[19]

Carroll's message is socially oriented, a philosophy of charity and universal love: "Sylvie will love all." Arthur sacrifices himself to the sick during an epidemic as an act of charity; Sylvie and Bruno care for others, Uggug only for himself. Carroll's view of sin is also socially focused, and, because it takes environment into account, surprisingly modern: a desperate criminal's major crime may be a lesser sin than an apparently minor failing in one who is advantaged (from which Arthur takes heart: "millions whom I had thought of as sunk in hopeless depths of sin were perhaps, in God's sight, scarcely sinning at all"). Similarly, Carroll opposes the ritualization of religion. It is the spirit of religion that is foremost for him. Indeed, his philosophy of universal love amounts to an homage to vitalism, to the spirit that propels life, to that same energy that enlivens his own unequaled nonsense. So it is here that, in the end, his nonsense and his Victorian philosophizing meet. As Gattégno writes: "Sylvie and Bruno's song about 'love' is really a hymn to the universal power of sexuality, as the source of everything that exists:"[20]

> For I think it is Love,
> For I feel it is Love,
> For I'm sure it is nothing but Love!

---

19 Gattégno, *Fragments of a Looking-Glass,* 235.
20 Gattégno, *Fragments of a Looking-Glass,* 186.

A Horace Reading

~~~

MOUSEBENDER: I was sitting in the public library in Thurmond Street just now, skimming through *Rogue Herries* by Horace Walpole, when suddenly I came over all peckish.
WENSLEYDALE: Peckish, sir?
MOUSEBENDER: Esurient.
WENSLEYDALE: Eh?
MOUSEBENDER: Eee, I were all 'ungry, like!
WENSLEYDALE: Oh, hungry.
MOUSEBENDER: In a nutshell. So I thought to myself "a little fermented curd will do the trick." So I curtailed my Walpolling activities, sallied forth and infiltrated your place of purveyance to negotiate the vending of some cheesy comestibles.
WENSLEYDALE: Come again?
MOUSEBENDER: I want to buy some cheese!
  — "Monty Python's Flying Circus"

Not a tribute to Horace Walpole exactly. Yet the eighteenth-century earl would probably not have felt out of place in this sketch, for the Pythons continue a peculiar strain of British tradition distinguished by absurdity, ridicule, wordplay, wit, wickedness, and plain madness (not to mention cheesiness) that unquestionably reached one of its peaks in these extraordinary (and little known, even in England) *Hieroglyphic Tales.*

In a word: fermented curd. (Okay, two words.) Herewith a few field notes for going Walpolling:

He was about as odd as you would expect.

He lived (comfortably, thanks to a variety of sinecures — his father, Robert, had been prime minister of England under King George I) in a house on the banks of the Thames near Twickenham;

◀ The gallery at Strawberry Hill (Horace Walpole's estate; detail), 1784, by Edward Edwards. Ink and watercolor.

he called the house Strawberry Hill and made it into "a little Gothic castle" decked out with fake pinnacles, battlements, ornamental facades, and gargoyles of lath and plaster and crammed to overflowing with all manner of antiquities, curiosities, and objets d'art. Toward the end of his life and for some time thereafter (at least until a famous auction of its contents in 1842), Strawberry Hill was a tourist attraction. According to his memorandum book, Walpole personally ushered some four thousand visitors through it (complaining all the while of the inconvenience). Often criticized as a cheap, slipshod sham, it has also been lauded as a "subjunctive" edifice, an "architecture of the 'as if,'"[1] and as a creation that overturns conventional "rigid and stately rules of architecture."[2]

Besides being an extremely prolific writer ("When will it end?" wrote a reviewer in 1851 of Walpole's posthumous letters, well before they had attained their present mass of forty-eight volumes), he was a publisher (depending on your point of view, his publishing was "simple and restrained"[3] or characterized by "rather indifferent printing;"[4] in any case, his Strawberry Hill Press is hailed as the first major privately held printing press in England). Yet Horace Walpole, publisher, had a peculiar attitude to being published:

> In August 1796, six months before his death, Horace Walpole wrote a memorandum requesting his executors to "cord up strongly and seal" a large chest containing his memoirs, a

---

1   Diane S. Ames, "Strawberry Hill: Architecture of the 'as if,'" in *Studies in Eighteenth-Century Culture* 8, ed. Roseann Runte (Madison: University of Wisconsin Press, 1979) cited in Peter Sabor, *Horace Walpole: A Reference Guide* (Boston: G. K. Hall & Co., 1984), 230.

2   "Strawberry Hill," *Builder* 41 (August 13, 1881), cited in Sabor, 76.

3   Douglas McMurtrie, *The Book: The Story of Printing and Bookmaking* (London: Oxford University Press, 1943), 464.

4   Daniel Berkeley Updike, *Printing Types: Their History, Forms, and Use*, vol. 2 (1937; reprint, New York: Dover Publications, 1980), 140.

vast, unpublished manuscript of some three million words. The box was to be opened only by the "first son of Lady Waldegrave who shall attain the age of twenty-five years," the key to be guarded by Lady Waldegrave herself. This oblique form of publication — a key to a box containing manuscripts in search of an editor — is emblematic of Walpole's authorial career. His most famous work, *The Castle of Otranto*, was first published spuriously as a translation from the Italian of "Onuphrio Muralto." His other principal imaginative writings, *The Mysterious Mother* and *Hieroglyphic Tales*, were issued only to a few close friends in private editions at Strawberry Hill. Walpole arranged for his collected works to be published only after his death; his collected correspondence has taken until 1983 to reach complete publication in the forty-eight volumes of the Yale Edition; while the memoirs, duly recovered from the sealed chest, were mangled by incompetent nineteenth-century editors and have not yet been published in full.[5]

He had a diabolical (and at times rather infantile) sense of humor, demonstrated in his passing off *The Castle of Otranto* as a translation from the Italian and in the evil comedy of one of the *Hieroglyphic Tales*, "The Peach in Brandy." He once faked a letter to Jean-Jacques Rousseau that purported to be from the King of Prussia, precipitating a heated public dispute in which Rousseau, Jacob Grimm, and others participated.

He is supposed to have composed "The Peach in Brandy," in which an archbishop accidentally swallows a human fetus, for a young girl of his acquaintance: "The preference exhibited by Walpole in his old age for the society of ladies had its corollary in his life-long preference for little girls over little boys," Dorothy Stuart assures us. "He was always a courteous knight to virgins of five; and for the delectation of one of them, Lady Anne Fitzpatrick, he

---

5   Sabor, 1.

wrote in 1771 the fable of the Peach in Brandy. This fable formed one of a series of five *Hieroglyphic Tales*. . . . The whimsicality of these tales," she adds uncertainly, "is such that the intended parable or satire sometimes becomes a little difficult of detection."[6] It is indeed hard to imagine the effect of this story on its original intended audience.

We may wonder too about the reaction of Lord Ossory, to whom Walpole sent a copy of the story on the occasion of Lady Ossory's miscarriage of twin sons.

In this context Kenneth Gross notes that "Walpole's tales start to take on the qualities of a nightmare."[7]

Besides *The Castle of Otranto,* the other major literary work Walpole published during his lifetime was his tragedy in blank (at first I inadvertently wrote "black") verse, *The Mysterious Mother*. Byron admired it, calling it "a tragedy of the highest order, and not a puling love-play." It concerns a young man who, through a series of mistaken identities and unfortunate misunderstandings (no fault of his own), ends up marrying the daughter he has fathered by his mother (a bewildering set of relationships outdoing Bill Wyman). Dorothy Stuart, always charmingly sympathetic to Walpole, remarks, "It is, indeed, a little curious that his imagination — though in *The Castle of Otranto* he had toyed with the theme of incest — should have been allured by a story so sombre and so revolting."[8] In a contemporaneous review (1797), William Taylor rhapsodized that the play "has attained an excellence nearly unimpeachable" and that it "may fitly be compared with the *Oedipus Tyrannus* of Sophocles." Not many modern readers would value it quite so highly.

Walpole was blamed by his contemporaries for the suicide of the poet Thomas Chatterton, who wrote a bitter poem addressed

---

6   Dorothy Margaret Stuart, *Horace Walpole* (New York: Macmillan, 1927), 191.

7   Kenneth W. Gross, in Horace Walpole, *Hieroglyphic Tales,* (Los Angeles: University of California Augustan Reprint Society, 1982), x.

8   Stuart, 181.

to Walpole before perishing in romantic despair (he drank arsenic). Walpole had concluded that the claims of the youth (Chatterton was sixteen when he wrote to him) to have discovered a collection of medieval poems by a certain "Rowley" were fraudulent. Ironically, this was, as Chatterton insinuates in a poem, just the sort of deceit one might have expected from Walpole himself.

> Walpole! I thought not I should ever see
> So mean a Heart as thine has proved to be:
> Thou, who in Luxury nursd behold'st with Scorn
> The boy, who Friendless, Penniless, Forlorn,
> Asks thy high Favour, — thou mayst call me Cheat —
> Say, didst thou ne'er indulge in such Deceit?
> Who wrote *Otranto*? But I will not chide,
> Scorn I will repay with Scorn, and Pride with Pride.
> Still, Walpole, still, thy Prosy Chapters write,
> And twaddling letters to some Fair indite,
> Laud all above thee, — Fawn and Cringe to those
> Who, for thy Fame, were better Friends than Foes
> Still spurn the incautious Fool who dares —
>
> Had I the Gifts of Wealth and Lux'ry shard
> Not poor and Mean — Walpole! thou hadst not dared
> Thus to insult, But I shall live and Stand
> By Rowley's side — when Thou art dead and damned.

The Castle of Otranto is the work by which most people know Walpole (it has been published in more than a hundred and fifty editions), because of its historical significance as the first Gothic novel. It is hard now to appreciate how innovative a book this was, since countless other works have been patterned after it. Walter Scott admired the book, praising its "Pure and correct English" as well as its status as "the first modern attempt to found a tale of amusing fiction upon the basis of the ancient romances of chivalry." In contrast, the writer of Walpole's obituary in *Gentlemen's Magazine* (1797), though finding much to praise in Walpole's writings, flatly dismissed

The Castle of Otranto as "miserable trash." The book had its genesis in a dream in which Walpole found himself in an ancient castle, facing an enormous hand encased in armor. The novel is filled with ghosts, giants, mysterious appearances, and violent emotions. "I gave rein to my imagination," Walpole said. "Visions and passions choked me." In this classic work Walpole began to develop his taste for the Gothic and the grotesque and, more fundamentally, to tap the turbulent world of his unconscious in a manner shocking for his time, to take us closer to the terrifying psychological substrata that have become a major literary subject in our own century. Nonetheless, *The Castle* remains a rather mechanical and distanced work. It was not until the hieroglyphic tales that Walpole began to discover a more radical way of writing that anticipated a direction taken in modern fiction.

Walpole wrote in his postscript to the *Hieroglyphic Tales* that the tales were an attempt "to vary the stale and beaten class of stories and novels, which, though works of invention, are almost always devoid of imagination. It would scarcely be credited, were it not evident from the Bibliotheque des Romans, which contains the fictitious adventures that have been written in all ages and all countries, that there should have been so little fancy, so little variety, and so little novelty, in writings in which the imagination is fettered by no rules, and by no obligation of speaking truth. There is infinitely more invention in history, which has no merit if devoid of truth, than in romances and novels, which pretend to none."

This is an attitude with which many editors and publishers will sympathize, for we know that fiction manuscripts are distinguished more than anything else by their striking similarity to one another. How hard it is to be truly imaginative! In the *Hieroglyphic Tales* Walpole worked out a number of ways of breaking from the mold:

First, he structured his stories on a firm "fairy tale" foundation. Kenneth Gross calls the tales representatives of a tradition of "oriental fables" that also found expression in such works of the period as Voltaire's *Zadig*, Crébillon's *Le Sopha*, and Johnson's *Rasselas*. "Judged for themselves, however," he adds, "the tales are a small miracle. The best of them distill from the Bible, the *Arabian Nights*,

Shakespeare, French romances, English politics, and antiquarian lore a comic fantasy of an urbane, hard-edged strangeness such as it is hard to find anywhere else...."[9]

The familiarity of this form enabled Walpole to make bold innovations in other aspects of his narrative. "Music rots when it gets too far from the dance," Ezra Pound admonished in *ABC of Reading*, and "poetry atrophies when it gets too far from music." By the same token, narrative fiction atrophies when it gets too far from the foundations of storytelling: myths and folktales. Walpole was wise to graft his grotesque elaborations on a sturdy folktale rootstock.

(We might add that typography atrophies when it gets too far from handwriting. Walpole set his first edition of the *Hieroglyphic Tales* in a typeface designed by and named for the eighteenth-century English typographer William Caslon. It was the last major example of the Old Style typefaces derived from the Renaissance scribal tradition until the appearance of twentieth-century revivals.)

Among the most innovative of Walpole's narrative effects was his radical subversion of the representational fallacy. He strewed impossibilities through the stories (*contes absurdes et hors de toute vraisemblance,* as the epigraph has it), leaving the reader to puzzle over the ability of narrative and of language itself to confound our understanding of the relation between language, storytelling, and reality. The tales are opaque, calling as much attention to the telling as to the stories themselves. They were written, he tells us in the preface, compounding impossibilities one upon another, "a little before the creation of the world, and have ever since been preserved, by oral tradition, in the mountains of Crampcraggiri, an uninhabited island, not yet discovered." He peopled the stories with dead suitors, daughters who were never born (or, being born, are proven not to exist), and such fancies as goats' eggs sought as a cure for freckles.

In addition, Walpole disrupted the narrative continuity of his stories with detours, denials, false starts, solipsisms, and asides. In

---

9   Gross, iii.

Dance Macabre

THE BALLETS OF CÉLINE

~~~

Céline's fascination with dance spans his career: his first ballet, "The Birth of a Fairy," was written a few years after he published his astonishing first novel, *Voyage au bout de la nuit*, which he dedicated to the dancer Elizabeth Craig; and at the time of his death he was, according to his wife, Lucette — also a dancer — planning a book devoted to dance. Céline did love dancers ("That's all I love, really," he wrote dancer Karen Marie Jensen. "Everything else I find horrible") and he loved dance ("A man who doesn't dance confesses some disgraceful weakness," he wrote Milton Hindus. "I put dancing into everything").

In 1936, after finishing his monumental second novel, *Mort à crédit*, Céline visited Russia, where he hoped to have some of his ballets performed at the Theater Mariinski in Leningrad. How much foundation he had for this hope is unclear, and to my knowledge none of his ballets has been performed. On his return from Russia (in the highly politicized ambience of the late thirties), Céline turned to pamphleteering, not publishing his third novel, *Guignol's Band*, until 1944. His hysterical wartime diatribe, *Bagatelles pour un massacre*, however, begins and ends with a ballet, so that the ballet could be said to represent his major published literary activity in this period. The ballets remained largely overlooked in the unpleasant context of Céline's offensive anti-semitic outpourings, although he returned to the form sporadically. (He continued to cherish hope of having his ballets performed. He thought that "Wicked Paul. Brave Virginie" might be performed at the 1937 Exposition Universelle in Paris. Around the same time, he lobbied to obtain a British performance of "The Birth of a Fairy." In 1945 he tried to get "Slings and Arrows" performed by the Copenhagen Opera.)

◀ Louis-Ferdinand Céline in 1932, Prix Renaudot press photo. *Bibliothèque Nationale de France.*

In 1959, when Céline was sixty-five years old, five ballets were collected in an edition of 5,500 copies published by Gallimard and nicely illustrated with line drawings by Éliane Bonabel. Bonabel was the daughter of an old friend. Her kind visit to Céline when he was imprisoned in Denmark (the "tiresomeness" that interrupted his work on "Slings and Arrows") had cheered him in that dark time: "Éliane's arrival is really something miraculous!" he wrote his wife. "The whole past flooding back in a whirlwind. I see myself as a young doctor in Clichy, she was five years old! And now she sees us again under such conditions!" The book was entitled *Ballets sans musique, sans personne, sans rien* — Ballets without Music, without Dancers, without Anything.

Dancing is a prominent element in Céline's fiction, figuring especially in *L'Église*, *Feérie pour une autre fois*, *Guignol's band*, and *Nord*. For Céline, dance serves three principal functions: it helps to ground his rhythmical prose in a firm musical mode; it offers a model for managing crowds and choreographing complicated, frenzied scenes of apocalypse and delirium; and it provides an example of ideal beauty that is a thematic counterpart to his obsessions with evil, deterioration, death, and the grotesque.

Céline's fiction, written in the first person (unlike the ballets), is intensely emotional and personal (in *Entretiens avec le professeur Y*, Céline said that he sought a stylistic means of achieving an "emotive subway" — the most direct conveying of emotion possible). "I am not a man of messages," Céline once claimed. "I am not a man of ideas, I am a man of style." One of his techniques for achieving his goal of direct emotion was the use of a comic rhythm that became increasingly intrinsic to his prose. He once gave a friend a copy of *Voyage* with the admonition, "It's all dance and music — always at the edge of death, don't fall into it." His elliptical style was suited to his writing for this reason, and in his later works he employed it more and more as a device to control phrasing and timing, breaking down his sentences into smaller

Illustration by Éliane Bonabel for *Ballets sans musique, sans personne, sans rien. Copyright © Éditions Gallimard.*

and smaller units. In a preface to *Guignol's band*, he defends his technique on musical grounds: "Three dots! . . . ten! twelve dots! help! Nothing at all if that's what's needed! That's how I am. Jazz replaced the waltz . . ." (Céline also uses the exclamation mark as a rhythmic device.) Here, on the level of the phrase, one senses the phantom presence of a Célinean ballet master, pounding out rhythms by beating on the floor with his cane, whipping the authorial voice to a furious climax.

Despite the personal quality of his writing, Céline very often takes the long view. He is to a large extent a wartime writer. He was hailed as a hero in the first world war (which figures prominently in his first book) and assailed as a villain — a scapegoat, he said — in the second (which figures prominently in his last books). Partly for this reason, Céline often describes scenes with great masses of characters. Dance suggested a way that such large groups could be choreographed and managed. Repetition and acceleration are his main devices. Typically, waves of "dancers" enter from various directions and goad each other to a kind of frenzy that culminates in a black comic apocalypse of almost sexual release. Such apocalyptic scenes can be viewed as the fulcrums around which the novels are balanced. In many of them, a destructive, satanic figure — a Grand Guignol, a diabolic ballet master — directs the action, whipping it into *délire,* frenzied excess, and finally destruction. Céline's dance is a dance of action and abandon — critics have described it as Dionysian (Céline approvingly quoted Nietzsche's assertion that he could only believe in a god who dances).

Céline lived through a time of madness and horror. All the rest of his life he was troubled by a ringing in his ears that was the result of a wound suffered in battle, which came to seem an internal airraid siren heralding the apocalypse. As a recruit in the first world war, as a doctor who worked among the poor, as a refugee in the second war and a prisoner afterward, Céline witnessed degradation, depravity, despair, decay, destruction. Against this overwhelming demonstration of sorrow and evil, he was only able to oppose a pallid, played-out romantic vision left over from a more vigorous Europe of a past, a vision that could hardly help seeming remote and unobtainable. Céline, says Frédéric Vitoux, "is a man of the past, i.e., despairing, like all nostalgics." Small wonder that this aspect of his work is overshadowed by his darker vision.

This kind of conflict grips Bardamu in *Voyage au bout de la nuit;* in *Mort à crédit,* the Krogold legend makes it explicit. The narrator of that book, Ferdinand, has written a work called *The Legend of*

Illustration by Éliane Bonabel for *Ballets sans musique, sans personne, sans rien.* Copyright © *Éditions Gallimard.*

Krogold: "an epic, sad to be sure, but noble . . . resplendent." This work is quite similar to aspects of the ballets in style, theme, plot, and setting. Ferdinand, a broken-down doctor, finds the beauty of the story a relief and respite from the foul and dirty world he actually inhabits. It is the story of Gwendor the Magnificent, Prince of Christiania, who betrays King Krogold and is killed in battle. As he expires on the battlefield, he converses with Death, who tells him, "There is no softness or gentleness in this world, Gwendor, but only myth! All kingdoms end in a dream…" (Against the dream of Krogold Céline's works give us the nightmare of an expiring Europe.) Ferdinand reads his *Legend* to a colleague — who promptly falls asleep. No one is interested in his legend: "The only one who cared was myself." Everyone turns away from beauty. Beauty is no longer possible in this world — it belongs to the world of myth. The world of the ballets.

"If the world were not so evil, if the author had been left the possibility of living the life he wanted, Céline would have sung touching airs of long-ago times, told beautiful stories of fairies and of King Krogold," says Maurice Nadeau. "He dreamed of transporting ballets in the moonlight, rustic phantasmagorias. More than novels, many of his books . . . are poems: they transform an unbearable reality into a kind of thick black dream." When the evil puppet master, the Grand Guignol, drives his characters into a destructive frenzy, the wispy grace of the dancers is hardly equal to the task of holding the spirit of destruction in check. In Céline's vision, beauty is ephemeral and elusive, and it rarely triumphs for long — the lovely dancers he dreams of represent a beauty that is unobtainable in a world that is irredeemably impure and destestable.

The five works in *Ballets sans musique, sans personne, sans rien* are explicitly ballets, but some are more formally balletic than others: the early ballets, such as "The Death of a Fairy" and "Wicked Paul. Brave Virginie," contain a fair amount of stage direction. By the time of "Slings and Arrows" and "Scandal in the Deep," Céline was writing something closer to fiction — not his usual fiction but something more like the romance of Krogold — and in fact "Scandal in the Deep" barely acknowledges its supposed ballet form, and it includes many passages that would pose real difficulties for staging. The longer, later works also have more involved and developed plots and a greater variety of settings and situations.

While ballet rehearsal scenes appear in "The Birth of a Fairy" and "Slings and Arrows," more common are dance hall interiors, street and dock scenes, even folk and ritual dance. In his youth, Céline was a habitué of dance halls and burlesque shows, and their influence can be sensed, especially in his decor and costumery. And surface elements such as these often seem his primary interest. In "Scandal," his description of the undersea kingdom of Neptune, for example, reads as a last gasp of the old European tradition of the court masque. Where once the masque represented what Russian critic Mikhail Bakhtin called a "dialogic open form," in which conventions and expectations were routinely undone and overthrown, in Céline's ballets the grotesque and the burlesque, though amply present, cannot overpower the picturesque and sentimental. Much as Harlequin's crude antics and coarse motley eventually gave way in the commedia dell'arte to stagey acrobatics and a merely decorative pattern of diamonds, so in Céline's ballets such traditional carnivalesque figures as the lord of misrule, the clown, the fool, the ogre, the juggler, the pedant, the parasite, lose much of their raw vitality and become elements in a largely decorative display. The use of the third person and an offstage vantage point further distance the work. Even as dark a piece as "Wicked Paul. Brave Virginie" — which satirizes and parodies the popular eighteenth-century Rousseauian novel *Paul and Virginie*, in which the shipwrecked couple find nobility among the native people of Maritius in contrast to a loss of innocence in civilized society — cannot achieve the emotional force of the novels.

If Céline's fiction chronicled what he regarded as the death of Europe, his ballets, though a positive counterbalance to his darker vision, also manifest a carnivalesque European tradition, but one that has declined and atrophied. Yet they remain unique, original, and revealing works from one of the twentieth century's most innovative writers.

Harmony of the Spheres

THE PASSION OF JOHANNES KEPLER

～～～

On January 1, 1616, the astronomer Johannes Kepler wrote a letter to the Senate of Leonberg, a town near the city of Stuttgart in southwest Germany, on behalf of his mother, Katharina, who stood accused of practicing witchcraft. Kepler was an exceptionally learned man, an inspired mathematician who worked out the laws of planetary motion that would lead Newton to formulate the principle of gravity; but his mother, like many women of the time, was illiterate. Now in her seventies, she was an herbalist, like her aunt, who had already been burned at the stake as a witch. While Kepler embodied the worldview of the male literati, whose ideas of the world were codified in written texts, his mother represented the old folk traditions, knowledge of which often resided in women, passed from mother to daughter. With the spread of literacy to a greater range of society, such folk knowledge became increasingly marginalized and demonized, and these women became popular targets of witch hunts. Witchcraft, not particularly gender biased during the medieval period, now became increasingly associated with women, and especially older women.

Kepler's mother's case was a typical one of petty village malice. Her accuser was another old woman, who had fallen ill after being given one of Katharina's herbal infusions. Kepler sought to discredit this woman's testimony and to use his influence at court to protect his mother. He wrote:

> There is a case before you concerning several people accused by the court, based purely on the fanciful rantings of your dear darling housewife and sister, Ursula Reinbold. Everyone knows that until this day, this woman has lived frivolously, and now, by your own account, she has become

◀ Witches' Sabbat, 1606, by Frans Francken II (1581–1642). Antwerp. Oil on oak panel. *Victoria and Albert Museum, London, bequeathed by Rev. Alexander Dyce*, Dyce.3.

mentally ill. Caught in the middle of this depressing web of suspicion, my own dear mother, who has lived honorably into her seventieth year, has been accused by you of giving this same crazy person some silly magic potion, which you say caused her insanity. . . .

I want you to know that I will seek the help of my friends and mentors, and that I will gain favors from well-known and respected persons I am acquainted with. I intend to contest this matter and bring to bear the full extent of my powers until it is finally remedied in accordance with the written laws. . . .

Kepler's family background and childhood situation gave little hint that he would one day acquire the kind of clout this letter implies. His father, Heinrich, was a mercenary soldier who was by all accounts a bitter and violent man; Kepler described him as "vicious, inflexible, quarrelsome, and doomed." When he was home he beat his wife and children, and he once tried to sell Johannes's brother — his namesake, Heinrich — into slavery. (The younger Heinrich was a teenager at the time, so maybe he had cause.) But he was usually off fighting some war, for whichever side offered the better price. When Kepler was a young child his mother left him in the care of his grandparents while she journeyed to the Netherlands — it cannot have been an easy trip for a woman presumably traveling alone. She was searching for her husband, who was fighting for the Duke of Alba of Catholic Spain. But ultimately she could not succeed in holding him within the circle of the family, and he drifted off to parts unknown, or perhaps was killed in battle; all contact with him was lost.

Born Katharina Guldenmann, Kepler's mother was the daughter of an innkeeper (her husband would also make a brief attempt at running a tavern in between his mercenary excursions). In a private document, at once narcissistic and self-excoriating as was typical of him, that Kepler wrote in his mid-twenties, he described himself and his family. His mother, he said, was "small, thin, swarthy, gossiping, and quarrelsome, of a bad disposition" (from this description she seems to have been the family member whom

Kepler himself most resembled, in appearance at least, and probably in personality). She had been raised by the aunt who would later be burned as a witch. In Kepler's birthplace, a town of some two hundred families, thirty-eight witches were burned between 1615 and 1629. In nearby Leonberg, where his mother now lived, six witches were executed in the year that she was accused.

Katharina was nearly among them. Her trial, which would drag on until 1621, six months before her death, was among the longest in the history of the witch hunts, which reached their peak between the 1580s and the 1630s — the span of Kepler's life. Only her son's influence — along with her own stubborn refusal to confess — seems to have saved her (most of the accused confessed under torture, but Kepler's success in preventing her from being tortured enabled her to hold firm).

Katharina and Ursula Reinbold, the wife of a glazier, had been companions, but they had a falling out. On one occasion, Ursula alleged, she had fallen ill after Katharina had given her a "potion." She blamed Katharina, though others whispered that her ailments were the result of a long-ago abortion, from the time when, it was said, she had worked as a prostitute. But the Reinbolds had connections with the local magistrate, and Ursula's charges against Katharina were soon acted upon. Then more witnesses came forward to testify that they too had fallen ill after accepting a drink from the old woman; that she had caused the deaths of their children merely by touching them; that she took wild midnight rides on neighbors' livestock; that cattle and pigs fell ill in her presence, or began to kick and tried to climb walls; that people merely passing her house would feel sudden sharp pains in their arms and legs; that she tried to seduce younger women to follow her devilish arts; that she questioned the idea of heaven, claiming that life terminated at death; that she had been known to pass through locked doors; that she attempted to make a drinking vessel out of her own father's skull (this one was true); and many other incriminating facts.

Kepler himself had inadvertently appeared to incriminate his mother through a story he had written called "The Dream" (Somnium). The story, sometimes called the first science fiction based on

Johannes Kepler, copy of an original oil painting, 1610.

something resembling modern science, imagined a trip to the moon. Kepler had drafted an early version during his student days at Tübingen University. He had not yet seen the work through to publication, but versions of it had circulated in manuscript. In the story a student is banished by his mother, a witch, to Denmark, where he studies with the Danish astronomer Tycho Brahe (for whom Kepler himself had been an assistant). On his return she reveals that she learned the arts of witchcraft from a demon who instructed her how to travel between the earth and the moon at times of a lunar eclipse. The story began as an attempt to imagine how the universe would look from another celestial body, but, under the circumstances, the portrayal of the Kepler-like protagonist's mother as a witch cut a little close to home.

In the early seventeenth century, before the heavens had been polluted by all the lights of modern technology, the stars and the planets were a more intimate part of daily life than they are today, when some people cannot even say what phase the moon is in — unthinkable ignorance by earlier standards. When Kepler was six, not long after his father abandoned the family for the final time, his mother led him to "a high place" to observe a famous astronomical phenomenon, the Great Comet of 1577; at age nine he was called outdoors to witness a lunar eclipse. These incidents suggest that his mother wanted to initiate him in the realm of heavenly mysteries; if so, the lesson took. Kepler, whom Carl Sagan called "the first astrophysicist and the last scientific astrologer," remained something of a mystic throughout his career. From his first major astronomical work, *The Cosmographic Mystery*, through the massive *Harmony of the World*, his writings chart an indefatigable, indeed almost a desperate, search for evidence of God's divine plan in the physical world, and especially in the heavens. "The diversity of the phenomena of nature is so great, and the treasures hidden in the heavens so rich," he wrote, "precisely in order that the human mind shall never be lacking in fresh nourishment." This quest to fathom the divine plan made him thirst for accurate astronomical data.

Today Kepler, despite his mystical leanings, has been claimed by science, and he occupies a prominent position in the pantheon of figures in the "scientific revolution" of the Renaissance and early modern period. His signal accomplishment, from the standpoint of science history, was his three laws of planetary motion: in brief, planets follow elliptical orbits around the sun, they move more rapidly when they are closer to the sun (technically, the radius vector of their orbits covers equal areas in equal times), and the square of their orbital periods is proportional to the cube of their mean distance from the sun. The first two laws appeared in *New Astronomy* in 1609, the third in *The Harmony of the World*, which was published in 1618. The discovery of these laws was doubly remarkable since Kepler did not have calculus as part of his mathematical arsenal (in fact, he didn't even have decimals) and had to derive his results by arduous trial and error, using traditional geometry.

He had achieved these results by working from data compiled by the Danish astronomer Tycho Brahe, whom he served as an assistant at Prague. Tycho had taken a position there as imperial astronomer to the eccentric Bohemian king Rudolf II, the Austrian Habsburg emperor. Rudolf had moved his court to Prague from Vienna in 583, and he had become a great supporter not only of science but of the arts as well; he was also deeply interested in the occult and the arcane. Some say Rudolf was mad, others that he was just deeply melancholic; certainly he was not as disturbed as his son Don Giulio Cesare, who dismembered his mistress and flung the parts out the windows of Frumlow Castle. Rudolf ruled what was called the Holy Roman Empire but which was really a loose confederation of cities, duchies, and principalities mainly located in modern Austria, Germany, and central Europe. (Control of the eastern Habsburg lands had gradually ceded to Rudolf's grandfather, Ferdinand I, from his brother Charles V of Spain in the first half of the sixteenth century, and the two branches had become effectively autonomous.) The political and religious strains of the early seventeenth century brought the two astronomers together. Tycho had been forced to abandon his home, where he had built the most elaborate astronomical observatory up to that time, located on the island of Hven in the Oresund strait between the Swedish region of Scania and Danish Zealand. (Historically a part of Denmark, the island has been part of Sweden since the second half of the seventeenth century.) The observatory, which Tycho called Uraniborg, doubled as a research institute, housing some hundred students, scholars, and workers. King Frederick II of Denmark (whose daughter Anne would marry James and become queen of England and Scotland) had been so pleased with Tycho's international fame that he had supported him with an amount equal to a full percent of the country's total wealth, but after Frederick's death in 1588, the situation changed dramatically. The new king, Christian IV, wanted to reduce the political power of the small but influential Danish aristocratic elite of which Tycho was a part; he seems also to have held some personal animus against Tycho. Tycho was forced to find a new location for his observations and a new patron; this turned out to be Rudolf of Bohemia.

At about the same time, Kepler too had to flee from his home. He had been living in Graz, in Eastern Austria, where he was employed as a teacher of mathematics at subsistence pay. (He was not an exceptional teacher. His mind tended to wander. In his first year a few students signed up for mathematics; in his second year not a single one took the course.) A crackdown on Protestants in the region forced him to look for a new situation, as he refused to renounce Lutheranism and convert to Catholicism. A similar stubbornness later in his life, when he rejected the concept of "ubiquity" — the idea that God's *body* is ubiquitous in the world and not just his spirit, as Kepler held — caused him to be excommunicated from the Lutheran Church. From the distance of the twenty-first century it can be difficult to understand how such distinctions could be so important as to expel a person who subscribed to all of the other official church doctrines from its community, or why it was so important to Kepler to maintain this position despite the serious consequences, but within a few years, in the Thirty Years War, a great many people would die for just such fine distinctions (ironically, the Lutheran Church itself would abandon the doctrine of ubiquity a few years later).

Kepler and Tycho had corresponded, and the result was Kepler's moving to Prague to serve as Tycho's assistant. The two were an odd couple. Tycho was aristocratic, rich, outgoing, and robust. He loved banquets and celebrations; Danes at this time had a reputation as the heaviest drinkers in Europe, and Tycho was no exception. (He had been raised by an uncle who had kidnapped him as a young boy from his parents; the uncle died of pneumonia after fishing the drunken King Frederick out of the icy Copenhagen waters into which he had toppled.) Kepler, on the other hand, could barely tolerate alcohol because of his perpetual poor health. Something of a tortured soul, he was solitary and inward-looking, and he shrank from social situations. Secretly believing himself the better astronomer, Kepler resented Tycho's wealth and popularity. He also coveted Tycho's data, which he needed to figure out why the planetary orbits refused to properly conform to his theories, but Tycho was not ready to share the information in more than a limited way. He had previously had his work stolen — a man calling himself Ursus ("Bear") had obtained some of his work and passed it off as his own; in fact, this is the man Tycho had now replaced as Rudolf's royal astronomer.

Brahe was a flamboyant figure, who combined his astronomical observations with alchemical experiments. Having lost part of his nose in a duel, he wore a prosthetic metal one. He is said to have kept a pet moose that died when it got drunk on beer and fell down the stairs. Among his household was a dwarf who was supposed to be clairvoyant: he would make portentous pronouncements from a position underneath the dining table during parties. Despite his personal eccentricities Tycho had compiled decades of data from his celestial observations that were far more meticulous and precise than anything previously available. His elevation of observation over speculation was one of the key developments leading to the modern concept of inductive scientific investigation. Kepler, though appreciative of the benefit of accurate data, was less capable of obtaining it directly. A bout of smallpox in childhood had left him frail and sickly, with a severe visual handicap: he was short-sighted and had double vision in one eye. Nor did he have the means to construct a large observatory like Tycho's Uraniborg. So he depended on Tycho for the data he needed to elaborate his theories of celestial harmony. How far would he go to obtain that data? In an odd echo of the case against his mother, Kepler was accused, nearly four hundred years after the fact, in a 2004 book by Joshua and Anne-Lee Gilder, of poisoning his mentor.

Traditionally, Tycho was said to have died of bladder failure after a banquet, because etiquette required him not to leave the table in the presence of royalty. Even today some Czechs who need to leave the table for a bathroom break may say "Excuse me, please. I don't want to end up like Tycho Brahe." This explanation never made much sense: Tycho was completely at ease with royalty and could have found some means of handling the situation. The Gilders' attempt to build a case against Kepler was based on then-recent forensic analysis of Tycho Brahe's hair that suggested he had ingested a potent dose of mercury shortly before his sudden, unexpected death in Prague in 1601. From this they deduce that he was murdered, and they go on to paint Kepler as a sociopath who would stop at nothing to obtain Tycho's data. With the case gone more than four hundred years cold, Kepler, like a number of others, cannot be ruled out as a suspect in the murder, if there was one. But the Gilders' case is speculative in the extreme. The mercury could have been administered as a form of euthanasia, or it could have been taken inadvertently. Mercury was used to treat various diseases, and an accidental overdose is a possibility championed by, among others, an archaeologist who exhumed Tycho's remains and a historian of science at Johns Hopkins University. The mercury could have been taken by Tycho himself or administered by his wife or any number of people other than Kepler.

A Danish scholar, Peter Andersen, has proposed that Tycho was killed by a visiting cousin in a plot concocted by Christian IV. (Contentious cousins bedeviled Tycho — it was another cousin who had removed the bridge of his nose in a duel. Four more of his cousins died in other duels, one killed by yet another cousin.) This particular cousin arrived in Prague from Denmark not long before the alleged murder, and Andersen says his diaries tend to implicate him. He also suggests that Christian resented Tycho for having had an affair with his mother, Queen Sophie. And, to add a bizarre Oedipal complication to the theory, he goes on to suggest that Christian could have been Tycho's son, and he has called for DNA testing of the king's remains to test this theory.

Finally, the conclusion reached by the forensic analysis was itself challenged by a professor of pharmacy and medicine at the University of Toronto. It appears he was right. In November 2010 Tycho's body was once again exhumed, and new tests were made; the results of those tests, according to separate teams of Danish and German scientists, indicated there was insufficient mercury to substantiate a charge of murder. Tycho "most likely," according to the Danish report, "died of a burst bladder."

Kepler may not have been a murderer, but he was in many respects an unpleasant personality. Despite his talents, he suffered from feelings of inadequacy, which made him by turns resentful, suspicious, calculating, fawning, and obsequious; he was opportunistic, duplicitous, and deceitful. As a young man he kept an enemies list, on which it seemed nearly everyone he associated with appeared—he never forgot slights but would not hesitate to shower praise on the offending party when it was beneficial to him to do so (while criticizing him behind his back). His correspondence with Tycho is marked by alternating fits of rage and cringing apologies. He did not believe in washing and bathing, and perhaps as a result complained constantly about boils and sores, as well as a variety of other ailments and afflictions; sitting was painful for him, so that he would often walk in preference to riding a horse. In a horoscope he cast for himself as a young man he compared himself to an annoying little dog that imitates the behavior of others, fawns on its masters but snaps at everyone else, and snarls when things are taken from it; like a dog, he liked to gnaw on bones and hard dry bread. "He is malicious," wrote Kepler of himself, "and bites people with his sarcasms."

And yet, he was more generous with the results of his work than were Tycho or Galileo with theirs. He would not bend his religious principles, even when faced with excommunication. He was inspired by beauty and motivated by the desire to understand the workings of God. He was relentless in pursuing a problem to its final solution. He combined brilliant intuition with a willingness for inexhaustible labor when needed.

By 1621, as the Thirty Years War was raging, the accused witch Katharina Kepler was being subjected to psychological torture. Kepler had prevented his mother from being physically tortured, through the implied threat of reprisal from his influential friends, and through generally making himself a pain to all concerned. The court scribe at one point set into the record, "The accused appeared in court, accompanied, alas, by her son, Johannes Kepler, mathematician." The defense's 128-page Act of Conclusion was mainly written by Kepler. The case was presided over by the Tübingen Faculty of Law. The faculty decided that the mildest form of torture should decide the old woman's fate. This involved the executioner confronting the accused, presenting his instruments one by one, and describing, presumably with disturbing relish, the exact methods in which they were used and their effects on the victim. Whatever satisfaction the executioner obtained from this charade, however, there would be little satisfaction for Katharina's accusers. The same stubbornness that kept her son pursuing twenty years of calculations to determine the orbit of Mars, the stubbornness that had seen her follow after her husband's army for many hundreds of miles to bring him home, remained strong in her. The provost reported that

> I led her to the usual place of torture and showed her the executioner and his instruments, and reminded her earnestly of the necessity of telling the truth, and of the great grief and pain awaiting her. Regardless, however, of all earnest admonitions and reminders, she refused to admit and confess to witchcraft as charged, indicating that one should do with her as one liked, and that even if one artery after another were to be torn from her body, she would have nothing to confess; whereafter she fell on her knees and said a paternoster, and

demanded that God should make a sign if she were a witch or a monster or ever had anything to do with witchcraft. She was willing to die, she said; God would reveal the truth after her death, and the injustice and violence done to her.

Katharina was freed, but others accused of witchcraft, lacking her resources, were not so lucky. In January 1616, the same month that Kepler wrote his initial letter in defense of his mother, a large number of women in Spa de Ban, in the Walloon region of what is now Belgium, were accused of witchcraft. The sorcery was manifested in illnesses and deaths of children and livestock, failed pregnancies, and other misfortunes. Fourteen persons were found guilty; at least ten were executed (the other four may not have survived their torture in order to be executed). All were women.

Women accounted for somewhere around three-quarters of all witchcraft accusations. Of those accused, women were more likely to be convicted, and of those convicted, women were more likely to be executed. To a large extent this was the result of their relative lack of power. Particularly if the woman was widowed, she might lack male relatives available or willing to defend her. Despite notable exceptions, by and large victims of witchcraft trials tended to be among the poorer, less educated, and more remotely located of citizens.

The number of people accused, convicted, and executed as witches is difficult to determine. Some witch hunters claimed extraordinary results — one, Nicolas Rémy, boasted of having convicted nine hundred witches over about a decade. This number seems vastly inflated, but at the height of the witch trials, between the mid-sixteenth and the mid-seventeenth century, somewhere between fifty and one hundred thousand trials may have been held. There is a tendency among contemporary historians to question the enormous numbers sometimes given, but whatever the tally, the fact remains that a lot more supposed witches were killed during this period than in others, and more in Europe than elsewhere.

Johannes Kepler's quest to uncover the secret of celestial harmony — the music of the spheres — was but the latest in a long

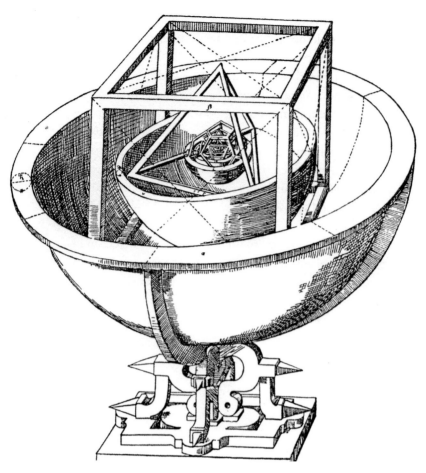

Model of the "Cosmic Cup," by Johannes Kepler, from *The Cosmographic Mystery,* 1596. On July 9, 1595, the twenty-three-year-old math teacher Johannes Kepler had a eureka moment while diagramming a problem on the blackboard for his small, bored, and restless class. In his off hours Kepler had been working on fathoming the divine order of the universe, but he couldn't make his theories match observations of planetary motion. Now it struck him: he was working in two dimensions and needed to be working in three — the orbits must be related not to the proportions of flat forms but to the five Platonic solids. Young Kepler was so taken with his revelation that through sheer enthusiam he managed to convince Frederick, Duke of Württemberg, to construct his model of the universe in the form of a drinking cup. The solids, each representing a planet, would be cut with different stones: diamonds for Saturn, jacinth for Jupiter, and so on. The cups would serve various beverages: Mercury would be brandy, Mars would be vermouth, Jupiter a white wine. The project dragged on for several years before petering out.

tradition that sought to unveil the mathematical and musical secrets of the universe. It would not be the last: in the twentieth century it would bear fruit in a verse by Leonard Cohen. In his "Hallelujah" he sings of a "secret chord" that "pleased the Lord." According to a reviewer in London's *Sunday Times,* the song succeeds "through some mysterious alchemy," and to judge from the number of times it has been covered — 1818, according to one database of musical covers — it is among the most popular of the songwriter's works. In an interview, Cohen explained that "'Hallelujah' is a Hebrew word which means 'Glory to the Lord.' The song explains that many kinds of Hallelujahs do exist. I say: 'All the perfect and broken Hallelujahs have an equal value.'"

According to Cohen's lyrics, the secret chord was made up of a particular mixture of fourths and fifths and of major and minor keys. Kepler, calculating proportions among the varying velocities at which the planets orbit the sun, thought that he had discovered just such a secret chord: it was made up of intervals of a fourth, an octave, a major third, a minor third, and a fourth. For example:

Kepler's first interest was theology. He was deeply disappointed when the University of Tübingen, where he had studied, would not find him a post as a professor of divinity but instead shunted him off into the backwater position of teacher of mathematics at Graz. Mathematics and theology were inextricably bound for him. "Geometry," he insisted, "existed before the Creation, is co-eternal with the mind of God, *is God himself.*" He explores this theme most fully in the work that he considered his magnum opus, the one he was working on even as he was defending his mother against the witch hunters, his *Harmony of the World.*

In times of disorienting and disturbing change, of turmoil and strife, there are people who are driven to search for the opposite: for signs of harmony in the world. So it was for Kepler. *Harmony* was published in 1618, while Kepler was defending his mother. He had recently been excommunicated. The daughter he had named after his mother had died. At his moment of triumph Kepler had been cut adrift — to support himself he had been forced to resume publishing and selling yearly astrological calendars after having abandoned the practice for more than a decade. And now war was breaking out.

Yet Kepler's *Harmony* unveils the hidden beauty of creation. Astronomical considerations take up only a part of the work (buried among its hundreds of pages is the revelation of the Third Law of Planetary Motion). The book's main impulse, the culmination of the inspiration that had driven him to write his early *Cosmic Mystery*, was the desire to reveal that geometrical patterns and harmonies govern all things: "Geometrical things," he wrote, "have provided the Creator with the model for decorating the whole world." The harmonies that we perceive with our human senses are echoes of the larger harmony that we are unable to hear. By attuning oneself to the correspondences among things, one's soul resonates with the cosmic harmony. In the tradition of Pythagoras, Kepler saw mathematics as the key to universal harmony, the unheard music of the universe. "The more anyone falls in love with mathematics," he said,

> the more fervent will be his dedication to God, and the more he himself will make every effort to practice gratitude, the crown of virtues, so that he will join me in prayer to the merciful God that much more sincerely: let him crush the warlike confusion, eliminate devastation, sniff out hatred, and venture forth to discover that golden harmony once again.

Kepler completed his book the same week that the Defenestration of Prague occurred — the incident that triggered the long war that would eventually suck in all the major nations of Europe, leaving central Europe a wasteland. "I cast the die and write a book for the present time," he wrote, "or for posterity. It is all the same to me.

It may wait a hundred years for its readers, as God also waited six thousand years for an onlooker."

In 1611, following a long and exhausting but ultimately indecisive war against the Ottomans, Rudolf II had been forced to cede power over the Empire to his younger brother Matthias; nine months later Rudolf died at the age of sixty. With Rudolf's death Kepler lost his powerful patron, and he left Prague for a position as provincial mathematician in Upper Austria. The childless Matthias reigned for only a few years. In 1617 he was succeeded by his nephew Ferdinand as king of Bohemia (the region around Prague that is now the western half of the Czech Republic). That's when all hell broke loose.

Ferdinand was an ardent Catholic who had won the support of the Spanish Habsburgs. Restive Bohemian Protestants called a diet to press the new king for guarantees of religious rights. Ferdinand forbade the diet from meeting. It assembled anyway in May 1618. A deputation marched to Hradschin Castle and confronted the king's regents, demanding an explanation for the diet's having been declared illegal. Dissatisfied with the response, the delegates seized the two regents and their secretary and threw them out an upper-story window. Landing in a mound of manure, all three survived. Catholics subsequently claimed the three men had been saved by the intervention of angels, while Protestants attributed their survival to the horse dung into which they fell. This grotesque incident, known as the Defenestration of Prague, is traditionally marked as the beginning of the Thirty Years War.

Protestants gathered around Frederick, the son-in-law of James I of England, Catholics around Ferdinand. Largely because of its religious implications, the initially local conflict escalated, eventually involving the nations of Denmark, Spain, Sweden, and France, among others; the pacifistic King James was one of the few leaders with a potential stake in the outcome to hold back from military involvement.

By the time Denmark entered the conflict in 1625 the Empire's finances had been strained to an alarming degree. At that point a Bohemian Catholic convert from Lutheranism, Albrecht von

Wallenstein, recruited more than thirty thousand men at his own expense and led them in battle. Wallenstein, who became supreme commander of the empire's armies, was a military strongman whom Ferdinand, wary of his ambition and fearful of his changing sides, would eventually have assassinated. This was the man to whom Johannes Kepler attached himself in the later years of his life.

Rejecting invitations from Italy and England, Kepler remained in Germany through the years of warfare. "Am I to go overseas?" he wrote of an invitation from England. "I, a German? I, who love the firm continent and who shrink at the idea of an island in narrow boundaries of which I feel the dangers in advance?" In 1624 Kepler did a ten-year forecast of the generalissimo's fortunes that concluded with a prediction of "dreadful disorders" in 1634. That February Wallenstein would be murdered. Meanwhile, in 1628, Wallenstein hired Kepler as his full-time personal astrologer and mathematician.

For Kepler these were years of painful wandering. Perhaps he recalled his father's distant wartime service during this time, or his mother's difficult journey to the Low Countries in search of her husband. Her story anticipates that of Mother Courage, a character in a tale by the greatest seventeenth-century German novelist, Hans Jakob Christoffel von Grimmelshausen. Grimmelshausen's narrator, the title character, is a camp follower who refuses to bow to the slings of fortune but schemes her way through the Thirty Years War and prospers from it. For Bertolt Brecht, who would base his play of the same name on Grimmelshausen's character, Mother Courage was both complicit in and victimized by a capitalist system that profited from war. In the same way, Kepler, a committed Lutheran who had scant faith in astrology, spent his final years wandering war-torn Germany making horoscopes for the military commander of the Catholic forces.

Finally, in 1630, in a Bavarian town at the confluence of the Danube and Regen rivers that was then called Ratisbon, now Regensburg, Kepler took to bed, delirious and raging with fever. He was bled, but it didn't help. After a time he stopped raving, and in the end he spoke little, only pointing first to his head and then to the sky. Attended by Lutheran priests, he would be buried in a church cemetery. The churchyard would be desecrated by Swedish forces, and his bones scattered and lost. His epitaph, however, survives:

> I measured the heavens, now I measure the shadows of the earth
> My mind was of the heavens, here my body's shadow lies

It is estimated that a quarter of the population of the Holy Roman Empire — around eight million people — died over the course of the Thirty Years War, the most devastating in central Europe before World War II. More than three hundred years later, in 1939, as Europe was again descending into the madness of all-encompassing war, and new, even more ruthless and senseless witch hunts were beginning, German composer Paul Hindemith was, like Kepler before him, thinking about the harmony of the world, despite, or perhaps because of, the coming conflict. Also like Kepler, Hindemith (whose wife was Jewish) had a somewhat compromised relation to political power, accommodating the Nazi regime in small ways before fleeing Germany in 1938.

Hindemith researched Kepler's life and work for an opera that he would call *Die Harmonie der Welt* — "The Harmony of the World." Through the cataclysmic war years the music of that opera coalesced and reverberated in Hindemith's head. Finally, in 1951, he prepared a symphony based on passages from the as-yet-unwritten opera; the symphony was performed to acclaim by the Basel Chamber Orchestra. Then, in 1956, during the chill of the cold war, Hindemith completed the libretto of the opera, which premiered in Munich the following year. It portrays Kepler as a spiritual seeker in a violent and senseless world. Kepler's spiritual quest is contrasted with the furious efforts of General Wallenstein to impose harmony by force. Yet Kepler does not succeed in hearing the harmony of the world until, at the last moment, with death approaching, in a surreal final scene in which Hindemith pulls out all the dramatic and musical stops, he relinquishes his own striving. Then he gives himself up to the world as it truly is.

LATIN AMERICA

La Tempestad

࿊࿊࿊

> . . . this thing of darkness
> I acknowledge mine.
> — Shakespeare, *The Tempest*

The action of *The Tempest* takes place on an enchanted island that appears by turns idyllic and desolate. If the island can be situated anywhere, the story would suggest that it lies somewhere in the Mediterranean — closer to Corsica than to Cuba — yet it has come to be strongly associated with the post-Encounter Americas. It has become the foundation myth of the New World.

And so it is seen as a narrative about colonialism. The magician Prospero comes to this new land and enslaves its sole flesh-and-blood resident, the fishlike wildman Caliban. He gives Caliban language, which the creature uses to curse him.

> You taught me language; and my profit on't
> Is, I know how to curse. The red plague rid you
> For learning me your language!

Prospero also wields power over a more compliant slave, the air-sprite Ariel, whom he manipulates with alternating threats and promises.

The play is colored with language that appears to have been borrowed from early accounts of English adventures in the New World. The shipwreck in Bermuda of the Jamestown-bound *Sea Venture*, reported by William Strachey, seems one of the prime sources; the play alludes to the "still-vex'd Bermoothes." Caliban's name is a near anagram of "cannibal," which derives from the same source as "Caribbean." The fool Trinculo comments on the English interest in new lands that makes them willing to pay "to see a dead Indian."

But insofar as the play can be read as a narrative about colonialism,

◀ Djimon Hounsou as Caliban in Julie Taymor's *The Tempest*.

it is more prophetic than historical, for in 1610–1611, when it was probably written, the British had little colonial presence. Some scholars have scoffed at the notion that Shakespeare intended any comment at all on colonialism. Harold Bloom has repeatedly complained of "mock scholars moaning about neocolonialism" who had turned Shakespeare's "salvage and deformed slave" into "an African-Caribbean heroic Freedom Fighter." The critic E. E. Stoll insisted that "there is not a word in the *Tempest* about America or Virginia, colonies or colonizing, Indians [he was wrong there] or tomahawks, maize, mocking-birds, or tobacco."

But others read the play differently. Leslie Fiedler (best known for *Love and Death in the American Novel*) felt no need for restraint. He saw in *The Tempest* "the whole history of imperialist America . . . from the initial act of expropriation through the Indian wars to the setting up of reservations, and from the beginnings of black slavery to the first revolts and evasions . . . fugitive white slaves, deprived and cultureless refugees from a Europe they never owned, which D. H. Lawrence was so bitterly to describe . . . the revolt against the printed page, the anti-Gutenberg rebellion for which Marshall McLuhan is currently a chief spokesman." Wow.

For the Barbadian novelist and essayist George Lamming, who explored themes from *The Tempest* in his 1960 collection of essays, *The Pleasures of Exile*, the play was "prophetic of a political future which is our present. Moreover, the circumstances of my life, both as a colonial and exiled descendant of Caliban in the twentieth century, is an example of that prophesy."

The debate turns on two different modes of reading: one historical, the other symbolic. One searches for sources and contexts, the other for effects and subtexts. Should we look forward or should we look back? I would like to think that the approaches could coexist, or that a middle way is possible. Maybe the past is present, the present past. Laozi said:

> in innocence we see the beginning
> in passion we see the end
> two different names
> for one and the same

The Afro-Caribbean Caliban that Bloom detests owes a debt

to the Martinican Aimé Césaire and other Négritude writers. In 1969 Césaire wrote a play he called *Une Tempête*, set in Haiti. In Césaire's version of the story, Caliban is a black rebel, while Ariel is a mulatto who accommodates and collaborates with the colonizer Prospero. (Similar incarnations of Caliban subsequently appeared in works by many Caribbean and African writers.) Historically oriented readers might object that there were no black slaves in English North America — which Shakespeare seems to have mainly had in mind — at the time *The Tempest* was written. But the truth of this kind of reading is not so much historical in the strictest sense as symbolic. It may not be exactly *vrai* but it is what the French would call *juste* — fair and right. Césaire wrote:

> To me Prospero is the complete totalitarian. I am always surprised when others consider him the wise man who "forgives." . . . Prospero is the man of cold reason, the man of methodical conquest — in other words, a portrait of the "enlightened" European.... Let's not hide the fact that in Europe the world of reason has inevitably led to various kinds of totalitarianism.

Literary critics, especially those associated with the approach called "New Historicism," took up the colonialist interpretation with enthusiasm. (New Historicism, if I've got it right, looks at literary texts as nodes in a network of "texts" — in the broadest sense — of all sorts, both influenced by and contributing to the flow of culture, often focusing on the intersection between historical context and modern response.) In 1988 the Shakespeare Association of America hosted a conference on "Shakespeare and Colonialism." Over the years, scores of learned articles were published, with titles like "Learning to Curse: Aspects of Linguistic Colonialism in the Sixteenth Century" (Stephen Greenblatt), "'This thing of darkness I acknowledge mine': *The Tempest* and the Discourse of Colonialism" (Paul Brown), "Hurricanes in the Caribbees: The Constitution of the Discourse of English Colonialism" (Peter Hulme), "Prospero in Africa: *The Tempest* as Colonialist Text and Pretext" (Thomas Cartelli), and so on. These critics "emphasize the discursive strategies that the play shares with all colonial discourse, and the ways in which *The Tempest* itself . . . fosters and even 'enacts' colonialism by mystifying or justifying Prospero's power over Caliban," according to Meredith Anne Skura in "Discourse and the Individual: The Case of Colonialism in *The Tempest*." "The new point is that *The Tempest* is a political act."

It is odd (isn't it?) that many Anglo scholars are eager to highlight colonialist discourse in *The Tempest* yet display little interest in how the play has been perceived by Latin Americans. Is it significant that several of the shipwrecked characters — including Ferdinand, to whom Prospero contrives to marry his daughter, Miranda — are citizens of Naples? When *The Tempest* was written, Naples had been part of Spain for more than a hundred years ("Italy" did not exist), and Spain and Portugal were by far the best-established colonial powers in the Americas. For Shakespeare's audience, the overtones of language and imagery taken from British accounts of its incipient overseas adventurism would likely have mixed with recollections of Spain's extraction of New World wealth. England, which had been at peace with Spain since 1604, looked to Spain as a model for its colonialist aspirations. (Shakespeare's sources were not only British: Setebos, the god worshipped by Caliban's mother, takes his name from that of a Patagonian deity mentioned in Pigafetta's account of the voyage of Magellan.)[1]

As it turned out, it was English-speaking North America that inherited Europe's imperialist worldview, while Latin America bit-

---

[1]   Recent research suggests that Shakespeare was the author of 320 lines of "additional passages" that were added to the popular potboiler *The Spanish Tragedy*, attributed to Thomas Kyd. The play is thought to allude to the tensions between England and Spain, and possibly to the defeat of the Spanish armada in 1588 — Sir Francis Drake's flagship was named the Revenge. *The Spanish Tragedy* is a revenge drama featuring a play within a play, so it is often compared to *Hamlet*. The additional passages were published in a 1602 version of the play but probably written earlier. A reprint was published in 1610, around the time Shakespeare was probably working on *The Tempest*.

terly felt the pain of having been liberated from its European colonizers only to become subject to economic, political, and military domination by its New World neighbor. Carlos Fuentes saw the birth of
imperial North America in the invasion of Mexico in 1846 (a conflict
contrived by President Polk in order to gain a port on the Pacific). But
it was the Spanish-American War of 1898 that particularly concerned
Latin Americans — a concern expressed in terms of *The Tempest,*
which provided core imagery for the pan-Hispanic movement that
took hold in Latin America near the turn of the century in response
to the aggressive posture of the colossus to its north.

From our present vantage point it seems surprising that in the
beginning most Latin American writers identified not with Caliban
but with Ariel. The great Nicaraguan poet Rubén Darío wrote an article called "The Triumph of Caliban" in 1898 in which he denounced
the crudity and avarice that he associated with American capitalism,
and with Caliban. He compared North Americans to "buffaloes with
silver teeth . . . red-faced, heavy, and gross" who were "like animals in
their hunt for the dollar." (In an earlier essay on Poe, Darío had written
that "Caliban reigns on the island of Manhattan, in San Francisco, in
Boston, in Washington, in the whole country.") Argentine writer Paul
Groussac picked up the motif, calling the U. S. "Calibanesque." Along
with similar currents in French thought, he influenced the important
Uruguayan author José Enrique Rodó (who was from Catalonia and
sympathetic to Spain in the war). Rodó composed a widely read essay
called "Ariel." In it he championed the virtues of truth and beauty he
saw in Ariel and rejected the materialism of the Caliban-like North
Americans. For him Ariel represented "the soaring nobility of the
spirit," while Caliban epitomized "the sensual and the obtuse." He
associated the earthy Caliban with materialism and wispy Ariel with
the higher realm of ideas. Rodó's *arielismo* dominated Latin American letters throughout the first half of the twentieth century. Arturo
Torres-Rioseco (who was born in Chile and taught Latin American
literature at the University of California, Berkeley, for more than
forty years) went so far as to call "Ariel" "the ethical gospel of the
Spanish-speaking world."

While Rodó's complaints about the U. S. were particular to

Latin America, his Caliban-Ariel contrast was largely an inherited one, a latter-day version of old disputes between Catholic southern Europe and Protestant northern Europe. His literary models and values were drawn from the traditional Western canon, and he showed scant interest in indigenous American culture. But by the mid-twentieth century, in the postwar period when many African countries were winning their independence, writers in colonized nations began to seek alternatives to European models, and to reclaim Caliban. In contrast to Rodó, George Lamming spoke of the need to get "out from under this ancient mausoleum of [Western] historic achievement." "Caliban's history," he said, "belongs entirely to the future."

The Cuban writer Roberto Fernández Retamar helped to overturn Rodó's *Tempest* symbolism through an influential essay, first published in Spanish, that appeared in English in a special Latin American issue — entitled *Caliban* — of *The Massachusetts Review* in 1974. He flatly rejected Rodó's reading of the play, saying that "the identification of Caliban with the United States . . . was certainly a mistake." His own reading of the *Tempest* story is unabashedly in the symbolist rather than the historical mode — "Caliban is our Carib," he asserts. "We, the *mestizo* inhabitants of these same isles where Caliban lived, see with particular clarity: Prospero invaded the islands, killed our ancestors, enslaved Caliban. . . ."

Critic Emir Rodríguez Monegal, author of *José Enrique Rodó en el Novecientos* ("José Enrique Rodó in the Twentieth Century"), complained that Fernández Retamar's reading of Rodó was "superficial and biased." (Fernández Retamar called Rodríguez Monegal, who taught at Yale, a "servant of imperialism.") Nonetheless, Rodó's symbolism had been emphatically overturned. "The new reading of *The Tempest*," Fernández Retamar observed, many years later, "has now become a common one throughout the colonial world."

And not just the colonial world. Fernández Retamar is right. The identification of the colonized with Caliban — the symbolist, prophetic reading of the play — is now complete. You don't need to see the film to know which part in Julie Taymor's recent version of *The Tempest* was given to the African actor Djimon Hounsou.

▲ *Caliban, Miranda, and Prospero*, 1875, by C. W. Sharpe (English, 1818–1899). Engraving on paper.

A NOTE ON SOURCES: I became interested in this topic on reading Enrique Krauze's essay on José Enrique Rodó in his *Redentores: Ideas y Poder en América Latina* (New York: Vintage Español, 2012). Among works I subsequently consulted were the following: Bruner, Charlotte H., "The Meaning of Caliban in Black Literature Today," *Comparative Literature Studies* 13, no. 3 (September 1, 1976): 240–253, doi:10.2307/40246045; Carey-Webb, Allen, "Shakespeare for the 1990s: A Multicultural Tempest," *The English Journal* 82, no. 4 (April 1, 1993): 30–35, doi:10.2307/820844; Frey, Charles, "The Tempest and the New World," *Shakespeare Quarterly* 30, no. 1 (January 1, 1979): 29–41, doi:10.2307/2869659; Griffiths, Trevor R., "'This Island's Mine': Caliban and Colonialism," *The Yearbook of English Studies* 13 (January 1, 1983): 159–180, doi:10.2307/3508119; Khoury, Joseph, "'The Tempest' Revisited in Martinique: Aimé Césaire's Shakespeare," *Journal for Early Modern Cultural Studies* 6, no. 2 (October 1, 2006): 22–37, doi:10.2307/40339571; Langhorst, Rick, "Caliban in America," *Journal of Spanish Studies: Twentieth Century* 8, no. 1/2 (April 1, 1980): 79–87, doi:10.2307/27740921; Márquez, Antonio C., "Voices of Caliban: From Curse to Discourse," *Confluencia* 13, no. 1 (October 1, 1997): 158–169, doi:10.2307/27922583; Marshall, Tristan, "The Tempest and the British Imperium in 1611," *The Historical Journal* 41, no. 2 (June 1, 1998): 375–400, doi:10.2307/2640111; Monegal, Emir Rodríguez, "The Metamorphoses of Caliban," *Diacritics* 7, no. 3 (October 1, 1977): 78–83, doi:10.2307/464886; Nixon, Rob, "Caribbean and African Appropriations of 'The Tempest'," *Critical Inquiry* 13, no. 3 (April 1, 1987): 557–578, doi:10.2307/1343513; Reid, John T., "The Rise and Decline of the Ariel-Caliban Antithesis in Spanish America," *The Americas* 34, no. 3 (January 1, 1978): 345–355, doi:10.2307/981311; Retamar, Roberto Fernández, "Adiós a Calibán," *Guaraguao* 2, no. 6 (January 1, 1998): 103–114, doi:10.2307/25596045; Retamar, Roberto Fernández, Lynn Garafola, David Arthur McMurray, and Robert Márquez, "Caliban: Notes Towards a Discussion of Culture in Our America," *The Massachusetts Review* 15, no. 1/2 (January 1, 1974): 7–72, doi:10.2307/25088398; Sanchez, Marta E., "Caliban: The New Latin-American Protagonist of the Tempest," *Diacritics* 6, no. 1 (April 1, 1976): 54–61, doi:10.2307/465034; Skura, Meredith Anne, "Discourse and the Individual: The Case of Colonialism in 'The Tempest'," *Shakespeare Quarterly* 40, no. 1 (April 1, 1989): 42–69, doi:10.2307/2870753; Vaughan, Alden T., "Caliban in the 'Third World': Shakespeare's Savage as Sociopolitical Symbol," *The Massachusetts Review* 29, no. 2 (July 1, 1988): 289–313, doi:10.2307/25089981; Vaughan, Alden T., "Shakespeare's Indian: The Americanization of Caliban," *Shakespeare Quarterly* 39, no. 2 (July 1, 1988): 137–153, doi:10.2307/2870626; (n.d.); and Vaughan, Alden T. and Virginia Mason Vaughan, *Shakespeare's Caliban: A Cultural History* (Cambridge: Cambridge University Press, 1993). Of these, the works by Alden T. Vaughan and Virginia Mason Vaughan, although I consulted them late in my process, are probably most similar to the approach taken here.

New World / New Words

~◇~◇~◇~

The original is unfaithful to the translation.
  —Jorge Luis Borges, 1943, on Samuel Henley's 1786
    translation of William Beckford's *Vathek,* which was
    published before the original

BROKEN WORLD, BROKEN WORDS

In the *Popol Vuh,* one of the handful of Mayan texts to escape the auto-da-fé of the Spanish missionaries of the sixteenth century, the story is told that the first people who had speech sufficient to praise the gods were made of maize. Their language was the language of the gods themselves. When those first people gazed into the distance, they could see clear to the edge of the world and the end of time. But the perfection of the people of maize alarmed the gods, especially when they began to multiply and overrun the earth. Their perfect speech was withdrawn, and instead each group was endowed with its own language.

So we live in a broken world, the world of Babel. Our world is broken, because our language has been shattered into thousands of fragments. Words are no longer the perfect, transparent embodiment of things themselves but instead are mere pointers, signs by which we grope to know the world from multiple viewpoints. To the translator falls the Sisyphean task of rejoining those shards and restoring the limitless world, a seamless world again, as it once was, whole.

WHAT IS TRANSLATION?

Any time we read literature, we perform an act of interpretation. Where interpretation fades into translation is difficult to establish. If in reading Chaucer we perform an act of translation into modern English, how are we not also translating when we interpret

◁ La Malinche translates for Cortés, detail from the "Lienzo de Tlaxcala," painted mid-1500s to support a petition to King Charles of Spain. Tlaxcalans had allied with Cortés against the Aztecs, and they imagined that might count for something. A tracing was produced in the mid-1800s, but the original has been lost. There is a good source on the Lienzo at *http://bit.ly/14drMfG.*

Shakespeare? To try to draw a line where translation begins is to confront a form of Zeno's paradox. George Steiner believes that because language is constantly changing, "when we read or hear any language-statement from the past, be it Leviticus or last year's best-seller, we translate. Reader, actor, editor are translators of language out of time." But what about writing that is not distant in time but is distant in other ways, such as idiom or social milieu? Is our interpretation of such texts also an act of translation?

In a sense, language itself is a kind of translation — the transmission of messages from a speaker to a listener, just as translation, in the strictest sense, is the transmission of messages from a source language to a target language.[1] Language, and especially translation, is the fundamental expression of the recognition of the other. "Language," Tzvetan Todorov said, "exists only by means of the other, not only because one always addresses someone but also insofar as it permits evoking the absent third person. . . . But the very existence of this other is measured by the space the symbolic system reserves for him." In this way, translation performs a quintessentially diplomatic function, for in the recognition of equality despite difference lies the basis of cooperation and hope for peaceful resolution of conflict. "Translation," Robert M. Adams said, "is simply a special instance of the general, but terribly fragile, power of language to cross gaps, to communicate. It leads across a somewhat wider and more precisely defined gap than everyday speech tries to cross, but attempts to connect one mind with another in much the same way."

Yet, as the Quiche authors of the *Popol Vuh* saw, language is also a means of exclusion. In contemporary jargon, languages serve not just

---

[1]   And if thought is a form of internalized language, as some claim — the Russian neuropsychologist Alexander Romanovich Luria, for example, who said that "apart from being a means of communicating, language is fundamental to perception and memory, thinking and behavior. It organizes our inner life" — then the labors of translators are like the synapses of collective cross-cultural cerebration, working at the planetary level to, as E. M. Forster said, "only connect."

to communicate but also to define in-group and out-group status.[2] An extreme example of this are esoteric and private "languages," such as those found in the Kabbalah or Tantric Buddhism. Language is a fundamental element of social cohesiveness and identity, and the other side of that coin is separation and estrangement. So the meeting of languages through the mediation of speech or writing — of *langues* through instances of *parole,* in Saussure's terms — is also a meeting of social groups. Through the act of translation, in other words, the translator draws together not just two texts, the original and the translation, but two cultures, represented by all the embodied history and intertextuality implied by those texts. Consequently, the alert translator must be sensitive to the implications of a multitude of specific choices, artfully balancing manifold references and connotations.

CULTURAL TRANSMISSION

Though one may imagine utilitarian origins of translation as a vehicle for trade and exchange,[3] some of the earliest written translations are of religious texts. (The extant *Popol Vuh* is a kind of translation, or bilingual edition. The Mayan text was transliterated in the Roman alphabet and accompanied by a Spanish crib.) Translations of sacred texts from Sanskrit and Pali into Chinese, for example,

---

2   In a recent study, researchers at Harvard and the École des Hautes Études en Sciences Sociales concluded that young children were suspicious of foreign-language speakers even before they themselves had learned to talk. Linguistically defined identity can be clearly observed in cases where nations contain sharp language divisions, such as French and English speakers in Canada, for example. Linguistic subversion often appears in such situations — James Joyce addresses this in *A Portrait of the Artist as a Young Man.* Black English might be another example of a subversive idiom employing private signifiers.

3   The distinction between utilitarian and nonutilitarian exchange is evasive. The structuralist critic Jacques Ehrman has argued "that all literature constitutes an economics of language, that literature is language's economy. . . . Every rhetorical structure is therefore an economic system."

were instrumental in spreading Buddhism and other elements of South Asian culture into China and elsewhere. As a result, the Chinese were among the first to systematically confront some persistent issues in translation, and by the end of the fourth century a number of state-supported translation bureaus were actively addressing these questions.[4] The bureaus developed in great part from the efforts of a Buddhist monk of the Eastern Jin dynasty named Dao An (314–385), who compiled a catalogue of scriptures and directed their translation. Dao An himself, however, did not know Sanskrit, and perhaps this limitation lay behind his demand that the translations should be literal, word for word. Still, he invited the Indian monk Kumarajiva (350–410) to join him in Changan to assist in the massive translation project, even though Kumarajiva advocated a free approach to translation that disregarded the surface in an effort to reach the essence of the Sanskrit sutras.

One more Chinese translator should be mentioned before we return to the Americas. His name was Xuanzang (600–664), and his struggles to bring sacred texts from India are the subject of the popular Ming-dynasty classic *A Journey to the West* (which features the marvelous character Monkey). Xuanzang insisted that translation be both "truthful" and "intelligible to the populace." In these terms we may hear echoes of the literal and the free approaches of his predecessors, Dao An and Kumarajiva. Xuanzang sought to construct a culturally equivalent text in the target language — and, incidentally, he worked both ways, not just translating into Chinese but also producing Sanskrit versions of Chinese classics such as the *Daode jing* (*Tao Te Ching*). He is therefore the model for the middle way of translation, which seeks a balance between the strict and the free.[5]

---

4 The translators were "usually furnished with spacious quarters within the royal precincts or in some famous temple," according to Kenneth Ch'en.

5 John Dryden said that translations fall into three classes: metaphrase, paraphrase, and imitation. Metaphrase is literal translation, the way of Dao An. Imitation is free translation that does not closely follow the source text; this is the way of Kumarajiva. Paraphrase is the middle way, the way of Xuanzang. This some-

Among the American heirs of Xuanzang was the Mexican writer Octavio Paz. Paz maintained that poetry must balance the traditional and the innovative. At either extreme, Paz said, lies failure: a poem that is too traditional offers nothing new and is not worth communicating, whereas a poem that is too inventive loses its common reference and cannot be communicated.[6] So the poet must strike a balance, and, Paz added, the translator must likewise strike a balance between the literal and the interpretive. This is one way in which translation is an art form, not a mechanical process.

Here is Adams again: "There is, at one extreme, a sort of parodic parallel which maintains just the least shred of trivial equivalence in one minimal respect, so that it may violate equivalence the more outrageously in all other respects. There is, at an opposite extreme, the technique of exact literal translation, which renders the meaning of the original word for word, without respect for the violence done to the idiom of the new tongue — which is, so to speak, abjectly faithful. Between these two rapes — one of the From-language, the other of the To-language — all sorts of more agreeable and equable arrangements are possible. They can very well be conceived as bargains,[7] in which one sort of equivalence is accomplished at the expense of others."

The German philosopher Friedrich Schleiermacher put it this

---

what schematic discussion of Chinese translation owes a debt to Weihe Zhong's "An Overview of Translation in China," *Translation Journal* 7:2 (April 2003). For fuller and more nuanced views, see Kenneth Ch'en, *Buddhism in China*; Chen Fukang, *A History of Translation Theory in China*; and Wang Kefei and Shouyi Fan, "Translation in China: A Motivating Force," *Meta: Journal des traducteurs* 4:1 (1999).

6   In our post-Babel world, the limits of Paz's equation will be determined differently by each reader.

7   This recalls Ehrman's assertion that rhetorical structure is an economic system, as cited in note 3 above. It's curious that the economic model should so often emerge in discussions of translation, considering that a career in translation today is akin to a vow of poverty. Could cultural transmission be an epiphenomenon of trade and exchange?

way (in 1813): "Either the translator leaves the author in peace, as much as possible, and moves the reader towards him; or he leaves the reader in peace, as much as possible, and moves the author towards him." Schleiermacher voted for the author, and he advocated a style of translation that highlighted the translated text's foreignness rather than seeking to assimilate it as a plausible target-language creation. That might be a working strategy but it is a theoretical impossibility, for to retain the text's foreignness in its totality would be to encounter Borges's paradox of a map in which one inch equals one inch.[8]

TRANSLATION AND BETRAYAL

At least by the time of Muhammad (born in Mecca around 570), translation of sacred texts came to be viewed with suspicion.[9] Muslims believe that the Qur'an embodies the direct word of God, presented to his prophet through the angel Gabriel. God was literally the author of the Qur'an — his prophet, who was illiterate, was merely his vehicle. God's language was Arabic; therefore a true Qur'an can only be read in that language. Copying God's work is a sacred act, with the result that some Qur'ans are dazzling examples of book arts. But once the Word is translated, it stops being the direct word of God and becomes merely a sort of commentary, which is how translations of the Qur'an are usually viewed by believers. This attitude to translation reflects the recognition that all translations introduce new aspects and omit original aspects of the source text. It cannot be otherwise, for each language is a unique

---

8   Or perhaps his account of Pierre Menard, who happened to author a perfect duplicate of Cervantes's *Quixote*. Borges's map is indebted to Lewis Carroll. Schleiermacher is quoted in Lawrence Venuti's *The Translator's Invisibility*.

9   No doubt suspicion has always clung to the translator, who, crossing borders, travels dangerous territory. Dao An's insistence on literal translation, noted above, might be seen as an expression of such suspicion.

The translator's complicity: Cortés and La Malinche, 1926, by José Clemente Orozco. Mural, Colegio de San Ildefonso, Mexico City, Mexico. *Photo by William Navarrete, http://bit.ly/1lvYf6V.*

Negotiating with the Other. The Aztec god Huitzilopochtli, from the title page of the *General History* of the conquest (known as the *Décadas*), 1601, by Antonio de Herrera y Tordesillas.

medium that carries an implicit corpus of intertextuality. Hence the Italian proverb *traduttore, traditore* (translator, traitor).

With the secularization of literature, it is a small step from the word of God the Author of All Things to the word of the author, writ small, of a particular text, and many authors have lamented the fallibility of translation.[10] Voltaire said that poetry couldn't be translated,

---

10 Sometimes the failures of translation are immediately evident. Carlos Fuentes told me once about visiting Russia and being presented with an elegantly slim volume said to be the Russian version of *Cambio de Piel* (*A Change of Skin,* which exceeds five hundred pages in the original Spanish). "We took out all the parts that wouldn't work for Russian readers," his hosts assured him. This is free translation at an extreme.

demanding: "Can you translate music?" Robert Frost echoed that sentiment, calling poetry "what gets lost in translation." Samuel Johnson thought such untranslatability a good thing: "Poetry cannot be translated; and, therefore, it is the poets that preserve the languages; for we would not be at the trouble to learn a language if we could have all that is written in it just as well in a translation. But as the beauties of poetry cannot be preserved in any language except that in which it was originally written, we learn the language."

Is poetry really what gets lost in translation? "I should say that poetry is what gets transformed," Paz argued. "Poetry is 'impossible' to translate because you have to reproduce the materiality of the signs, its physical properties. Here is where translation as an art begins: since you cannot use the same signs of the original you must find equivalents." Of course, the translator cannot completely reproduce the identical poetic effects of the original or we would have not a translation but a copy. Instead, new poetry must be created in the target language that is equivalent to the poetry of the original. The goal is equality in difference, which again is the ideal of the relation between the self and the other.

Perhaps the definitive example of encountering a previously unknown other is the encounter between the Old World and the New World. At the heart of this fateful encounter lies the figure of a translator. Todorov, whom I quoted earlier, has argued that Cortés's triumph in Mexico was above all a linguistic triumph. It was a triumph that could not have been easily accomplished without the assistance of the woman the Spanish called Marina, popularly known as La Malinche (or *La Chingada*, "the fucked one"). She epitomizes the two sides of the translator: the facilitator and the betrayer. Paz, in *The Labyrinth of Solitude*, argues that for Mexicans La Malinche (who was Cortés's mistress)[11] represents the violated mother. Through

---

11 "We touch here," to quote George Steiner (in *After Babel*) from a somewhat different, though related, context, "on one of the most important yet least understood areas of biological and social existence. Eros and language mesh at every point. Intercourse and discourse, copula and copulation, are sub-classes of the

her son with Cortés she is said to have given birth to modern Mexicans, who are *hijos de la chingada* — sons of the bitch.

More recently, Chicana writers have reclaimed the figure of Malinche. After all, she was a slave (she had already been exchanged among native peoples at least twice before she was given up to the Spaniards). Moreover, some say her efforts did more to save native Mexicans than to destroy them. "Any denigrations made against her," the Chicana writer Adelaida Del Castillo insists, "indirectly defame the character of the Mexicana/Chicana female. If there is shame for her, there is shame for us; we suffer the effects of these implications."

Malinche — whom Bernal Díaz del Castillo called a "great lady" without whose help "we would not have understood the language of New Spain and Mexico" — is the First Translator of the Americas,[12] and I hold her to be the patron saint of American translators, those faithless and heroic slaves to the uncompromising text.

THE POETICS OF EQUIVALENCE

If poetry is, as Paz maintained, what gets transformed in literary translation, how is this to be achieved? The translator must create new poetic effects equivalent to those of the original — but what constitutes "equivalence"? To answer these questions requires a sophisticated understanding of the various ways in which literature signifies, a topic to which there is no end.[13] In general, texts

---

dominant fact of communication. They arise from the life-need of the ego to reach out and comprehend, in the two vital senses of 'understanding' and 'containment,' another human being. Sex is a profoundly semantic act."

12 Not chronologically first. But Cortés's first translator, Jerónimo de Aguilar, a Spaniard who had been shipwrecked and lived among the Maya before the arrival of Cortés, played a more limited and less profound role.

13 John Hollander says that "a theory of translation would have to be a theory of literature in general." This statement and some others I have quoted from Octavio Paz are drawn from *The Poet's Other Voice* by Edwin Honig.

acquire meaning through their relation to other texts, through a variety of literary allusions and effects.

The notion of "equivalence" in translation is imprecise and falls upon the translator to determine as a personal judgment. If one adheres to the relativistic anthropological view of Edward Sapir and Benjamin Whorf that each language determines a fundamentally distinct worldview, then translation might entail the explication of a succession of puzzles at the surface level. (For example, how does one translate the word *machismo*, for which English has no exact equivalent, without elaboration?)[14]

If, on the other hand, one subscribes to the view of transformational linguists such as Noam Chomsky and Steven Pinker that there is a universal language instinct,[15] of which each particular language is a kind of fractal manifestation, then the translator would pay less attention to surface detail, viewing translation as an alembic reduction of the original to the deep level of universal language, followed by its transmutation into the target language.

Behind the *Popol Vuh*'s account of the fragmentation of languages — and similar myths and legends from other cultures — is the notion of a universal primal language, or *Ur-Sprache*, that has been lost. Using the transformational model, the translator is one who dives deep into the primal stream to carry the message of the text from one shore to the other. Translation then involves in effect not two but three texts, counting the invisible mediation of the implicit shared grammar that underlies both the source and the target.

---

14 The practicing translator will probably choose from possible choices ranging approximately from "manliness" to "balls" (or retain a degree of foreignness and leave "machismo" untranslated) and then try to balance what is lost or gained from that with other choices — or "bargains," in Robert M. Adams's vocabulary — elsewhere.

15 In *The Descent of Man*, Darwin called language "an instinctive tendency to acquire an art."

Discovering Columbus

❧❧❧

In a Latin American village, native dancers peer through wooden masks painted with fair skin, blue eyes, and blond beards. They are decked out in the elaborate fashions worn by Spanish conquistadors expecting to meet the Grand Khan of the Indies. So begins, in the eternal present of the festival, a new discovery, a ritual reenactment of the conquest of the Americas. It is an incongruous but not unusual scene, for in Latin America the conquest remains a part of daily life, and signs of it are everywhere: in Mexico, Christian churches rise on the foundations of Aztec temples; in Central America, Maya praise the resistance hero Tecun Uman; in South America Inca gold, melted and recast in the form of saints, adorns the most glorious cathedral altars.

In North America, by contrast, the conquest often seems an abstraction, obscured by Hallmark images of *Mayflower* landings and blunderbuss-and-buckle-bedecked forefathers dining thankfully with feathered, moccasined noble savages who have stepped from the pages of Lamartine and Cooper. We have forgotten our origins, rejected and expunged our native heritage; our imagination only really takes hold centuries later, with the pioneer movement west.

"Latin American culture, the culture in which we write, in which we create today, is permeated by the event of the conquest and by the world preceding the conquest, which is not true of North America," Carlos Fuentes once remarked. "In Mexico and the Andean countries and Central America, the Indian world is alive, one way or another. Even if it's only alive in a corrupt religious ceremony, it is there. One can see it, one can visit it. Our language is permeated with Indian words, so it is not something of the past. The past is present in Latin America; the past is past in the United States."

So maybe it's not surprising that for us Christopher Columbus

◀ Masks at Chichicastenango, Guatemala (detail). *Photo by cotaro-70s, flickr.com/photos/cotaro70s.*

tends to be little more than a name, a list of ships, and a date recited by schoolchildren. Of the man himself we know next to nothing. Yet his arrival on our lands determined the course of our history. "It is in fact the conquest of America that heralds and establishes our present identity," Tzvetan Todorov writes in *The Conquest of America*. And he adds, "We are all the direct descendants of Columbus." (Likewise, all American translators are descendants of La Malinche, Cortés's native translator.) Because the discovery and conquest are experienced almost as contemporary events in Latin America, its writers have been the most astute interpreters of those events. Among modern novelists, Miguel Ángel Asturias and Fuentes have produced notable works on the theme, and Gabriel García Márquez was strongly influenced by the fabulous chronicles of the Spanish explorers; recently, the Brazilian João Ubaldo Ribeiro traced consequences of the conquest down to the present in his sweeping novel *An Invincible Memory*, while in Argentina Abel Posse produced a new take on the Columbus story, called *The Dogs of Paradise*.

But *The Harp and the Shadow* (*El Arpa y la Sombra*, 1978), the last major novel by the Cuban writer Alejo Carpentier, remains the prototype. (Eduardo Galeano, in *The Memory of Fire*, his interpretive history of the Americas, quotes from it at the beginning of his account.) The encounter of the Old and New Worlds, the give and take of colliding cultures and traditions, has been a recurring theme in Carpentier's work. In *The Lost Steps* (*Los Pasos Perdidos*, 1953), for example, a Spanish American musicologist returns from Europe to make a visit to one of the sources of native American culture, traveling up the Orinoco River to dwell with an Indian tribe. In *Explosion in a Cathedral* (*El Siglo de las Luces*, 1962), the guillotine, gruesome symbol of the French Revolution, arrives in the New World, where it is reshaped by a tangle of indigenous secret societies, voodoo, and other assimilated local traditions. And in another historical novel, *The Kingdom of This World* (*El Reino de Este Mundo*, 1949), the nineteenth-century Haitian ruler Henri Christophe finds himself torn between French and Afro-Caribbean cultures.

Columbus's encounter represents the quintessential encounter of the self with the other, an other that is completely unknown and seemingly unknowable, unfathomable, and uninterpretable. In this postlapsarian confrontation, language itself has no referents — the other becomes a mirror to the self, harshly exposing the flaws that lie at the foundation of our American culture. In Columbus's fall, we sinned all.

Mexican historian Edmundo O'Gorman proposes in *The Invention of America (La Invención de América)* that America was not discovered but invented. The invention begins with Columbus. Discovering unknown peoples, Columbus shapes them by turns into Edenic innocents, sickly Moors, and villainous cannibals — even the name he gives them, "Indios," is based on a fundamental misconception (or preconception). New World fruits, birds, trees, people — Columbus lacks the words to understand or to convey much of what he has discovered; in this sense he might be said to have failed to discover anything. "I say that the blue mountains I can see in the distance are like those of Sicily, though they are nothing like those of Sicily," he explains in Carpentier's novel. "I say the grass is as tall as that of Andalusia in April and May, though there is nothing here that is anything like Andalusia. I say nightingales are singing when I hear twittering little gray birds with long black beaks that are more like sparrows. I allude to the fields of Castile, here where not a single thing recalls the fields of Castile. I have seen no spice trees, and I suggest that there may be spices here...."

Instead of an unspoiled tropical paradise, Columbus sees, finally, a monstrous mine of gold, which exists only in his imagination. In desperation, unable to produce gold from this mine, he transfers its wholly imaginary value to the human resources he has found, balancing his mental ledgers by means of the institution of slavery and firmly planting greed, deceit, and oppression in the fertile ground of our hemisphere. So, Carpentier suggests, begins the modern history of the Americas.

Eva Perón in Life and Myth

Long after the death of Argentine icon Eva Perón at thirty-three, her enigmatic image continued to blaze through the tenements of Buenos Aires, accompanied by the prophetic legend, "I will return and I will be millions." And so, in a way, it has come to pass, as performers turned politicians have popped up everywhere in the years since: in the U.S. one thinks of George Murphy, Ronald Reagan, Fred Thompson, Sonny Bono, Clint Eastwood, Jesse Ventura, Arnold Schwarzenegger, Al Franken — the list goes on and on.

From 1944, when she first met Juan Perón, until her death from uterine cancer in 1952, Eva played her role as a public figure to perfection. (Critics did not give her film work quite such high marks. Maybe actors who excel at playing themselves do better as politicians than those who can inhabit a wider range of characters.) Upon her death there were some, like Jorge Luis Borges, who were glad to see her go. Others called for her canonization. That's when things got weird — it would take another two decades before she would be laid to rest.

The cancer that ate away at Eva's body seemed simultaneously to feed her myth. As the frail body of Eva Ibarguren wasted away and expired, the myth of Evita swelled, until it was too big to fail.

Eva's origins are so obscure, the details of her life so intentionally concealed and falsified, and her story so compounded by legend that any account of her life must be some admixture of hagiography, celebrity gossip, detective story, fantasy, and exposé. There are more questions than answers: Did the youthful Evita leave her dusty hometown to run off to Buenos Aires with aging tango singer Agustín Magaldi? Did the struggling actress turn tricks in the city's squalid backwaters to see her through tight stretches? Or (unlikely as it seems) did she remain virginal, saintly, through everything? Where did she go when she disappeared from sight for

◀ Official portrait of Argentine president Juan Domingo Perón, with his wife María Eva Duarte de Perón, ca. 1948, by Numa Ayrinhac (1881–1951). Oil on canvas. *Museum of the Argentine Bicentennial, Buenos Aires* (*www.museo.gov.ar*).

several months? How did she win Perón, whose military colleagues could never accept their marriage? Did she help to transfer Nazi wealth into Swiss bank accounts? Was it Perón or was it Eva who really goaded the masses — those she called *descamisados* (shirtless ones) or *gracitas* (greasers) — to carry him into power? As death approached, did she become a leftist?

Ibarguren was the name of her unmarried mother, who worked as a seamstress and cook. Eva and her sisters and brother were the illegitimate children of a married man, a wealthy rancher named Juan Duarte. Her parents were both of Basque descent. Her mother, like Eva, was illegitimate. When Eva was one, her father returned to his wife and cut off support to the family. When she was seven, he died in a car accident. Her mother caused a scene when she took her children and tried to attend his funeral.

In 1935, at the age of fifteen, she took her leave of the pampas and left for Buenos Aires, where she adopted her father's name, becoming "Eva Duarte" (or sometimes "Eva Durante"). She modeled, competed in beauty contests, and got bit acting parts. She became a blonde. Somehow she won the support of a succession of male patrons. Eventually she got a contract with a leading radio station to play great women of history such as Elizabeth I of England, Sarah Bernhardt, Isadora Duncan, Empress Carlota of Mexico, and Catherine the Great. (Later she would express a wish to "enter history" on her own.) By 1943 she was the best-paid actress in the country. The next year she met an up-and-coming politician named Juan Perón, who was then Secretary of Labor (under a junta that had assumed power through military coup), at a party. He was forty-eight, she was twenty-four. They left the party together. She stuck to him the remaining eight years of her life. Around the same time, she became (like another famous actor-politician) the head of an actor's union, beginning her political career.

Alicia Dujovne Ortiz, in her biography *Eva Perón*,[1] has traced

---

1   Alicia Dujovne Ortiz, *Eva Perón*, tr. Shawn Fields (New York: St. Martin's, 1996).

the evolution of Eva's several names. Originally Eva Maria Ibarguren, once married to Perón she took the traditional, deferential, and legitimizing name of Maria Eva Duarte de Perón. (She presented a forged birth certificate with the name Duarte on her wedding day.) That name would not confine her for long. Soon Perónist propagandists would christen her Eva Perón, emphasizing the strongman's name. But in the end she would overshadow Perón. She would cast off his name to become simply Evita.[2]

In 1946, with the support of the *descamisados*, Perón became president. The political program he initiated, called Perónism, can be difficult for North Americans to comprehend. Politics in Argentina have not generally been aligned along conventional liberal and conservative blocs but rather by competing strains of populism. Perón's was a populism of the right, which drew its support from the lower-middle-class masses who were elsewhere associated with the left. He was strongly influenced by Mussolini, but the differing attitudes of the two tyrants toward labor was telling. Mussolini sought to repress organized labor; Perón sought to co-opt it. In Argentina a variety of interest groups competed for seats at the table, and Perón played them off against each other. He nationalized corporations and granted quasi-governmental authority to some labor organizations, blurring the boundaries between government, industry, and labor. Still in her mid-twenties, Eva was put in charge of the Ministries of Labor and Health. Soon she would direct her own charitable foundation, whose finances would become mixed up with those of the government — and of the Peróns themselves.

Eva gathered trusted friends and colleagues around her to help her create an independent center of power that in time would seem to rival that of Perón. Her brother was named Perón's press secretary. Her brother-in-law was appointed to the supreme court, replacing a justice Perón had impeached for supporting the junta under which he himself had served as labor secretary. She moved

---

2 *Evita*: "Little Eva." Not the Little Eva who was a one-hit wonder with "The Loco-Motion," a different one.

into the same office Perón had worked from when he had held that post.

Gradually she gained power and influence. She became a celebrity. She was constantly in the public eye. "A series of different Evitas, innumerable Evitas," says Dujovne Ortiz, "began to emerge, one after another — frivolous Evita, greedy Evita, manipulative Evita, Evita who dreads blunders, insolent Evita who shows off to hide her fear, sensitive Evita, the protagonist of a beautiful story." With a loan from the Central Bank, she bought control of a newspaper, the *Democracia*, which chronicled all of those Evitas, and its circulation soared. Meanwhile, the independent press was virtually shut down through government intimidation and false claims of a paper shortage.

Eva proved savvy at propaganda. She attended receptions, presided at ceremonies, gave speeches, made radio broadcasts. She encouraged the adoption of the new technology of television, making Argentina the first American country after the U.S. to get television.

In 1947 she embarked on a grand tour of Europe. She characterized herself as a "rainbow" between Argentina and Europe, so the tour was dubbed the Rainbow Tour. When she left for Spain, it was her first time in an airplane. One hundred fifty thousand *descamisados* saw her off at the airport. A second plane followed, bearing the clothes she would wear to meet the heads of state.[3] According to Eva, no one wanted to follow a dowdy leader. What people wanted was a figure who would embody their dreams. And indeed, Madrileños flocked to catch a glimpse of her in Spain. "Any time you want to attract a crowd this size," she is said to have told Generalissimo Franco, "just give me a call." Carried away by the enthusiastic reception, she raised her arm to the crowd in what was taken to be a fascist salute. In Italy, where political opinion

---

3   The *New York Times* reported that in Europe "Señora Perón's wardrobe continues to be a rich source of conversation. In her many public appearances she has not worn the same outfit twice, and often she changes three or four times in a day." But of course any actor is accustomed to costume changes.

was polarized, the reception was mixed. Rome prepared a lavish reception. The pope received her courteously. She presented herself as a feminist, telling a crowd that "women have the same duties as men and therefore should have the same rights." (The Perón regime established women's suffrage in Argentina; Eva announced the news on the radio.) But in Milan she was met with a mix of cheers and taunts. And in Bern, Switzerland, a rock thrower broke the window of the car she was riding in, while the next day she was the target of a volley of tomatoes.

A visit to England failed to materialize over a series of diplomatic miscues and slights. France received her warmly, though with smaller crowds than she had seen in southern Europe — everyone was watching the Tour de France. In Monte Carlo she apparently met Aristotle Onassis, who would later boast (implausibly) that she had slept with him there, in exchange for a donation to charity. It's not altogether clear how much the trip accomplished for Argentina on the diplomatic front, but it did wonders for the cult of Evita. She made the cover of *Time* and other magazines.

The trip seemed to change her. Throughout it, she had displayed scant interest in European art, culture, and history, with the exception of its high fashion. She became a client of Parisian couturiers, spending more than $25,000 a year on clothes by Dior, Fath, and Balmain. Her story was like that of Cinderella, and she had to dress the part of a princess. She bedecked herself in opulent jewelry, wore jewels in slums. "I am taking the jewels from the oligarchs for you," she assured her *descamisado* supporters. "One day you will inherit the whole collection."

On her return from Europe in August 1947 she threw herself into social work with a fury. She called it "social aid," and took pains to distinguish it from the sort of charity that she had once received from blue-haired ladies who looked down their noses at her. "Charity humiliates," she said, while "social aid dignifies and stimulates." Her foundation's work could not have been more direct. People would write to Eva. She would send a note in reply, and a meeting would be scheduled. John Dos Passos described one of these sessions for *Life* magazine: "At the end of each hard-luck story the

Señora reached with jeweled fingers under the blotter on the desk and took out two fifty-peso notes," he wrote. "Then she made out with a rapid scratch on a pink slip an order for a doctor or a doll for the baby girl."

She received 12,000 letters each day. Her foundation employed 14,000 people. In a year it would give away 400,000 pairs of shoes, 500,000 sewing machines, 200,000 cooking pots. For Christmas in 1947 she gave away five million toys. She liked to give dolls to little girls, dentures to their parents. She ordered a thousand schools to be built, doubled the number of hospitals in Argentina, provided training for countless nurses. She had homes built for single mothers, the elderly, and the homeless. She established parks and orphanages. She ordered that birth certificates no longer register births as "illegitimate."

With colleagues she could be humorless, rancorous, and vindictive. Several observers characterized her as sexless. But to her clients she was unfailingly respectful and generous. Her confessor, Father Hernán Benitez, wrote, "I saw her kiss the leprous. I saw her kiss those who were suffering from tuberculosis or cancer. I saw her distribute love, a love that rescues charity, removing that burden of injury to the poor which the exercise of charity implies. I saw her embrace people who were in rags and cover herself with lice."

The money came from the workers themselves, in the form of taxes, and from businesses who were extorted into giving large sums. A donation would be requested, and if it was refused inspectors would find health or labor violations that would require shutting the company down. Fleur Cowles, the American writer, editor, and artist who was publisher of *Flair* magazine, asked Eva how she kept track of all of her giving. "Keeping books on charity is capitalistic nonsense," Eva replied. "I just use the money for the poor. I can't stop to count it."[4]

A lot of the money ended up among the Peróns' personal

---

4   John Barnes, *Evita: First Lady* (New York: Grove, 1978), 115.

Eva Perón with supplicants in the offices of her foundation. *Http://bit.ly/SqZJXU.*

assets. By the early 1950s they were worth more than $20 million. At her death Eva owned more than a thousand brooches of silver and gold, a hundred gold clocks, a glittering mound of emeralds and diamonds.

Her adoring supporters ate it all up. She seemed to be becoming a bigger presence than Perón himself, and there was talk of her running for vice president. There she overstepped. Army generals insisted that Perón withdraw the meddlesome woman from public life. The threat of a coup was constant and, indeed, Perón would be overthrown by the military in 1955. She tearfully announced her withdrawal in August 1951, in a speech that would be known as "The Renunciation." Legend has it that she spoke from a balcony before a crowd of *descamisados* who clapped and whistled and demanded her candidacy. In fact, the announcement was made on the radio.

It only added to her myth, to the image of her as self-sacrificing. She applied herself once more to her foundation, and seemed to work constantly. She grew pale and thin. She refused a medical examination because she did not trust the doctors. Eventually, though, she had to give in. She was diagnosed with uterine cancer, the same disease that had killed Perón's first wife. The mutilation of a botched abortion in 1943 can't have helped. She continued getting thinner. By June 1952 she weighed only eighty pounds.

In her agonizing final days, Evita dictated a little book called *Mi Mensaje* ("My Message," published in English under the title *In My Own Words*). The book was a kind of sequel to an earlier work called *La Razón de Mi Vida* (*My Mission in Life*), which had been conceived and ghostwritten by a Spaniard named Manuel Penella de Silva. He theorized that the disaster of the Nazi regime was caused by a lack of women in political power, and he envisioned a political system in which women would control one of the houses of government.

With this in mind, he traveled to Argentina, interviewed Eva, and wrote *My Mission in Life*. But de Silva's views were not those of Perón or the Perónists, and the book was substantially sanitized by their propagandists. It is difficult to know to what extent it reflects Eva's thoughts (little of the writing sounds like her voice).

Upon her death Evita left *My Message* unfinished. It was almost forgotten until it surfaced in 1987 in the garage of Perón's chief archivist. Its text is as doubtful as that of *My Mission in Life*, and it has been disavowed by Eva's surviving sisters. Yet in some ways it is a more plausible representation of Eva's views, and it is possible that it reflects to some degree her final thoughts. It gives us a left-leaning Evita, and is of value in helping us to understand how young Argentine radicals could have taken the wife of Perón as a precursor.

Perón himself had moved on. Without Eva he gave in to self-indulgence. He collected hundreds of motor scooters, on which he would cruise local playgrounds looking for appealing young girls. He formed a relationship with one of these, a fourteen-year-old named Nelly Rivas, and he was unable to keep gossip about it out of the press. In September 1955 he would have to leave her behind as he fled the country, but in exile in Panama he would meet a woman named María Estela Martínez, who was thirty-five years his junior, and he continued to Spain with her in tow. They married there, and like Eva she was renamed — she would be Isabel Perón.

Nine months after Eva's death, her brother was found with a bullet in his head and a gun by his hand. It was termed a suicide. But the bullet in his head was .45 caliber and the gun by his hand was .38 caliber. It was rumored that Eva had deposited Nazi wealth in Swiss bank accounts during her trip to Europe, and that her brother was one of the keepers of the accounts. He had been killed so that the Nazis could have unfettered access to them. Certainly Perón's Argentina had been exceptionally welcoming to Nazi refugees from the war — it is estimated that by 1947 90,000 had taken refuge there. Perón traveled in the other direction, enjoying the comfortable exile of a villa in Spain. (He would return to power in Argentina in 1974 but die within a year. His vice president — his new wife, Isabel — would succeed him.)

Eva's last words before her death in July 26, 1952, were said to have been the nearly palindromic *Eva se va* — "Eva is leaving." But in fact she didn't leave. She remained as much a symbol after her death as before it. The Vatican received 40,000 letters calling for her canonization. (It would not consider it because of her questionable past.)

Nor did her body leave. Her hair was re-dyed blonde, her fingernails polished. After she died a Spanish embalmer worked feverishly to preserve the body, the internal organs intact, until he pronounced her "completely and definitively incorruptible." He spent subsequent years perfecting his work. The result was exhibited to the public by Perón, but after his overthrow it fell into the hands of the junta. Fearful that the perfectly preserved cadaver might be used to rally the masses, yet also afraid to destroy it, they formulated elaborate ruses to elude Perónists and hide the corpse in a foreign cemetery. Compounding this black farce, several identical wax and vinyl copies of Evita were created to mislead her devoted followers.

In his remarkable novelized treatment of the peregrinations of

Eva's embalmed body, entitled *Santa Evita*,[5] Tomás Eloy Martínez reconstructs the journeys of the true and false Evitas as they passed from one corrupt, wicked, and demented hand to another. As they were hidden, stolen, and swapped again and again, they were mysteriously accompanied by the candles and flowers of the faithful, eerily appearing as if by a mummy's curse.

At times Martínez addresses the reader in his own, rather confessional voice, at times he presents what he says are almost verbatim interviews, at times he imagines events in a weirdly compelling narrative style (perfectly rendered by translator Helen Lane). Martínez shows how for so many of those who became involved with Evita — even after her death — she became an obsession.

The colonel charged with hiding her body, for example, driven mad by his feelings for Evita, came to believe that her corpse made its way to the moon, buried by Neil Armstrong as an international television audience looked on. This strange, sad character was the main player in the machinations surrounding Evita's corpse, and he plays a corresponding role in Martínez's book.

Martínez interviewed many survivors, among them Evita's hairdresser, the wife of the mad colonel, and a bizarre, dwarfish confidant of the secret service called Tom Thumb, who is like a character from Günter Grass. How much of what Martínez tells us is imagined and how much is real? In the end, it is impossible to say, for Martínez himself fell under Evita's spell. For him too she became an obsession, an obsession so powerful that it bursts the formal boundaries of the novel, obliterating the distinction between fiction and nonfiction. So why does Martínez present the result as a novel? "The novel is the most effective way of telling the truth," he has said, "especially about a person like Eva Perón, whose character has taken on mythical qualities in Argentina."

The truth is that Eva was herself a kind of fiction. In his story "The

---

5   Tomás Eloy Martínez, *Santa Evita*, tr. Helen Lane (New York: Knopf, 1996).

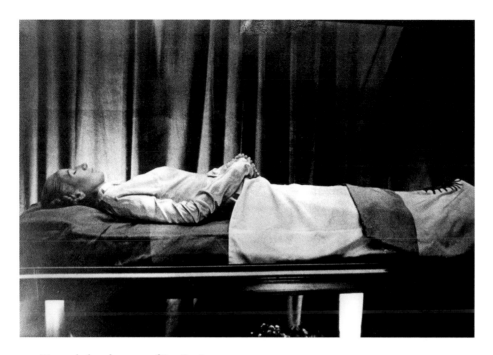

The embalmed corpse of Eva Perón.

Sham," Jorge Luis Borges describes a "mourner" in a small town who displays a simple cardboard box with a blonde doll inside it. Soon townspeople were lining up, and for a fee of a couple of pesos they paid their respects to the doll and offered sympathy to the "general." What kind of man, the narrator wonders, could dream up such a "funereal farce"? But then he reflects, "The mourner was not Perón and the blond doll was not the woman Eva Duarte, but neither was Perón Perón, nor was Eva Eva. They were, rather, unknown individuals — or anonymous ones whose secret names and true faces we do not know."

MENDOZA

Double-Crossed

THE INVENTION OF THE CHICANO

~~~

We didn't cross the border, the border crossed us.
— José Antonio Burciaga

"Who remembers," asked Gary Snyder in one of his poems, "the Treaty of Guadalupe Hidalgo?" Mexicans remember. The treaty that ended the U.S.–Mexican War radically redrew the map of North America. Together with the earlier annexation of Texas, the U.S. acquired a million square miles of territory, including the present states of California, Arizona, New Mexico, Nevada, and Utah, as well as parts of Wyoming, Colorado, and Oklahoma. Mexico lost about half of its territory, and the U.S. acquired the Pacific seaports it coveted. But U.S. citizens mostly have forgotten the treaty — unless they happen to be Chicano or Chicana. *El pueblo que pierde su historia, pierde su destino*, goes a Latino folk saying: a people who lose their history lose their destiny.

Many people associate Chicanos with the "immigration debate." It's a pertinent association, but not so much in the way a lot of people think. For it was Anglo immigration into Mexico that led to the invention of the Chicano.[1]

In 1824, in an effort to better utilize its land assets, Mexico passed a colonization law that sought to encourage immigration to its province of Texas by offering exemption from taxation. The immigrants, termed *empresarios*, would receive grants of land if they swore to take up farming and Roman Catholicism, and to conduct their business in the Spanish language. Eventually thousands of

---

[1]   The current wave of immigration from Central America is mostly the result of U.S. drug policies, which have not had much affect on demand here but have resulted in supply being controlled by violent rival criminal gangs that have terrorized citizens there.

◀ Lydia Mendoza (1916–2007), "La Alondra de la Frontera" (The Lark of the Border). In 2013 the U.S. Postal Service inaugurated its Music Icons series with a stamp devoted to the Tejana 12-string guitar legend. Thirty million copies of the stamp (detail shown) were printed.

Anglos poured into Texas from the U. S. to take advantage of this offer — though few observed the oaths regarding religion and language. They congregated in communities where they grew cotton, raised cattle and pigs, and kept slaves. By 1827, reported one observer, "the ratio of Mexicans to foreigners is one to ten."

Mexico at this time was a loose confederation of provinces, and some had tested their ability to assert some degree of independence, or even to break away entirely, from the central government. California threw out a governor sent from Mexico City. Yucatan was for a time an independent nation, though it later rejoined the confederation.

In Texas, Anglo settlers grew tired of Mexican restrictions, even if they weren't rigorously enforced. An uprising in 1827 was put down, but after bloody battles involving atrocities on both sides, the Mexican president, General Antonio López de Santa Anna, was captured in 1836 and forced to sign a document called the Agreement of Velasco, removing Mexican troops from the province. In fact, he signed two versions of the document, one public and one private. The private version committed Santa Anna to advocating for Texan independence. After his release, however, Santa Anna disavowed the agreement and claimed that it obliged him only to try to arrange a hearing for Texas commissioners. Mexico never accepted the agreement, and it did not recognize the independence of Texas until it was forced to sign the Treaty of Guadalupe Hidalgo in 1848.

But Texas now considered itself an independent republic, and it was recognized as such by several other nations. In 1836 it approved a constitution that was based on the U. S. model but explicitly forbade the emancipation of slaves. Slavery was entrenched in Texas. Four-fifths of those who had voted to secede from Mexico had come from U. S. slave states.

The republic occupied an uneasy position between Mexico and the U. S., and other foreign powers were threatening to become involved in its affairs. So Texans voted to petition the U. S. for statehood. But the matter of slavery stood in the way. Admission of Texas would upset the balance of free and slave states.

Anti-slavery advocates opposed annexation. Ralph Waldo Emerson compared acquiring Texas to taking a dose of arsenic: it could be swallowed, but eventually it would harm the nation. He might have had a point.

In 1844 the election as president of James Polk of Tennessee, a protégé of Andrew Jackson who had campaigned with a pledge to add Texas to the Union, was the tipping point that resulted in its admission as a state. Polk believed that westward expansion was God's will for the nation. His sense of its manifest destiny (a phrase coined in 1845 by pro-expansionist journalist John L. O'Sullivan) was strongly colored with a sense of racial superiority. Americans would bring civilization to the lands they annexed.[2]

Polk attempted to purchase Mexico's northern provinces. Though sparsely populated, they offered access to valuable trade routes, such as the Santa Fe–Chihuahua Trail. A special prize was the California port of Monterey — it would provide access to the Pacific, which was shaping up to be the next international battleground (the first Chinese Opium War had recently concluded; a second phase was brewing). As an incentive, he put various kinds of pressures on Mexico, such as sending a "peace ambassador" to press for "unpaid damage claims." He moved troops near the southern border of Texas. But where was that exactly? Most maps of the time showed the border at the Nueces River. But Polk claimed the border was further south, at the Rio Grande (Rio Bravo). A Mexican ambassador to Washington had warned officials at home about this. "The project will seem delirium to any rational person," he said, "but it certainly exists."

Inevitably, the presence of U.S. forces south of the Nueces resulted in skirmishes with Mexican troops. That was the provocation Polk had looked for as a rationale for war. Illinois state congressman Abraham Lincoln opposed the conflict, arguing that Polk had purposely

---

2   Ironically, opposition to expansion was also often racial in tone. Senator John C. Calhoun of South Carolina argued that the U.S. "never dreamt of incorporating into our Union any but the Caucasian race — the free white race. To incorporate Mexico would be the very first instance of the kind of incorporating an Indian race; for more than half of the Mexicans are Indians, and the other is composed chiefly of mixed tribes."

provoked a crisis. "There is something of an ill omen among us," he said, referring to "the growing disposition to substitute the wild and furious passions in lieu of the sober judgments of the courts." After the war, Ulysses S. Grant described it as "one of the most unjust wars ever waged by a stronger against a weaker nation."

But the majority of Americans supported hostilities. "Let our arms now be carried with a spirit which shall teach the world that, while we are not forward for a quarrel, America knows how to crush, as well as how to expand," Walt Whitman thundered. "What has miserable inefficient Mexico — with her superstition, her burlesque upon freedom, her actual tyranny by the few over the many, what has she to do with the great mission of peopling the new world with a noble race? Be it ours to achieve that mission."

Under the command of generals Winfield Scott and Zachary Taylor — Taylor would succeed Polk as president — and with the help of officers such as Grant and Robert E. Lee, U.S. forces invaded from the north, blockaded Mexican ports and besieged Veracruz, and marched to the capital. Mexico, vanquished, was forced to sign the Treaty of Guadalupe Hidalgo. Later, Mexican president Porfirio Díaz would sigh, "Poor Mexico! So far from God, and so close to the United States."

Many people in the U.S. tend to think of the movement westward as a process of settlement of a vast empty frontier. Mexico's northern territories — California, New Mexico, Texas — were, it is true, sparsely populated, but they had a long history of civilization under Spanish and Mexico rule, not to mention pre-Columbian native America. By the 1840s, most of their people spoke Spanish and observed Roman Catholic rituals and feast days, but their collective ancestry was far more native than Spanish: in the early years after the Columbian encounter, a small group of Spanish men had come to the Americas and taken women from the native population. The prototypes were Cortés and his translator Malinche, who are like Adam and Eve figures for post-Columbian Mesoamerica. Today there is a tendency to call their descendants "Hispanic" (a term invented by the U.S. census office), but that designation defines them by their language and privileges a few male progenitors while ignoring more substantial native lineages.

Fandango: Spanish Dance, San Antonio, by Theodore Gentilz (1819–1906), ca. 1848. "For three centuries under Spanish colonial rule," according to historian J. Patrick McHenry, "provincial towns . . . nurtured a regional pride in their costumes, customs, cuisine, songs and dances." *Gift of the Yanaguana Society, Daughters of the Republic of Texas Library.*

What the conclusion of the U.S.–Mexican War meant for the residents of what is now the American Southwest is that — although many belonged to families that had resided there for generations — they had now become second-class citizens of the new nation into which they were subsumed, a nation whose language, dominant religion, and customs were different from those they had observed for centuries.

Cuando la fuerza ríe, la razón llora (when force laughs, reason cries). *Al más potente, cede el más prudente* (the prudent yield to the powerful). *Hay que aprender a perder, para empezar a juego* (you have to learn how to lose before you can start to play). Those are Latino folk sayings collected by José Antonio Burciaga in *In Few Words / En Pocas*

Palabras, a book I published when I headed a publishing company called Mercury House.[3] The American Southwest is, Burciaga said, "the northernmost link of America Latina." Some refer to this region as Aztlán, the word the Aztecs used to describe the northern region where their people were supposed to have originated.[4] In Nahuatl, the Aztec language, Aztlán can mean "The Place of the Heron" or "The Place of Whiteness." Burciaga riffed on the latter meaning in an essay called "The White Gospel":

> In the beginning was the word and the word was seized by the white man and the word was white and all who wrote were expected to write like a white man. All things said were through the white word and without the white word nothing was said. The white word shone in the darkness; but the darkness grasped it not.
>
> There were prophets of color with red words, blue words, and yellow words. They came from the four winds to bear witness to the white word concerning the truth that all might believe the true word. It is the true word that enlightens every man and woman who comes into the world, regardless of color.[5]

Regardless of color. The residents of what had been Mexico's northern provinces now found themselves in a nation that looked

---

3 José Antonio Burciaga, *In Few Words / En Pocas Palabras* (San Francisco: Mercury House, 1997).
4 *Aztec* is a word that means "People from Aztlán."
5 José Antonio Burciaga, *Weedee Peepo* (Edinburg, TX: Pan American University Press, 1988). Some Chicano writers have gone over to the white side, linguistically speaking: Lázaro Lima, then associate professor of Spanish and Latino Studies at Bryn Mawr College, wrote in *The Latino Body: Crisis Identities in American Literary and Cultural Memory* (New York: New York University Press, 2007) that "the term 'Latino' reimagines itself as a signic space outside the bleachable and assimilable location of privilege in majoritarian culture, all the while asserting its referential locus of agency within those parameters."

Chicano Phone Call, by José Antonio Burciaga (1940–1996). It's easier to be "Hispanic" than "Chicano." From *Last Supper of Chicano Heroes: Selected Works of José Antonio Burciaga* by José Antonia Burciaga. *Copyright © 2008 The Arizona Board of Regents. Reprinted by permission of the University of Arizona Press.*

down upon them because of their ethnicity, in particular their Indian heritage, which made them look more like Malinche and less like Cortés.

When Mexicans invited Anglo settlers across the border between Texas and the U.S., they imagined it would improve the nation's economy and the lives of the territory's residents. Instead, it set the province on the path to U.S. statehood. President Polk pushed the border of Texas south. The conclusion of the war continued the redrawing of the border between the U.S. and Mexico all the way from the Gulf of Mexico to the Pacific Ocean. The residents of the new U.S. regions who had made it their home the longest were no longer to be Mexicans. They had become Chicanos. They had "immigrated" to the U.S. without moving an inch. The border hadn't simply crossed them. It had double-crossed them.

NORTH AMERICA

Pocahontas in London

~~~~

In June 1616 a desk clerk in a London hotel checked in a party of travelers that was remarkable even to his jaded eyes. The lodgers were a mixed group of about ten or twelve men, women, and children. The most startling was a shaman named Uttamatomakkin. His face was boldly painted in bright colors. His hair was shaved on one side of his head, and braided to a length of several feet on the other. He wore a breechcloth and carried a long, notched stick, on which he had tried for a time to record an estimate of England's population before giving up the attempt as hopeless. He was probably traveling in the company of his wife, a daughter of the *mamanatowick*, his people's paramount chief, Powhatan. The clerk must have eyed him nervously, because Uttamatomakkin was in a foul mood — he found everything about London annoying, especially the condescension of its citizens. He would be unimpressed with its King James, about whom he had heard so much, for when English colonists had given Powhatan a white dog the chief himself had fed it. But after Uttamatomakkin had crossed the ocean the English king had given him nothing, proving that he was ignorant of the standards of diplomacy of civilized people. "I am better," he said, "than a white dog!"

Also among the party was a Virginia tobacco farmer named

◀ Illustration to *The Tempest* from Rowe's Shakespeare, 1709. Tobacco farmer John Rolfe and his first wife were among the passengers on the *Sea Venture*, a merchant ship bound for Virginia. The ship was caught in a hurricane and was wrecked off the coast of Bermuda. Rolfe survived and continued to Bermuda, but his wife and a daughter born on the island both died. Survivors' descriptions of the storm that wrecked the ship probably inspired Shakespeare's play *The Tempest*. In Virginia Rolfe would remarry to a young Powhatan captive who had been abducted by the English settlers. In 1616 they would travel together to London.

John Rolfe. He was traveling with his young son, Thomas, and his nineteen-year-old wife, whose name prior to her marriage was Matoaka but who would be known in London by her Christian name, as the Lady Rebecca. She was Uttamatomakkin's wife's half-sister; both were daughters of Powhatan. The group, led by fire-brand Virginia governor Sir Thomas Dale — who had hanged a man on board ship during the ocean crossing — had been assembled as a promotion on behalf of the managers of the Virginia Company, a joint business venture financed by a group of London shareholders who were increasingly impatient to see a return on their investment. But it was Matoaka, whose childhood name had been Pocahontas ("Mischief"), who was to be the celebrity of the party.

It is said that the inn the travelers checked into was the Bell Savage, which was located on London's Ludgate Hill, not far from St. Paul's Cathedral; the site is now mostly a parking lot. The inn had doubled as a playhouse since about the 1560s, making it one of the first stages of the Shakespearean era, and one of the few that somehow managed to operate within the city walls, despite prohibitions against such entertainments. The inn could not have offered the most tranquil lodging experience, as the playhouse had presented martial arts exhibitions by the London Company of the Masters of Defense along with such entertainments as bear baiting and demonstrations of song and wit by actors such as Richard Tarlton. Theatrical "enterludes" were also part of the fare. In 1579 a writer critical of theatrical entertainments made an exception of "the twoo prose Bookes plaied at the Belsauage" (whose name derived from that of an early owner of the establishment), "where you shall finde neuer a woorde without wit, neuer a line without pith, neuer a letter placed in vaine." By the turn of the century, however, the entertainments had been suppressed. Yet the alien, noisy, and aromatic London setting must still have made sleep difficult for the American visitors accustomed to the green forests of the Chesapeake Bay river drainage.

The party's stay at the Bell Savage is presented as fact in many sources, including P. L. Barbour's *The Three Worlds of Captain John Smith*; Anthony Parr's *Ben Jonson, The Staple of News*; Camilla Townsend's *Pocahontas and the Powhatan Dilemma*; Alden

An early inn and playhouse, the White Hart at Southwark. The Virginia Company's delegation to London, including the Powhatan maiden Matoaka (Pocahontas), probably stayed in an inn similar to this one — a long tradition maintains that it was the Bell Savage in London's Ludgate Hill. The arrangement of such inns made them suitable for performances: the yard served as a stage and the stables as dressing rooms for the actors. Lower classes craned for a view from the outer edges of the yard while the more privileged looked down from the upper levels.

Vaughan's *Transatlantic Encounters: American Indians in Britain, 1500–1776*; Ben Weinreb's *The London Encyclopaedia*; Grace Steele Woodward's *Pocahontas*; and many more. Yet not a single comment exists from the time of her visit that mentions Pocahontas staying there. Rather, the story's persistence reflects an enduring association that was deeply held among the colonizing powers.

Europeans had long viewed America as a "belle savage." The word *America* is a feminized version of the name of the Italian explorer and cartographer Amerigo Vespucci. The feminization was not inadvertent. On early maps the continent is often represented by a naked native woman. Columbus had set the tone at the outset, when he claimed to have discovered the Garden of Eden on the Caribbean coast of South America — it was shaped, he said, like a nipple on a woman's breast. Much later, when England entered the Caribbean, Walter Raleigh still saw the region as a woman ripe for taking: "Guayana," he said, "is a country that hath yet her maidenhead." The travel writer Sam Purchas, an active cheerleader for the Virginia Company, saw Virginia in similar terms, as "a virgin . . . not yet polluted with Spaniards' lust"; the name *Virginia* (honoring England's Virgin Queen) encapsulates this point of view. The role of the colonizers, Purchas advised, was to woo her and make her "not a wanton minion, but an honest and Christian wife." Needless to say, as a wife she would serve in a subordinate position. If the early returns from the Virginia colony were not impressive, William Crashaw, in a sermon to "Adventurers and Planters of the Virginia Company," advised, the suitors should not lose heart. Crashaw urged the "adventurers" (investors) to be patient with the results of the "planters" (settlers), on the grounds that even great leaders were once infants "carried in the arms of sillie women."

In an elegy entitled "To His Mistress Going to Bed," John Donne inverted the conceit of colonialism as sexual conquest, comparing his mistress to the continent:

> Licence my roving hands, and let them go
> Before, behind, between, above, below.
> O, my America, my Newfoundland,
> My kingdom, safest when with one man mann'd,
> My mine of precious stones, my empery;
> How am I blest in thus discovering thee!
> To enter in these bonds, is to be free;
> Then, where my hand is set, my soul shall be.

Elsewhere, however, the poet's imperious conceit breaks down, and his lover appears a more treacherous continent:

> The hair a forest of ambushes,
> Of springes, snares, fetters and manacles;
> The brown becalms us when 'tis smooth and plain,
> And when 'tis wrinkled shipwrecks us again.

For Londoners, Matoaka — the Indian "princess" who as a naked girl had once turned cartwheels on the quad in Jamestown but now was making the rounds as a Christian lady bedecked in London finery — embodied and validated their paternalistic vision. Matoaka herself addressed John Smith, the man she was to become famous for rescuing from execution by her father, on this theme. According to Smith, he visited her with several other people in the country home outside London where she and her son and husband had relocated. Upon seeing him "she turned about" and "obscured her face, as not seeming well contented." She was left alone to cool off. When — hours later — she had collected herself and returned to the group, she confronted Smith, telling him, "You did promise Powhatan what was yours should be his, and he the like to you; you called him father being in his land a stranger, and by the same reason so must I do you." Smith replied smoothly that it would not be right for her to call him "father" because she was nobility, the daughter of Powhatan, a king. To this Matoaka answered that Smith was "not afraid to come into my father's country, and cause fear in him and all his people (but me)." Yet, she said, "you fear you here I should call you father. I tell you then I will, and you shall call me child . . ."

The encounter between Matoaka and John Smith in England is one of history's palimpsests. Virtually all of the many writers on the Pocahontas story mention it, and all interpret it according to their perceptions of the participants, particularly of Smith. He is the only source for this incident, which nonetheless has the flavor of authenticity and is one of the few times we hear Matoaka speak.

Smith's admirers tend to believe that Matoaka was flustered by a

John Smith, adventurer, creator of the legend of Pocahontas, and, by his account, lady's man. Smith's rousing tales, such as his report of beheading three Turks in combat, gave rise to a satirical poem by a Welsh clergyman named David Lloyd called "The Legend of Captain Iones." Published in 1631, the year of Smith's death, it parodied his autobiography. The poem proved popular and went through six printings. According to Lloyd, "nor need we stir our brains for glorious stuff / to paint his praise, himself hath done enough."

surprise encounter with a man she had loved, when she had thought him dead. Smith encouraged this reading. Over the years he gradually upped her age in retelling the story, presumably to make a romance more plausible, or less prurient; in fact she was no more than ten or eleven years old when Smith was held captive by Powhatan. Throughout his writings Smith tells of admiring women coming to his assistance when he is in tight spots. He reports that as a slave in Turkey he was protected by a young Muslim princess named Charatza Tragabigzanda. On his escape, Callamata, the wife of a Cossack chief, came to his aid. After he was shipwrecked in France a Madame Chanoie befriended and tended to him. In Virginia, Smith reported, "thirty young women came naked out of the woods (only covered behind and before with a few green leaves), their bodies all painted, some white, some red, some black, some parti-colored" and danced a ring around a fire, offering themselves to him, each in turn crying, "Love you not me?"

Despite this suspect pattern in his narrative, Smith has many champions, especially among those who think of him as one of the founding fathers of America. In historian J. A. Leo Lemay's assessment, for example, Smith was "energetic, disciplined, assertive, brave, independent . . . practical yet idealistic, studious and learned as well as a man of action, a social visionary as well as a pragmatist, and a kindly humanitarian . . . [with] nearly universal competence." Lemay and others tend to have faith in the veracity of Smith's stories, many of which have indeed been substantiated from other sources.

There are problems, however, with Smith's account of his rescue by Pocahontas. According to Smith, in December 1607 he and two companions were exploring (or perhaps trying to extort corn from the Indians — his story varies) upriver from the English settlement at Jamestown when they were attacked by Powhatan Indians. Smith was captured and taken to the confederacy's leader, Powhatan, father of Pocahontas (somewhat confusingly he was known by a throne name that was the same as the name of his people, and not by his regular name, Wahunsenacawh). As Smith told and retold this story, his part in it swelled with the passage of time — and the passing of witnesses to his Virginia adventures. In a 1608 account of his capture, for example, Smith reported that he held off a small group of Indians with a pistol until being overwhelmed by a force of two hundred men. In 1612 he revised the story and now held off two hundred men until getting mired in a bog. By 1624 the party had grown to three hundred men, with Smith suffering several wounds not previously mentioned. In this version he single-handedly held off the warriors even after falling into the bog, being captured only after he had become too numb with cold to continue.

Powhatan, believing Smith to be a leader of the English colony, tried to co-opt him into his confederacy, as he had done with other vassal chiefs. The two men shared a banquet, and then Smith was released back to Jamestown. The entire legend of Pocahontas's rescue of Smith while he was Powhatan's prisoner stems from this brief passage from his *Generall Historie of Virginia, New-England, and the Summer Isles*, 1624 (Smith refers to himself in the third person):

> At last they brought him to Meronocomoco, where was Powhatan their Emperor. Here more than two hundred of those grim Courtiers stood wondering at him, as he had beene a monster; till Powhatan and his trayne had put themselues in their greatest braveries. Before a fire vpon a seat like a bedsted, he sat covered with a great robe, made of Rarowcun [raccoon] skinnes, and all the tayles hanging

by. On either hand did sit a young wench of 16 to 18 yeares, and along on each side the house, two rowes of men, and behind them as many women, with all their heads and shoulders painted red; many of their heads bedecked with the white downe of Birds; but every one with something: and a great chayne of white beads about their necks. At his entrance before the King, all the people gaue a great shout. The Queene of Appamatuck was appointed to bring him water to wash his hands, and another brought him a bunch of feathers, in stead of a Towell to dry them: having feasted him after their best barbarous manner they could, a long consultation was held, but the conclusion was, two great stones were brought before Powhatan: then as many as could layd hands on him, dragged him to them, and thereon laid his head, and being ready with their clubs, to beate out his braines, Pocahontas the King's dearest daughter, when no intreaty could prevaile, got his head in her armes, and laid her owne vpon his to saue him from death: whereat the Emperour was contented he should liue to make him hatchets, and her bells, beads, and copper; for they thought him as well of all occupations as themselues.

The only source for the legend is Smith himself, and whether it happened at all has been the subject of lively debate since the nineteenth century. Because the story is difficult to prove or disprove, the debate will doubtless continue. But it is hard to reconcile Smith's romantic tale of rescue with what is known of Powhatan practices, and it promotes a ten- or eleven-year-old girl to a position of power that has no precedent in this context. Anthropologist Helen Rountree, the leading researcher on Virginia Indians and an honorary member of the Nansemond and Upper Mattaponi tribes, has written that "the 'rescue' is part of a sequence of events that would be farcical if so many people did not take it seriously as 'Virginia history.'... Pocahontas did not rescue John Smith. Even if she had been inside the house at the time, he would not have needed rescuing from anything other than overeating."

Smith also reported a conversation with Powhatan that curiously echoes one of the themes of his exchange with Matoaka in London. As was so often the case, the occasion was a meeting where Smith attempted to coerce Powhatan into providing the colony with corn, as the settlers had proven unable to survive without native assistance. Smith told Powhatan he was acting as an emissary from Captain Christopher Newport. He pointedly reminded Powhatan that the English had a great advantage in arms, but assured him that they would not use them because of the fellowship they felt with Powhatan. To this the chief cogently replied,

> Captain Newport you call father, and so you call me. But I see, for all us both, you will do what you list, and we must both seek to content you. But if you intend so friendly as you say, send hence your arms, that I may believe you.

All of this talk of fathers reminds us that the history of Virginia comes down to us from the Englishmen who recorded it. The paternalistic English society typically spoke of both religious and civil leaders as fathers. James I said, "Kings are compared to fathers in families: for a king is truly *parens patriae*, the political father of his people." The position of women was distinctly subordinate; often, as with John Rolfe's first wife, who died during the couple's passage to Virginia, we do not even know their names. While the native Virginians also esteemed fathers, their society was matrilineal, and this led to confusion and misunderstanding. Friends of Smith, for example, proposed that "he would have made himself a king by marrying Pocahontas, Powhatan's daughter," but this was not the case. The English were mistaken in thinking her a princess. Upon Powhatan's death his "kingdom" would fall first to his brothers and then to his sisters (the society was matrilineal, not matriarchal — inheritance passed through the mother's line, but it went to the sons before the daughters). Thereafter his nephews and nieces would be next in line. Since the mother of Pocahontas was not one of Powhatan's important wives, neither she nor her brothers would ever be in the line of succession, despite his having been their father — in fact, with each succession Matoaka's proximity to power would grow more distant. She was just an ordinary girl, though one whose bold and inquisitive personality found favor both with her father and with the newcomers to Powhatan lands.

Still the settlers persisted in their notion that the girl was a princess of the highest value. It appears that Powhatan played along with the idea, often sending his daughter along with messengers to the fort at Jamestown in a show of good will. Finally the colonists seized their chance and kidnapped her for use as a diplomatic pawn, though they rationalized the action as bringing her the benefit of the Christian religion. Kidnapping children was an explicit strategy of the English. Biblical precedents were cited in sermons in London, and the Virginia Company had issued a directive to the settlers "to procure from them some of their Children to be brought up in our language and manners if you think it necessary . . . by a surprise of them and detaining them prisoners and in case they shall be willful and obstinate, then to send us some 3 or 4 of them into England, we may endeavor their conversion here." It is conceivable that the kidnapping was not unforeseen by Powhatan, who still hoped to convert the newcomers into vassals of his confederacy. Marriage of women into outsider groups was as much a component of diplomacy for the American natives as it was for the Europeans. Powhatan himself was reported to have had a hundred wives, and this created many kinship ties that enabled him to secure his base of power.

The well-known phenomenon whereby hostages feel sympathy with their captors is called the Stockholm syndrome, after a 1973 bank robbery in Sweden. FBI data suggests that such sympathy is felt by more than a quarter of hostages. It is most common where the aggressor holds power over a victim who feels grateful for the occasional small kindness. Something similar must have affected some of the early modern women who, to restore their honor, became the wives of men who had raped them. It may also have affected the Powhatan maiden Matoaka, who was kidnapped and subsequently married to

Pocahontas Saving the Life of John Smith (detail), 1870. New England Chromo. Lith. Co. Color lithograph. This nineteenth-century lithograph perpetuates the legend of Pocahontas's saving John Smith from the block; many scholars question whether the event happened at all. In any case, Pocahontas would have been a girl of ten or eleven years old at the time and not the nubile maiden imagined by the artist (nor, of course, did the Powhatans live in teepees or dress up as Aztec kings).

John Rolfe, a member of the colony that abducted her. Consistent with Stockholm syndrome behavior, she complained that her father Powhatan would not exchange her for weapons (he did pay part of the ransom the colonists requested but felt he could not in good conscience give up the weapons and tools requested of him), and she was reported to have been reluctant to leave England and return to Virginia after her visit. In the broadest sense, a large percentage of the female population of the early modern period, essentially held subject by their brothers, fathers, and sons, may have experienced aspects of something like the Stockholm syndrome. Some women exhibited the feelings of shame, self-blame, subjugation, paradoxical gratitude, and resignation that have been identified as symptoms of a victimization syndrome that may be thought of as a subset of post-traumatic stress disorder. (Reading the above, my daughter Ellen suggests it could be argued that "attitudes that seem to be gratitude and indebtedness were carefully crafted written and public expressions in line with social mores of the time, rather than innermost feelings." She says I should grant women more "subtle autonomy" than the passage might imply.)

More is known about John Rolfe than about his wives, as is typical of the time. Matoaka is, to a degree, an exception, but even in her case we have only a few remarks in her own voice, whereas we have extended texts from her husband. Her brief moment of celebrity in London was in a sense artificially generated as an aspect of the public relations efforts of the Virginia Company, whose directors wanted to show a reformed heathen as an example of their good work. Apart from that moment, she does not often appear in contemporaneous writings related to the Virginia Colony and does not become a prominent part of its history until John Smith's romanticized story about her became popular in later centuries.

Matoaka was the second of John Rolfe's three wives. The first was a woman known to history only as Mistress Rolfe. In 1609 Rolfe, then in his mid-twenties, decided to take passage to Virginia on a newly built three-hundred-ton armed merchant ship called the *Sea Venture*. One hundred forty men were aboard, along with ten women, among them Mistress Rolfe, who was with child. The expedition, funded by the Virginia Society, was intended to bring resources of people and supplies to the new, struggling Jamestown colony. In July the vessel was hit by a hurricane. The ship took water and everyone aboard patched cracks with anything they could find, cast off possessions and cargo, and bailed furiously for thirty-six hours. Just as the travelers had reached the end of their strength and were preparing for death, the ship crashed on a reef off the coast of Bermuda. Everyone aboard was able to reach the island in the ship's boats; there the castaways happily discovered a population of hogs left by early explorers.

Among the travelers was William Strachey, who left an account of the voyage. "The storm in a restless tumult had blown so exceedingly as we could not apprehend in our imaginations any possibility of greater violence; yet did we still find it not only more terrible but more constant, fury added to fury. . . . Winds and seas were as mad as fury and rage could make them," Strachey wrote. "The sea swelled above the clouds and gave battle unto Heaven. . . . I had been in some storms before. . . . Yet all that I had ever suffered gathered together might not hold comparison with this: there was not a moment in which the sudden splitting or instant oversetting of the ship was not expected." Although the Virginia Society tried to suppress his account as bad press, it probably inspired Shakespeare's *Tempest*, which was first performed in 1611.

The Rolfes' daughter, christened Bermuda, was born on the island but died shortly after. Over the following months the enterprising colonists constructed two pinnaces, which they called the Deliverance and the Patience. The Rolfes took ship for Virginia on one of these vessels, but Mistress Rolfe died on the way, or soon after arriving. Women's lives were short, so marriages seldom lasted more than a couple of decades.

In Virginia Rolfe now found himself without a family, and Matoaka caught his eye. When she was captured, she was a married woman. What became of her husband, a man named Kocoum, is unknown. Among the Powhatans separation could dissolve marriage bonds, but it is curious that little was made of her first marriage by the English. Possibly they considered it nonbinding because of its non-Christian nature, or maybe they just chose to ignore it because it did not suit the message of native conversion that they were trying to convey back to England in order to garner additional support for the colony.

Matoaka was kept captive for more than a year. She was placed in the care of the women of the colony, who dressed her in the English fashion and instructed her in appropriate female behavior. A clergyman named Alexander Whitaker was charged with making her literate and teaching her the Christian religion. She learned the Lord's Prayer, the Ten Commandments, the Apos-

tles' Creed, and the Catechism. Whitaker baptized her with the name Rebecca. Around this time she attracted the attention of Rolfe, who was beginning to make tobacco farming in Virginia a viable business (his breakthrough had come when he imported *Nicotiana tabacum* seeds from Trinidad to replace the harsher native strain; how he obtained the seeds is not known). Rolfe wrote a long, anguished letter to the governor of the colony in which he struggled with his apparent guilt at feeling lust for a heathen but concluded that his religious duty justified marrying the captive woman. "What should I doe?" he wrote. "Shall I be of so untoward a disposition, as to refuse to leade the blind into the right way? Shall I be so unnaturall, as not to give bread to the hungrie? or uncharitable, as not to cover the naked? Shall I despise to actuate these pious dueties of a Christian? Shall the base feare of

▲ Design for a masque by Inigo Jones, 1609. On January 1, 1616, several significant events occurred. An enormous galleon filled with luxury goods from China arrived at the port of Acapulco — Pacific trade marked a new maritime globalism. On the same date, the astronomer Johannes Kepler sent a letter to officials in Germany defending his mother against charges of witchcraft — that case exemplifies the growing conflict between emerging science and magical thinking.

Also on this date, King James I of England and his queen, Anne of Denmark, attended a royal masque entitled *The Golden Age Restored*. The masques, a sort of combination pageant, drama, ballet, and ballroom dance, represented a new taste for theatrical spectacle that was making the old Shakespearean theater seem outdated.

In this same year Matoaka (Pocahontas) arrived in London. The following January she would have a place of honor at another royal masque, *The Vision of Delight*. Many such extremes of dislocation occurred during an age of unprecedented movement and unsettling change.

displeasing the world, overpower and with holde mee from revealing unto man these spirituall workes of the Lord, which in my meditations and praiers, I have daily made knowne unto him? God forbid."

God forbid indeed. There is no record of Matoaka's feelings for Rolfe, but he need not have been so troubled. The marriage fit perfectly with the Virginia Company's public relations plans, and was approved. The couple were married in April 1614 (the discovery of the remains of the wooden church where they were wed was called one of the top archaeological discoveries of 2010), and Matoaka gave birth to a son, Thomas, nine months later. In London in 1616 Matoaka was exhibited as a princess and made the rounds as American royalty. Her portrait was done by a young Dutchman, Simon van de Passe. Latin and English inscriptions on the engraving he produced identify her as "Matoaks als Rebecka," princess, daughter of Powhatani, emperor of Virginia, "converted and baptized in the Christian faith, and wife to the worthy Mr. Joh Rolff." Not everyone, however, bought the Virginia Company's line. One Londoner sent a copy of the engraving to a friend with the bitter comment, "Here is a fine picture of no fayre Lady and yet with her tricking up and high stile and titles you might thincke her and her worshipfull husband to be sombody, yf you do not know that the poore companie of Virginia out of theyre povertie are faine to allow her fowre pound a weeke for her maintenance."

As a visiting princess Matoaka attended the royal Twelfth Night masque in the Banqueting House at Whitehall Palace in January 1617. An observer reported that "the Virginian woman Poca-huntas, with her father counsaillor hath been with the King and graciously used, and both she and her assistant well placed at the maske." Although the English regarded Uttamatomakkin as Matoaka's assistant, from the Powhatan point of view it was he who should have been regarded as the visiting dignitary.

The masque, by Ben Jonson and Inigo Jones, was called *The Vision of Delight*. Like all royal masques it exalted the king. *The Vision* celebrated the advent of spring in his kingdom, with dancers representing Delight, Harmony, Grace, Love, Laughter, Revel, Sport, and Wonder. The antimasque figures were comical pantaloons and phantasms, drawn from the Italian commedia dell'arte, who represented vices of gluttony and lechery. To begin the concluding dance, courtiers descended from a Bower of Spring; the featured dancer was George Villiers, the king's new favorite (famous for his shapely legs), who had recently been named Earl of Buckingham.

What might Matoaka have thought of this spectacle? Again, she leaves no record of her feelings. But shortly after the performance the Rolfes prepared to return to Virginia — "sore against her will," according to an observer. She did not get far. Many of the visitors from Virginia had most likely been infected with a form of dysentery known as the "bloody flux" (some sources say their affliction was a lung disease, pneumonia or tuberculosis). The ship had to stop before it had exited the Thames. Matoaka was taken ashore. There she died within hours and was buried in an unmarked grave in a churchyard in the town of Gravesend.

Having lost his second wife, Rolfe prepared to continue to Virginia with their son. But Thomas too was ill. Rolfe left the boy on shore to be retrieved by a relative and went on alone. He would never see his son again, but Thomas survived. After his father's death he would return as an adult for the first time to his birthplace, where he would fight against his mother's people and become a person of influence.

After his return to Virginia John Rolfe married for a third time, to a daughter of original Virginia colonists. His tobacco enterprise prospered, and he became a wealthy landowner. In his lifetime he was highly regarded, while Matoaka, like most women of her age, had been thought of little consequence — except as a pawn, first in the interplay between the colonists and the Powhatans and then as a public relations symbol for the Virginia Company in London. But by 1995, when Disney Studios made an animated film of her story (presenting her, one critic said, as a "buckskin Barbie"), the situation had become reversed. The film company wrote Rolfe entirely out of the story.

Matoaka als Rebecca, 1616, by Simon van de Passe. Copper engraving. The inscription under this portrait made from life reads *Ætatis suæ 21 A. 1616*, Latin for "at the age of 21 in the year 1616." In fact Matoaka, better known as Pocahontas, was only nineteen at the time. The Virginia Company exaggerated her age because they wanted to show off a convert to Christianity who was beyond what was considered the age of consent.

This World Makes Trickster

❧❧❧

In *Trickster Makes This World*, Lewis Hyde, author of *The Gift: Imagination and the Erotic Life of Property* (1983), looks at the trickster figure in folklore and mythology, extrapolates a sort of universal trickster impulse, and considers expressions of that impulse in modern art and literature.

THE TRAP OF APPETITE

> "What is a sermon that surpasses the teaching of the Buddha and the Patriarchs?" Yunmen was asked.
> "Cake!" he replied.

Hyde divides his analysis into four parts, beginning with the "Trap of Nature" and ending with the "Trap of Culture" — an organization that reflects the basic movement of his argument from natural to cultural history. Viewing the trickster as an inevitable cultural outgrowth of natural law, Hyde portrays Trickster as a basic response to inescapable traps of the human condition. The first and most basic of these traps is the "trap of appetite," from which "the trickster myth derives creative intelligence." "Trickster starts out hungry, but before long he is master of the kind of creative deception that, according to a long tradition, is a prerequisite of art." Hyde thinks that "trickster stories . . . preserve a set of images from the days when what mattered above all else was hunting." He sees, in other words, the trickster impulse as a throwback to our most ancient conditions, a sort of vestigial tale that we wag behind us even as we evolve more sophisticated cultural forms.

Hyde takes a sort of fractal approach, drawing big conclusions from minute details. In fact, in one of his longest reaches, he takes us all the way back to the protazoan *Trypanosoma brucei*, the

◀ The trickster figure Coyote canoeing, from Edward S. Curtis, *Indian Days of the Long Ago* (Yonkers-on-Hudson: World Book Company, 1915).

"predatory" microbe that causes sleeping sickness. The microbe changes its outer protein coat, Hydes tells us, to escape human antibodies: it "is like a con man at a masquerade."

So Hyde proposes a biological basis for shiftiness, which eventually finds expression in trickster stories — Trickster represents an essential striving, a basic life force like that posited by Freud. Advancing from the microbial level, Hyde explicitly relates Trickster to natural evolution, citing several examples from the animal world where predators and their prey evolve new tricks to outwit each other in the eternal game of appetite. What Hyde seems to be getting at in his discussion of appetite is that tricks or lies are a basic survival mechanism, and that they become more sophisticated as one ascends the evolutionary ladder from primitive to complex and from prey to predator — indeed, trickery is what propels such evolution: "The mythology of trickster figures is, by one reading, the story of intelligence arising from appetite."

Hyde concludes this part of his argument with some paragraphs on Melville's *The Confidence-Man,* suggesting that this book, in which "a confidence man appears in a series of masks and roles, never as himself," is in some sense an outgrowth of the evolutionary dodginess he has detailed. If the microbe was "like a con man," then the con man must be like the microbe. It is a prodigious and perhaps unprecedented leap from the microbial to the literary — a leap that is fascinating to watch, but one we might hesitate to follow. Hyde's commentary may not much help us to better understand either *Trypanosoma brucei* or *The Confidence-Man.* Before considering to what extent it helps us to better understand Trickster, let's look at the rest of Hyde's argument.

A NET TO CATCH CONTINGENCY

> Chance is the fool's name for fate.
> — Fred Astaire, in *The Gay Divorcee*

Hyde continues his evolutionary approach to the trickster phenomenon in a discussion of accident and chance. "Theories of evolution have shown us," he says, "that, even though it is difficult at first to imagine how a process that depends on chance can be creative, nevertheless it is by such a process that creation itself has come to be." Trickster is a figure of the doorway, the byway, the cross-roads — one who wanders or who waits for the opportune accident, who capitalizes on the flukes of chance. One of the ways that Trickster "makes this world" is by taking us out of established patterns and following unexpected pathways. "Accident is needed for certain kinds of change," Hyde says. "Chance operations can change the mind because they circumvent intention." Being open to this kind of mental change is the key to Trickster's creativity: "The ability to create or work with contingency I take to be a mark of trickster's intelligence."

Hyde looks at Hermes (god, among other things, of roads), the Norse mischief maker Loki, the Yoruba trickster Eshu, and other folk and mythic figures, noting that often a chance meeting or an unexpected incident proves the vehicle for opportunistic creativity. Although Hyde does not discuss it, there is an affinity between trickster stories and the picaresque in literature, both in its narrow definition as an early Renaissance Spanish literary genre and in its wider common usage. Perhaps this is because of the element of chance that appears in both stories: the *pícaro*, like Trickster, is swept from incident to incident and from master to master, always surviving by tricks and pranks. But Hyde moves from the mythic (and the classical) to the modern without lingering much on intervening literary history.

As modern expressions of this tendency of Trickster to capitalize on chance, Hyde rounds up the usual suspects, focusing mostly on Marcel Duchamp and John Cage. Of Cage he writes that he

> was not blind to the fact that cultures and selves guard and
> replicate their ideals, their beauties, their masterpieces, but
> he did not cast his lot with durable structures, he cast it
> with perturbation. He turned toward chance to relieve the
> mind of its protective garment of received ideas so that it
> might better attend to the quietly stirring wind of the rain

patterning the roof. He made an art that was a net to catch contingency. He cocked his ear for noise, not the old harmonies, sensing that noise can lead to something so remarkable as this world, and believing that, in a civilization as complex and shifting as ours has become, a readiness to let the mind change as contingency demands may be one prerequisite of a happy life.

Chance, in culture as in nature, is a force for evolution and for change. Cage, like a trickster, stirs things up, refusing to submit to the established order.

PLAYING IN THE DIRT

> Degradation digs a bodily grave for a new birth; it has not only a destructive, negative aspect, but also a regenerating one.
> — Mikhail Bakhtin, *Rabelais and His World*

Hyde calls the third section of his book "Dirt Work," but I prefer (in the subhead above) to emphasize the play element in Trickster's bawdy and excremental exploits — what Hyde would call his "shameful" behavior. Throughout his analysis, Hyde gives little attention to the comic element in trickster tales (which enables him to track the trickster spirit in such sober figures such as Frederick Douglass). But in traditional storytelling, trickster tales are often greeted with laughter. Certainly, behind the laughter there is a serious side to the tales, but this only recalls Johan Huizinga's dictum that "the child plays in deadly earnest" — that is, that play can be a serious business.

The long trickster lineage tends to get wrapped up with the fool and the clown, both in performance and in literature. In carnival, the commedia dell'arte, the pantomime, and slapstick we might see a modern expression of the trickster impulse. Paul Radin, whose work is the lodestone of trickster studies (and whom Hyde quotes often), observed that "many of trickster's traits were perpetuated in the figure of the medieval jester, and have survived right up to the present day in the Punch-and-Judy plays and in the clown."

Farce (as would fit Hyde's theories of appetite since it was originally a cooking term) and maybe laughter itself are ways of "breaking the frame," of opening closed systems to allow new forms to evolve. Like Trickster, the clown and the fool stir things up; they overturn the established order. The clown crashes through the boundaries of the stage and rushes and somersaults through the audience, bringing the periphery, at least for the moment, to the center and turning convention on its head. This side of the topic might have been interesting to explore.

In "Dirt Work," Hyde considers the transgressive quality of Trickster's activities, his use of obscene, licentious, and offensive materials. He does not spend much time here on traditional trickster tales, preferring instead to look at modern manifestations of the trickster principle in works by Maxine Hong Kingston, Richard Rodriguez, Allen Ginsberg, Andres Serrano, and Robert Mapplethorpe. Hyde says, "Trickster's freedom with dirt means he can operate where fastidious high gods cannot and as a result heaven's fertility and riches enter this world."

That Trickster is transgressive is agreed upon, but Hyde's argument takes an unusual turn when he focuses on the "shame" such trangression entails. I have always tended to think of Trickster as shameless, and indeed Hyde himself says, "They're all the same, these tricksters; they have no shame and so they have no silence. Hermes should bite his tongue when he's hauled before the assembly of the gods, but instead he wiggles his ears and tells a bold-face lie, wearing — his mother says — 'the cloak of shamelessness.' Loki once had his lips sewn shut by an irritated dwarf, but Loki ripped the thongs out and went right on talking." Yet Hyde goes on to consider shame as a major element in the work of Kingston, Rodriguez, and Ginsberg.

I have some trouble following this part of Hyde's argument, but I think that he is shifting his focus to a psychological/social level in order to consider the dilemma of contemporary writers who have not been ordained as representatives of the sacred and so are shamed when their work is transgressive. But because transgression is necessary to open up the closed social system in which they live, such writers take upon themselves the shamelessness of Trickster (as Kingston adopted the East Asian trickster Monkey as her psychic ally in writing *The Woman Warrior*) in order to find voice for their shameful visions. While the mythological Trickster lives in a world of gods, where shamelessness is allowed him, these writers are caught between the ordinary social world and the mythic world of their art; as a result they are caught between shame, which causes one to be silent, and shamelessness, which encourages one to speak. "A kind of collective magic activates a shame threshold," Hyde writes. "The group marks a boundary and those who try to cross it, if they feel the communal Argus eyes upon them, will suffer shame's physical seizure, the flushed skin, the bound tongue." By taking this stance, Hyde finds more to say about these authors than others he has considered, but he also broadens his subject so greatly that it seems to encompass everything and nothing. (David Foster Wallace says, in a blurb on the promotional band that wraps around the book, "This book . . . ends up being about . . . well, everything.")

In one of the best commentaries in the book, Hyde looks at Andres Serrano's *Piss Christ* as an attempt at revitalizing faith, and he considers how it fell afoul of political attack. "The old wisdom would say that this debasing of the god is a necessary part of his periodic renewal," Hyde explains. Serrano intervenes "to save the divine form from its own too elevated purity. But we currently have no collective form, no agreed-upon narrative, to guide us in such operation." His comments on this subject are among the freshest moments in his book. Still, I'm not sure that simply transgressing social boundaries or taboos makes Serrano a trickster. Again I am intrigued by the connections between the trickster and the clown, and I think of the performances of Zuni clowns described by Jerrold E. Levy: "At the height of public performances, these clowns will eat excrement, throw bowls of urine on each other, eat the heads of living mice and the intestines of living dogs torn limb from limb.

Their sexual antics . . . were of an indescribable lewdness." Maybe the tradition of clowning could offer another context for viewing Andres Serrano's work.

THE TRAP OF CULTURE

> The clown, the early counterpart of the trickster, would have in ritual the role of evoking the violation of taboo, hyposta-sized in myth. These two imaginary figures would thus share a common origin in the experience of society, i.e., in the transgressive activities of magicians engaged in prohibited operations and manipulations to gain magical power.
> — Laura Makarius, "Ritual Clowns"

By evoking the shamelessness of the mythic trickster, the creative artist overcomes shame and breaks through the shackles of social constraint. In so doing, the artist highlights and calls into question the constraints themselves, so that the social system as a whole evolves and develops, just as the individuals within it do. Trickster remakes the world, and remakes it again, and again.

He does this, says Hyde, through "artus-work" — Hyde traces back the roots of the word *art* to relate it to the word for *joint*. He has shown that the trickster, driven by appetite, strives for the pores or joints in a network of restraint. Now he concludes:

> I would like to suggest that we think of trickster artists as artus-workers, joint-workers. Not that they are much involved with making the firm and well-set joints that lead to classical harmony, of course. What tricksters like is the flexible or movable joint. If a joint comes apart, or if it moves from one place to another, or if it simply loosens up where it had begun to stiffen, some trickster has probably been involved. In several different ways, tricksters are joint-disturbers.

Hyde begins literally, by relating trickster stories to origin myths of meat carving and sacrifice. But his real subject is the way that trickster figures can reconfigure their worlds. By questioning and confronting the established order, they cause a revision in that order — a new configuration (perhaps articulation would be a better word) — of its joints, the web of meaning that makes the net of culture. This is wonderful, but not terribly new. In his essay "Liminality and Communitas," V. Turner called such figures "threshold people" and noted that their attributes "are necessarily ambiguous, since this condition and these persons elide or slip through the network of classifications that normally locate states and positions in cultural space." Hyde, however, prefers his own articulation, working directly from the traditional and modern texts and not getting bogged down in a lot of consideration of some existing bodies of theory and criticism.

One thing he does not much remark on is that while Trickster plays a trick on culture by attacking and reconfiguring its joints, the culture plays a similar trick on Trickster by wrapping him within its net of signification. By institutionalizing Trickster and the artist who reflects his spirit, it internalizes and contains the questioning spirit. In his study *The Fool and His Scepter*, William Willeford neatly observed that

> If the fool is "the spirit of disorder," he is necessarily "the enemy of boundaries," but since the disorder of which he is the spirit is largely contained in his show, he serves the boundary of which he is the enemy; and in doing this, he sometimes even demonstrates an authority proper to the central figure of an established order (such as the king, the president, the chief, the boss).

Despite this limitation on the scope of Trickster's activities (Hermes will always be a fringe figure; he will never depose Zeus — or if he does, he will cease to be Hermes), "when human culture turns against human beings themselves the trickster appears as a kind of savior," according to Hyde. "When we have forgotten that we participate in the shaping of this world and become enslaved to shapings left us by the dead, then a cunning artus-worker may appear, sometimes erasing the old boundaries so fully that only no-way remains and creation must start as if from scratch, and sometimes just loosening up the old divisions, greasing the joints so they may shift in respect to one another, or opening them so commerce will spring up where 'the rules' forbid it. In short, when the shape of culture itself becomes a trap, the spirit of the trickster will lead us into deep shape-shifting . . . to wake the possibility of playing with the joints of creation, the possibility of art."

WHO IS TRICKSTER?

> Then are we in order when we are most out of order.
> — *Henry VI*

Hyde brings a courageous willingness to follow his subject farther down some of its sidepaths than others have done — he is not afraid to move from the tales of native peoples to the autobiography of Frederick Douglass to the art of Andres Serrano.

In moving from the particular to the extremely general, I'm afraid Hyde's learned commentary cannot conceal a certain imprecision in his argumentation. The first and most frustrating of these is his failure to clearly define what he is analyzing. He is writing, he says, about Trickster. But what is a trickser? It is a figure with a trickster's qualities. What then are the qualities of a trickster? They are the qualities that a trickster has. In this maddeningly circular way, Hyde fails to nail down his subject — has Trickster evaded his traps? Nor is it altogether clear what Hyde is attempting in his analysis of the work of modern artists. He cannot be simply calling them out as tricksters, which would be pointless, and Hyde's work is not pointless. Instead he seems to be trying to extrapolate a universal trickster quality or attitude, which he considers a key component of all culture, or all healthy culture.

Is Hyde writing about tricksters (nominative) or tricking (active)? When he talks about what he is doing, he speaks in the nominative mode — what Trickster is — but the analysis he actually performs is in the verbal mode — what Trickster does. Look at one of the first examples Hyde gives us of what he considers a trickster tale, a Native American story in which Buffalo Bull gives Coyote a magic cow. Buffalo Bull tells Coyote:

> "Never kill this cow, Coyote. When you are hungry, cut off a little of her fat with your flint knife. Rub ashes on the wound. The cut will heal. This way, you will have meat forever."
>
> Coyote promised this is what he would do. He took the buffalo cow with him back over the mountains. Whenever he was hungry he would cut away a little fat and then heal the wound with ashes as Buffalo Bull had said. But after a while he got tired of the fat. He wanted to taste the bone marrow and some fresh liver. By this time he had crossed the plains and was back in his own country. "What Buffalo Bull said is only good over in his country," Coyote said to himself. "I am chief here. Buffalo Bull's words mean nothing. He will never know."
>
> Coyote took the young cow down to the edge of the creek. "You look a little sore-footed," he told her. "Stay here and rest and feed for a while."
>
> Coyote killed her suddenly while she was feeding. When he pulled off her hide crows and magpies came. When Coyote tried to chase them off, more came. Even more came, until they had eaten all the meat. . . .

Is there a trick in this story? Coyote has, it is true, disobeyed Buffalo Bull's injunction not to kill the cow, and he has hidden his intention to kill the cow from his victim. Coyote has been given a gift with a stipulation attached to it; he ignores the stipulation, and he is punished. The story would seem to fall into the category of "disobedience punished," like the story of Adam or Orpheus or Pandora. How are these trickster figures?

It can't be that Hyde figures that Coyote is a trickster, so therefore every story about Coyote is a trickster story. In fact, he points to this as a "typical" trickster story: "The trickster," he explains, "is given something valuable with a condition set on its use, time passes, and before long a trickster's hunger leads him to violate the condition. As a consequence the plenitude of things is inexorably diminished. . . . Such is one common plot in the mythology of trickster." A common plot, certainly. But if the protagonist were someone other than Coyote, would we still perceive this as a trickster story?

FOOLS AND FOLLY, CLOWNS AND CLOWNING, TRICKS AND TRICKSTERS

> This fellow's wise enough to play the fool.
> — Shakespeare, *Twelfth Night*

Suppose that our subject were not "the trickster" but "trickery" or "tricking" — that is, that we were interested in action rather than in subject, in the verbal rather than the nominative. The closest thing in the action of this story to trickery is Coyote outsmarting himself. It won't do to define tricking so broadly as to include every foolish or unwise action for which one pays a cost. What if we looked at Coyote in this particular story more as a fool than as a trickster? The clown and the fool share many of the same characteristics as Trickster; indeed, the same figure can variously play the fool, the clown, and the trickster, just as Coyote, who so often plays the part of the trickster, takes on the part of the fool in this story.

Among the literature on folly and clowning are such books as Enid Welsford's *The Fool: His Social and Literary History*, Willeford's *The Fool and His Sceptre*, Conrad Hyers's work on the comic in Zen and the Eastern tradition, and, closer to the present subject, the numerous studies of Native American clowns and clowning, such as Matilda Coxe Stevenson's work on Zuni clowning, Frank Bock and Jerrold Levi on Hopi Clowns, or E. T. Kirby on the shamanistic origins of clowning, to name but a few. In a short footnote Hyde writes, "Many, myself included, find the connotations of 'trickster' too limited for the scope of activities ascribed to this character," and he notes as "partly true" the argument that "the general term 'trickster' is an invention of nineteenth-century anthropology and not well fitted to its indigenous objects."

He mines a rich vein when he considers the social function of trickery, but I would find his conclusions more useful if his methodology and terminology were more precise. I suggest we try looking at tricksters, clowns, and fools (or trickery, clowning, and folly) and thinking about the overarching principles through which these figures cause social systems to be questioned, challenged, and modified. And maybe more attention could be given to the ways systems respond by incorporating, co-opting, and internalizing their challenge. Still, in its focus on traps and evasions, and through the links it draws between mythic and modern artistic expression, *Trickster Makes This World* opens appealing sidepaths to explore, which at times open up onto magnificent vistas.

rongna.   *Pernoualla*.

Cucorongna and Pernoualla, 1621, by Jacques Callot (French, 1592–1635). Etching. Two characters from the commedia dell'arte. Many of the characters were various admixtures of fools, tricksters, and clowns.

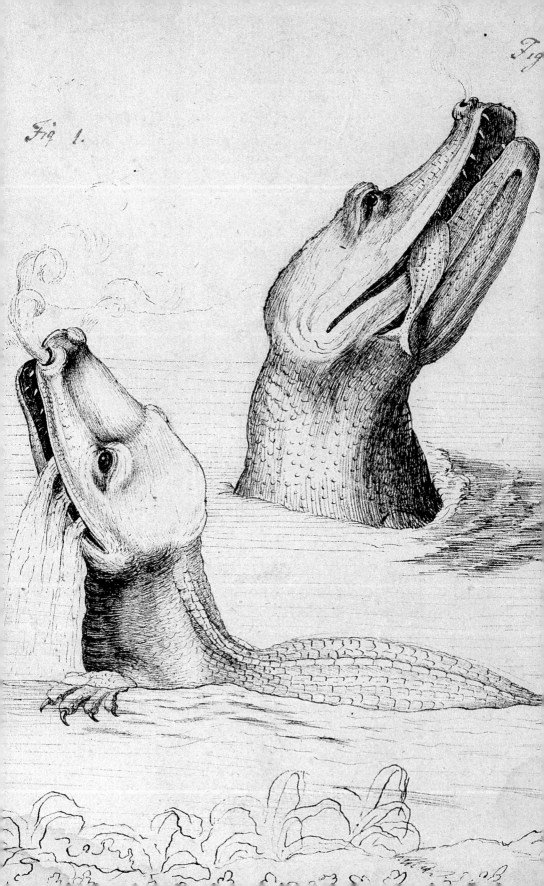

Fig 1.

Natural Man

WILLIAM BARTRAM'S *TRAVELS AND OTHER WRITINGS*

~~~

All things have roots and branches.
All affairs have beginnings and ends.
To know what is first and what is last
Will lead one near the way.
    — From the *Da Xue* ("Great Learning"), a classic Confucian text

When Georgia poet Jonathan Williams titled his selected poems *An Ear in Bartram's Tree* (1957–1967), his paperback publisher, New Directions, wrote that the title "celebrates the early American naturalist William Bartram's discovery of that rarest of native trees, *Franklinia alatamaha*, which has not been seen in the wild since 1803." For Williams, Bartram signified something rare, obscure, and unique — positive qualities in Williams's measure of things — but the sad fact was that by 1967, Bartram, like his tree, had long since stopped being associated with the wild. His remarkable book, *Travels through North and South Carolina, Georgia, East and West Florida, the Cherokee Country, The Extensive Territories of the Muscogulges or Creek Confederacy, and the Country of the Chactaws. Containing an Account of the Soil and Natural Productions of Those Regions; together with Observations on the Manners of the Indians* [1791], was seldom read. (Few will lament that Bartram's style in titles has gone extinct.) Acknowledged as the father of American nature writing, Bartram, like his tree, had become a cultivated relic, a reference point on the road to Thoreau, an obscure landmark in literary and botanical history. But with the Library of America's reissue of *Travels and Other Writings* in 1996 — admirably edited by Thomas P. Slaughter, who provides helpful notes, rare drawings, a chronology, a map, and a glossary of botanical and zoological names — perhaps more readers will return to this prolific American native.

◀ *The Alligator of St. Johns* (detail), 1773 or 1774, by William Bartram. St. Johns River, Florida. Drawing.

William Bartram grew up in the shadow of his stern and authoritarian father, John Bartram, a farmer and self-taught naturalist. John Bartram collected plant specimens for English sponsors — a practice in which his son Billy would later follow him — and is credited with identifying some 150 species of New World plants. Appointed Botanist for the North American Colonies by George III, the elder Bartram began a large botanical garden, which would later be sustained by his son. Such influential figures as George Washington, James Madison, and Alexander Hamilton would visit the gardens during William's lifetime. John Bartram's renown was so great it spread to Europe, where he was hailed by Linnaeus himself as "the greatest natural botanist in the world."

John's grandparents were part of the first wave of Quaker immigrants in 1683 (John's children were the third generation to have been born in America). The elder Bartram believed that "the creatures commonly called brutes possess higher qualifications, and more exalted ideas, than our traditional mystery-mongers are willing to allow them,"[1] a notion that Billy would champion and extend in his *Travels* (among the "brutes," in the prevailing view of the time, were Native American peoples). Apparently a kind of pantheist, John was disowned by his Quaker community for "denying the divinity of Jesus," a censure that seems to have troubled him not at all.

John Bartram's dissension from the conventional beliefs of his community placed him at the beginning of the most fruitful tradition of American naturalism. Thomas J. Lyon has commented on the dissident strain in American nature writing:

> Naturalists and nature writers make up a distinctly noncomforming, even heretical minority. The principal cultural heresy expressed in American nature writing is the refocusing of vision outward from the self, individually, and from the corporate self, our species. A radical proposal follows on the

---

1 Quoted in Thomas J. Lyon, *This Incomperable Lande: A Book of American Nature Writing* (Boston: Houghton Mifflin, 1989), 36.

widened vision: that the environment, nature, is the ground of a positive and sufficient human joy. Nature writers and naturalists do not appear to have conceptualized America as "a vast body of wealth without proprietors," in the phrase of one student of the frontier period; on the contrary, they very often recognized the priority of the Indians' claims and sympathized with them.[2]

Both Bartrams fall into this latter group.

John must have been quite a forceful fellow. Billy, though judging from his *Travels* an athletic and resourceful man, seems to have been made of milder stuff, and he did not really escape his father's control until he was well into his thirties. As a boy he distinguished himself by drawing plants and birds when accompanying his father on botanical expeditions. Later, when Benjamin Franklin (with whom John founded the American Philosophical Society) offered him a printing apprenticeship, his father declined it for him on the grounds that it would be too difficult to succeed financially in such a trade; instead Billy was apprenticed to a Philadelphia shopkeeper. Yet a printing career could not have been less successful than his mercantile career, which resulted in his fleeing Philadelphia to escape creditors. He headed south, where he had previously traveled with his father on a plant-hunting expedition.

In 1772, Billy wrote to his father that he intended to travel to Augusta to pursue his botanical researches because he must "retreat within myself to the only business I was born for, and which I am only good for (If I am entitled to use that phrase for anything)." To this his father peremptorily replied, "I don't intend to have any more of my estate spent there or to ye southward upon any pretense whatever." Nonetheless, for four years, supported by his British patron, John Fothergill, who paid him fifty pounds a year plus expenses for the purpose of discovering "rare and useful productions of nature," Billy (then in his thirties) was able to

---

2   Ibid., 19.

pursue his more or less aimless rambles through the South, ranging from the Carolinas to Florida to Mississippi.

Those adventures, described in *Travels,* must in large part have been an effort to escape not only his creditors but also his domineering father. (After his father's death, Bartram returned to live placidly in the family home outside Philadelphia — bequeathed on his father's death to his younger brother, John — and resisted calls to travel, such as Jefferson's invitation that he accompany Lewis and Clark on their westward expedition.) The literary fashion of the time, combined with the cataloging demands of his patron, made it difficult for Bartram to inject much personal material into his account, but at moments the man reveling in freedom and discovery bursts through his scientific prose and formulaic courtesies.[3] As in much good nature and travel writing, we sense in *Travels* a man discovering not just the natural world but himself as well.

He recalls, for example, an epiphanic moment when he encountered a formidable rattlesnake at close range: "I stopped and saw the monster formed in a high spiral coil, not half his length from my feet: another step would have put my life in his power, as I must have touched if not stumbled over him. The fright and perturbation of my spirits at once excited resentment; at that time I was entirely insensible to gratitude or mercy. I instantly cut off a little sapling and soon dispatched him: this serpent was about six feet in length, and as thick as an ordinary man's leg." Companions had the snake served up for dinner, but Bartram "could not swallow it. I, however, was sorry after killing the serpent, when coolly recollect-

---

3   "The doctor received me with perfect politeness, and on every occasion, treated me with friendship" (28). "It was the seat of virtue, where hospitality, piety, and philosophy, formed the happy family; where the weary traveller and stranger found a hearty welcome" (29). "Han. B. Andrews . . . received and entertained me in every respect, as a worthy gentleman could a stranger" (p. 34). "A house, where I stayed all night, and met with very civil entertainment . . ." (35). "He seemed an active, civil, and sensible man" (38). And so on.

ing every circumstance. He certainly had it in his power to kill me almost instantly, and I make no doubt but that he was conscious of it. I promised myself that I would never again be accessory to the death of a rattle snake, which promise I have invariably kept to" (226–227).

Convinced of the magnanimity of natural creatures, Bartram became a preservationist, raising his voice against the prevailing view of the natural world as a resource to be consumed and exploited. He describes traveling the Mosquito River in Florida and coming upon a group of bears "feeding on the fruit of the dwarf creeping Chamaerops." Although his party had "plenty and variety of provisions," they resolved to shoot one of the bears.

> Finding ourselves near enough, the hunter fired, and laid the largest dead on the spot where she stood; when presently the other, not seeming the least moved at the report of our piece, approached the dead body, smelled, and pawed it, and appearing in agony, cried out like a child. Whilst our boat approached very near, the hunter was loading his rifle in order to shoot the survivor, which was a young cub, and the slain supposed to be the dam. The continual cries of this afflicted child, bereft of its parent, affected me very sensibly; I was moved with compassion, and charging myself as if accessary to what appeared to be a cruel murder, endeavoured to prevail on the hunter to save its life, but to no effect! for by habit he had become insensible to compassion towards the brute creation; being now within a few yards of the harmless devoted victim, he fired, and laid it dead upon the body of the dam. (20)

As travel writing, the most dramatic incident in *Travels* was one that severely tested Bartram's preservationist inclinations. Exploring the St. Johns River in Florida, he entered an area in which alligators were extremely numerous. Bartram set camp in a little clearing, from which vantage he observed a fierce battle between two large gators. Although his "apprehensions were highly alarmed after being a spectator of so dreadful a battle," Bartram, armed only with a club, decided to set out in his canoe for a nearby lagoon to catch some fish for his dinner — a project that put his intentions at odds with the gators'.

> Penetrating the first line of those which surrounded my harbour, they gave way; but being pursued by several very large ones, I kept strictly on the watch, and paddled with all my might toward the entrance of the lagoon, hoping to be sheltered there from the multitude of my assailants; but ere I had half-way reached the place, I was attacked on all sides, several endeavouring to overset the canoe. My situation now became precarious to the last degree: two very large ones attacked me closely, at the same instant, rushing up with their heads and part of their bodies above the water, roaring terribly and belching floods of water over me. They struck their jaws together so close to my ears, as almost to stun me, and I expected every moment to be dragged out of the boat and instantly devoured. But I applied my weapons so effectually about me, though at random, that I was so successful as to beat them off a little. . . . The horrid noise of their closing jaws, their plunging amidst the broken banks of fish, and rising with their prey some feet above the water and blood rushing out of their mouths, and the clouds of vapour issuing from their wide nostrils, were truly frightful. . . . I began to tremble and keep a good look out; when suddenly a huge alligator rushed out of the reeds, and with a tremendous roar came up, and darted swift as an arrow under my boat, emerging upright on my lee quarter, with open jaws, and belching water and smoke that fell upon me like rain in a hurricane. I laid soundly about his head with my club and beat him off. (115, 118, 119)

Though not above dispatching an alligator or two with his firearm back at the campsite, Bartram recalls his naturalism long enough to courageously investigate alligator nests and eggs. This is by modern standards one of the least politically correct moments in Bartram's adventures, and yet it is one of the most successful literary moments, for here the author as a man in nature emerges, and the classifying botanist recedes.

The smoke-belching alligators must have made quite an impression on Bartram. The Modern Library edition includes a number of Bartram's drawings, most of which are models of their kind. But his drawing of *The Alligator of St. Johns* bears little resemblance to the others: It appears to depict a medieval sea monster, belching water and breathing fire.

To a large extent, modern nature writing is a post-Romantic phenomenon. The Romantics' elevation of individuality, spontaneity, intuitive discovery, transcendent experience, and a kind of personal mysticism or sense of oneness with the natural world made possible the development of the personal nature essay. But the most valuable personal observations emerge from a deep knowledge of nature, whether from the scientific discoveries of the great civilizations or the traditional knowledge of native peoples. As a writer of the Enlightenment, Bartram is part of a large project of cataloging and inventorying the natural world (the first stirrings, perhaps, of an attempt to reclaim what had been lost following the ancient conversion to agricultural societies).

In Bartram's work, we see the beginning of an integration of natural science and personal "sensibility" (a word he favored), an integration that would provide the foundation for later American nature writing.

Bartram wrote at a time when Linnaeus's system of classification was still relatively new. Linnaeus (1707–1778) proposed the system of classifying the entire natural world through the use of only two Latin names. Although Linnaeus's elaboration of his own system was soon supplanted, the notion that living things, like humans, could be grouped in family structures suggested that the world should be viewed as a complex system of interrelationships. This notion was the necessary foundation for the discoveries of Darwin and later ecological perspectives.

Bartram was an enthusiastic proponent of Linnaeus's system. The question was how to incorporate this taxonomic knowledge into a personal view of the world, and Bartram did this with varying success. At times he can inventory a scene with deadening precision. When Bartram sets off west from Augusta, he proceeds through "a level plain, generally of a loose sandy soil, producing spacious high forests, of *Pinus taeda, P. lutea, P. squarrosa, P. echinata,* 1. *Quercus sempervirens,* 2. *Quercus acquatica,* 3. *Q. phillos,* 4. *Q. tinctoria,* 5. *Q. dentata,* 6. *Q. prinos,* 7. *Q. alba,* 8. *Q. sinuata,* 9. *Q. rubra, Linodendron tulipifera, Liquidambar styraciflua, Morus rubra, Cercis tilia, Populas heterophylla, Platanus occidentalis, Laurus sassafras, Laurus Borbonia, Hopea tinctoria, Fraxinus excelsior, Nyssa, Ulmus, Juglans exaltata, Halsea, Stewartra*" (p 49). This is surely invaluable information about the transitional plain of the late eighteenth century, but it is not compelling as literature. (Did you skip any on the list? You would have if I had typed out one of his longer catalogs.) The reader is left to wonder: what did the plain look like, feel like, sound like, smell like? What were the relationships between these plants? Did all those *Quercus*es grow together? What determined which might be found in a certain location? How were the plants related to animal life and human culture?

Again, in championing the bounty of the tropics, Bartram offers this passage: "It is difficult to pronounce which division of the earth, between the polar circles, produces the greatest variety. The tropical division certainly affords those which principally contribute to the more luxurious scenes of splendor, as *Myrtus communis, Myrt. caryophyllata, Myrt. pimenta, Caryophyllus aromaticus, Laurus cinnam, Laurus camphor, Laurus Persica, Nux mosch. Illicium, Camillia, Punica, Cactus melo-cactus, Cactus grandiflora, Gloriosa superba . . .*" (14–15). Can you feel the splendor?

Though every bit an American, Bartram was traveling in the service of English science, so his scientific catalogs helped fulfill the mission that was paying his way. His personal bent, however, might have been more appreciative and less analytical — witness, for example, his charming "Anecdotes of an American Crow," in which he writes, "We do not speak here of the crow, collectively, as giving an account of the whole race (since I am convinced, that these birds differ as widely as we do from each other, in point of talent and acquirements), but of a particular bird of that species, which I reared from the nest" — for often enough Bartram fashions a new model for integrating scientific observation with personal experience:

> It is very pleasing to observe the banks of the river ornamented with hanging garlands, composed of varieties of climbing vegetables, both shrubs and plants, forming perpendicular green walls, with projecting jambs, pilasters, and deep apartments, twenty or thirty feet high, and completely covered with *Glycine frutescens, Glyc. apios, Vitus labrusca, Virus vulpina, Rajana, Hedera quinquifolia, Hedera arborea, Eupatorium scandens, Bignonia crucigera,* and various species of *Convolvulus,* particularly an amazing tall climber of this genus, or perhaps an *Ipomea.* This has a very large white flower, as big as a small funnel; its tube is five or six inches in length, and not thicker than a pipe stem; the leaves are also very large, oblong, and cordated, sometimes dentated or angled, near the insertion of the foot-stalk; they are of thin texture, and of a deep green colour. It is exceedingly curious to behold the Wild Squash climbing over the lofty limbs of the trees; its yellow fruit, somewhat of the size and figure of a large orange, pendant from the extremities of the limbs over the water. (128–129)

Here is a riverbank one can visualize, with its fine description of that distinguished American plant, the morning glory. Small wonder that the Romantic writer François-René de Chateaubriand used this passage in his American fictions. Wordsworth and Coleridge are others influenced by Bartram's work, which by the turn of the century had been published in England, Ireland, Germany, and France as well as the new American nation.

Bartram's scientific observations could be quite precise and detailed. Note his description of the tree that Jonathan Williams invoked, *Franklinia* (or *Gordonia) alatamaha*:

It is a flowering tree, of the first order for beauty and fragrance
of blossoms: the tree grows fifteen or twenty feet high, branch-
ing alternately; the leaves are oblong, broadest toward their
extremities, and terminate with an acute point, which is generally a little reflexed; they are lightly serrated, attenuate down-
wards, and sessile, or have very short petioles; they are placed
in alternate order, and toward the extremities of the twigs are
crouded together, but stand more sparsely below; the flowers
are very large, expand themselves perfectly, are of a snow white
colour, and ornamented with a crown or tassel of gold coloured
refulgent staminae in their centre, the inferior petal or segment
of the corolla is hollow, formed like a cap or helmet, and entirely
includes the other four, until the moment of expansion; its
exterior surface is covered with a short silky hair; the borders
of the petals are crisped or plicated: these large, white flowers
stand single and sessile in the bosom of the leaves, and being
near together towards the extremities of the twigs, and usually
many expanded at the same time, make a gay appearance: the
fruit is a large, round, dry, woody apple or pericarp, opening
at each end oppositely by five alternate fissures, containing ten
cells, each replete with dry woody cuneiform seed. (375)

Compare this to the terser, generally less adequate description
from a modern reference work (Norman Taylor, ed., *Taylor's Encyclopedia of Gardening*):

A shrub or small tree, not over 25 ft. high, the branches erect.
Leaves oblongish, 5–7 in. long, remotely toothed, long persistent, but ultimately bright crimson in the late fall. Flowers
cup-shaped, fragrant, about 3½ in. wide. Fruit nearly globe-
shaped, ½–¾ in. in diameter. Ga. Sept.–Oct. Hardy from
zone 5, or, with protection, from zone 4 southward.

Bartram appends to *Travels* an "Account of the Persons, Manners,
Customs and Government, of the Muscogulges, or Creeks, Chero-
kees, Chactaws, &c. Aborigines of the Continent of North America,"

in which he applies the same cataloging and scientific spirit to his study of Native Americans, classifying species, families, and habitats, and treating anthropology like something akin to lepidopterology. This yields some serious data, and Bartram's work is still pertinent for specialists; it also introduces a view of the "noble savage" that would become all the rage for the Romantics. Bartram writes, for example, that these peoples "form a perfect human figure; their features regular, and countenance open, dignified and placid; yet the forehead and brow so formed, as to strike you instantly with heroism and bravery" (386). (He perceived a similar nobility in the rattlesnake.) In "Observations on the Creek and Cherokee Indians," Bartram writes:

> Even a white man, whom they have reason to know is their most formidable, cruel, barbarous, and unrelenting foe, they would cherish as long as he might choose to stay, or else guard him to his country. If he came peaceably to his town, or even if he met him alone in the dreary forest, naked, hungry, bewildered, lost, the Indian would give him his only blanket, half his provisions, and take him to his wigwam, where he would repose securely and quietly, and in the morning conduct him safe back to his own frontier — and all this, even though he had been the day before beaten, bruised, and shot at by a white man. Thus they are hospitable, forgiving, gentle, humane, and grateful, without precept or scholastic education; and this by nature or some other unknown cause, without the least desire or expectation of applause or reward. (553)

Bartram spent considerable time with native people. The Seminoles gave him the name Puc Puggy ("Flower Hunter"). In this way he gained firsthand knowledge of them that caused him to be regarded as an authority. The text quoted immediately above consists of his answers to questions posed by Philadelphia physician and naturalist Benjamin Smith Barton, and the state of anthropological knowledge of the time is clearly reflected in some of Barton's questions, such as whether Indians are white at birth and only later turn reddish, or whether Bartram ever encountered any polka-dotted species.

Bartram's stated purpose in traveling among native peoples was to "judge for myself, whether they were deserving of the severe censure which prevailed against them among the white people, that they were incapable of civilization" (24). Despite his worthy intentions, Bartram's writing on the subject calls to mind Thoreau's remark that if he heard a philanthropist was heading his way he would hurry in the opposite direction. When Bartram pronounces the Indian worthy "of becoming united with us, in civil and religious society" (24), he comes off as condescending. But his compassionate spirit and his sincere effort to understand others (unfortunately, he does not seem to have extended the same effort to African slaves) represent a landmark in American racial relations — a significant, if flawed, beginning.

As I was gathering specimens of flowers from the shrubs, I was greatly surprised at the sudden appearance of a remarkably large spider on a leaf, of the genus *Araneus saliens*: at sight of me he boldly faced about, and raised himself up, as if ready to spring upon me; his body was about the size of a pigeon's egg, of a buff colour, which, with his legs, were covered with short silky hair; on top of the abdomen was a round red spot or ocelle encircled with black. After I had recovered from the surprise, observing that the wary hunter had retired under cover, I drew near again, and presently discovered that I had surprised him on predatory attempts against the insect tribes. I was therefore determined to watch his proceedings. I soon noticed that the object of his wishes was a large fat bomble bee (*apis bombylicus*), that was visiting the flowers, and piercing their nectariferous tubes: this cunning intrepid hunter conducted his subtil approaches with the circumspection and perseverance of a Siminole when hunting a deer, advancing with slow steps obliquely, or under cover of dense foliage, and behind the limbs, and when the bee was engaged in probing a flower, he would leap nearer, and then instantly retire out of sight, under a leaf or behind a branch, at the same time keeping a sharp eye upon me. When he had now gotten within two feet of his prey, and the bee was intent on sipping the delicious nectar from a flower, with his back to the spider, he instantly sprang upon him, and grasped him over the back and shoulder, when for some moments they both disappeared. I expected the bee had carried off his enemy, but to my surprise, they both together rebounded back again, suspended at the extremity of a strong elastic thread or web, which the spider had artfully let fall, or fixed upon the twig, the instant he leaped from it: the rapidity of the bee's wings, endeavouring to extricate himself, made them both together appear as a moving vapour, until the bee became fatigued by whirling round, first one way and then back again: at length, in about a quarter of an hour, the bee quite exhausted by his struggles, and the repeated wounds of the butcher, became motionless, and quickly expired in the arms of the devouring spider, who, ascending the rope with his game, retired to feast on it under cover of the leaves; and perhaps before night, became himself the delicious evening repast of a bird or lizard. (22–23)

Bartram's open and inquisitive mind shows keen observation and a rare appreciation of the natural world and its interrelations. No doubt influenced to some extent by his father's incipient pantheism, he assembled Linnaeus's world of relationships into an almost mystical view of the natural world. Comments on the arrangement of the Creator's work were formulaic at the time, but passages in Bartram's writing read as genuine reverence for the natural world and a generosity of appreciation that extends to its smallest, most seemingly insignificant creations. If at times he wonders whether so many wolves and alligators and mosquitoes are really necessary, he still recognizes that "in every order of nature we perceive a variety of qualities distributed amongst individuals, designed for different purposes and uses; yet it appears evident, that the great Author has impartially distributed his favours to his creatures, so that the attributes of each one seem to be of sufficient importance to manifest the divine and inimitable workmanship."

Faint Praise

BOOK REVIEWING IN AMERICA

~~~~~

A critic is someone who enters the battlefield after the war
is over and shoots the wounded.
   — Murray Kempton

Book reviewing is the slum of American letters.
   — Guy Davenport

I began reviewing in the 1980s, and some years I wrote a fair number
of reviews. I was a member of the National Society of Book Critics and the Northern California Book Reviewers Association. As
a publisher I issued several volumes of film reviews by the National
Society of Film Critics, and occasionally saw reviews make their
way into collections of essays (like this one). But book reviewing
is for the most part not a distinguished sector among the literary
arts — my own efforts, I fear, were no exception — and I gradually
reduced my reviewing and my participation in review groups.

Reviewers have an important role to play in the literary marketplace, but only a few do the job really well. Ideally, a review should
contextualize, describe, and deconstruct the work. Judgment and
evaluation only have meaning if the reviewer brings something sub-
stantive to the task. The best reviewers are able to articulate a coherent and consistent point of view over time, which enables the reader
to rely on the review as a source of information and opinion. Probably only a small number of her readers shared Pauline Kael's exact
tastes, but many got to know her enthusiasms and enjoy her takes
on the films she wrote about.

Today there are not many reviewers who are producing work
that is meaningful. Most operate as offshoots of the publicity

◀ Stack of used books. *Photo by Indi Samarajiva, http://bit.
ly/1dhDMiP.*

networks of international entertainment corporations. As a publisher I knew that one reason to take care with catalogue, jacket, and press release copy was that it would quite often be parroted back in the form of book reviews, in many cases word for word. Lazy or deadline-pressed reviewers would lift ideas, phrases, and entire paragraphs, presenting them as their own thoughts and words.

Others subscribe to the solipsistic "shallow opinions" school of reviewing. To this lot, the most important thing about any work is whether they liked it, and so they point, seemingly randomly, to a succession of miscellaneous things that struck their fancy or turned them off. Frequently these judgments are uninformed and inconsistent. Almost always they are beside the point.

Some reviewers, perhaps under pressure from their editors, or aspiring to be promoted to the more influential and lucrative positions of film reviewer or TV critic, treat the book review as a form of entertainment. They jazz up their reviews with snarky witticisms and catty comments. A steady diet of that becomes wearying, so once or twice a week they churn out fawning reviews that tout the current literary star's latest work. (Besides, the reviewer wants to mingle with the glitterati at parties.)

Most positive reviews adhere to a familiar template. Seven or eight enthusiastic paragraphs hail the book's content and style, sometimes with a few short quotations, followed by a few crisp criticisms (demonstrating that the reviewer is exercising critical capacities), to be succeeded in turn by a remark along the lines of "but these flaws do not detract from the author's achievement." Then a big bombastic finish may follow in which readers are exhorted to rush to buy a copy of the same book everyone else is reading.

Having posted remarks similar to these on my primary website, rightreading.com, I received from Gail Pool a copy of her *Faint Praise: The Plight of Book Reviewing in America*. Even as I was being worn down by the banality and mediocrity of most book reviews, the resilient Pool had remained undaunted. She was determined that it didn't have to be that way. It was encouraging to hear that she still believes in reviews, thinks they matter, and imagines that significant industry-wide improvements are possible. I admire her attitude, and I'd like to think she is right. But I can't fully share her optimism — not, at least, as concerns what she calls "traditional book reviews."

Pool mainly does two or three things in this book: she details problems with book reviewing today and makes a call to action to help correct them. In the process she also provides an overview of how reviewing works in the U.S., and for some readers that might be the book's most valuable contribution.

Pool notes that book reviews are routinely criticized for dullness, bias, and inaccuracy — and such criticisms are as old as reviewing itself, which she says began in the late 1700s in the United States. Though the criticisms are often as laden with private agendas as the reviews themselves, one must wonder whether it is possible to repair an institution that has, by common consensus, been broken for centuries, in fact since its inception.

Pool's main focus is print reviewing in newspapers and magazines. Most such reviews are commissioned from a freelancer by an editor, who selects the books for review from a barrage of choices unleashed upon her by publishers' publicity departments. There are many reasons why the selection process is skewed toward mediocrity: the preference for reviews of well-known authors; the favoritism shown to publishers who take out ads; the marketplace imperatives of the host publication; the pressure of deadlines; the poor quality of the publisher's press releases, usually written by junior members of the staff; and so on. George Orwell perfectly described the result:

> A periodical gets its weekly wad of books and sends off a dozen of them to X, the hack reviewer. . . . To begin with, the chances are that eleven out of the twelve books will fail to rouse in him the faintest spark of interest. They are not more than ordinarily bad, they are merely neutral, lifeless and pointless. If he were not paid to do so he would never read a line of any of them, and in nearly every case the only truthful review he could write would be: "This book inspires in me no thoughts whatever." But will anyone pay

you to write that kind of thing? Obviously not. As a start, therefore, X is in the false position of having to manufacture, say, three hundred words about a book which means nothing to him whatever. Usually he does it by giving a brief resume of the plot (incidentally betraying to the author that he hasn't read the book) and handing out a few compliments which for all their fulsomeness are about as valuable as the smile of a prostitute (58).

And how was Orwell's Mr. X selected as the hack reviewer in the first place? There are no special qualifications, no particular training, required to break into reviewing. You just need to be willing to work for little pay and produce the particular flavor of pabulum that the reviewing publication requires — in the U.S. this usually means either some connection with the topic or a demonstrable ability to craft a flashy lead that will divert the attention of readers as they gulp down their morning coffee. Pool offers a telling contrast between a British review (in the *TLS*) and a U.S. review (in the *NYTBR*). (Strangely, Pool identifies neither reviewer by name.) The *TLS* reviewer begins

> Virginia Woolf claimed that there is no such thing as an objective biography. "Positions have been taken, myths have been made." This is unquestionably the case with Byron.... (89)

while the U.S. reviewer, needing something sexier and punchier, leads with

> Lord Byron was the Mick Jagger of his time, "mad, bad, and dangerous to know," in the words of his tragic admirer Carolyn Lamb.... (89)

To add a little glamour to their publication, review editors may not only review the books of well-known writers but also solicit reviews from them, commissioning a popular novelist to review another novelist's work, for example. But reviewing and writing fiction are very different things, and the result is often disappointing. Editors may also try to generate a bit of spark by soliciting a review from someone who has an interest in the subject that is so close as to preclude objectivity. (Objectivity is also lost when the reviewer has an agenda of which the editor is unaware, which is often the case.) I think most editors today would (unlike, apparently, Ms. Pool) gladly sacrifice impartiality for buzz. Conflict causes talk, and a catty, dismissive review might do more for circulation than a judicious one. Pool reports that in a survey of its members, the National Book Critics Circle found that 86 percent of respondents saw no problem with having a book reviewed by a "casual acquaintance" of the author; 30 percent would even allow the book to be reviewed by someone cited in its acknowledgments!

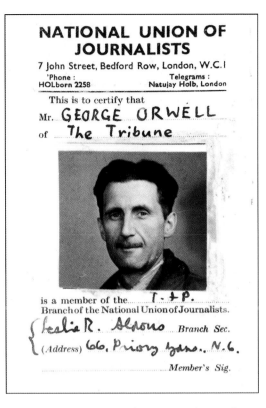

George Orwell, working journalist and author of "Confessions of a Book Reviewer," *http://bit.ly/105fqG*.

To overcome such problems, Pool suggests that the role of the assigning editor must be strengthened and reformed. She thinks the book review editor should be a more visible figure than the shadowy presence who often lurks behind review supplements. She calls for reviews to be organized "more coherently," with books of a similar type grouped together. She thinks the selection of books to be reviewed can be improved by the use of a cadre of critical screeners. She would like to see more reviewers do columns rather than one-offs. She would like more stringent consideration of who should be allowed to review, focusing mainly on critical thinking. She proposes establishing guidelines and codes of ethics for reviewers. She would like to see a relaxation of the publishing schedules of reviews.

This is mostly sensible advice. While I disagree with some particulars, I do agree that if reform is to occur review editors must take the lead. I just wouldn't hold out much hope. Book reviews occupy an uncomfortable crack between the grinding gears of the publishing industry. Book publishers provide books for review so long as the reviews tend to be favorable and promote sales — or at least engender the word of mouth that leads to sales, which requires reviews to be precisely timed relative to the ever-narrowing window of a book's shelf life in stores. Book reviews pander on the one hand to publisher advertising and on the other to an increasingly fickle readership, as literacy declines because of cuts in education funding, put through by demagogues who depend for power on the support of an ignorant electorate unable even to identify its own self-interest. When the majority of Americans fail to read even a single book in a year, the prospects of a healthy book review segment in the mainstream media will be dim regardless of the review editor's best efforts.

Nonetheless, Pool continues to place her faith in the traditional review. "The traditional review," she claims, "is the only kind of 'coverage' that focuses exclusively on the text and that is — or at least aims to be — written by a disinterested and qualified critic." Pool devotes a fair amount of space to online reviewing but does not, in my judgment, fully appreciate its potential. Instead, she focuses primarily on reader reviews on sites such as Amazon (which for all their flaws I find sometimes helpful), and of course has little difficulty highlighting their staggering weaknesses. But I think there is reason to place our hope for reviewing more in the Internet than in print (to generalize broadly, since there are heroic efforts in print as well). With respect to reach, online numbers can be much bigger than print numbers, and the connection between reviewers and readers is more readily customized online.

Rather than looking at Amazon, I would look at something like Ron Silliman's blog (ronsilliman.blogspot.com). Ron is able to review far more poetry there than he would be likely to cover in print. While his reviews are opinionated and even contentious, it does not take too long to get a general sense of where he's coming from. I happen not particularly to share his aesthetic, but I know I can rely on him to cover his topics with consistency and fairness within the parameters he has set down. I would place a larger share of my hope in these sorts of voices than in the prospect of mainstream reviewing rising from the muck.

That doesn't mean I want to see such reviewing fail. I would welcome reviewing that is inspirited with soul and focus (and that helped to sell books, or at least get them talked about and, ideally, read). I wish Ms. Pool all the best in getting her reforms adopted. Her earnest and informed book makes a good introduction to mainstream book reviewing in America.

#OccupyXmas

Christmas has always been politicized. Since 2005, when Fox News commentator John Gibson published *The War on Christmas: How the Liberal Plot to Ban the Sacred Christian Holiday Is Worse Than You Thought*, the focus has mainly been on a supposed progressive agenda to, in the words of Bill O'Reilly, "get Christianity and spirituality out of the public square." Last year the New York City YMCA drew criticism for replacing Santa Claus with Frosty the Snowman at a family event — children were forced, complained the *New York Post*, to "suffer the icy embrace of a talking snowman" instead of the warm hug of a fur-clad fat man. Now, for the 2011 Christmas season, the American Family Association has once again called out retailers who favor the word "holidays," placing them on its "Naughty" list.

But there is also something different going on this year. A popular hashtag on Twitter is #OccupyXmas. In Portland, San Francisco, and elsewhere, carolers dressed in Santa suits and elf outfits have been singing a new song. It goes in part like this:

> Arrest ye merry bankermen
> All profiting today
> You crashed the whole economy
> Yet nothing did you pay . . .

Through the centuries a spirit of rebellion has often colored the Christmas season. There is good historical precedent for thinking of Santa Claus and Christmas itself as icons of the 99 percent movement.

Next to nothing is known about St. Nicholas, a Greek who was the Christian bishop of Demre, a town on the southern coast of Turkey. As Christianity expanded northward he became a symbol that could be invoked for any variety of causes, such as the welfare

◀ "Old Christmas" by Robert Seymour, illustration for *The Book of Christmas* by Thomas K. Hervey (London: William Spooner, 1836).

of children. According to one persistent legend, he was a member of the affluent one percent who became disturbed by prevailing social inequities and sought to redistribute wealth to the less fortunate. Through the centuries the notion of wealth redistribution would be associated with the saint, and with Christmas.

The Catholic calendar assigned feast days for celebrating its saints, and Nicholas's day was December 6 — the same month in which the church had placed Christmas. While the actual date of the nativity (which was not celebrated until centuries after Christ's lifetime) was unknown, assigning it to the winter season enabled the church to co-opt ancient midwinter festivals. Because of their shared season of observance, St. Nicholas and Christmas became associated with each other.

In the pre-modern era, once the fall harvest and slaughter season had been completed, agricultural workers found themselves with time on their hands and a bountiful supply of fermented beverages. Rowdy celebrations were one result. An antiauthoritarian strain ran through these winter rituals. The Christmas season was a time of what the early-twentieth-century literary theorist Mikhail Bakhtin described as the spirit of carnival. A master of revels, called the Lord of Misrule, might be appointed or selected by chance (for example, by discovering a bean hidden in a cake) to govern over festivities in which the high and low exchanged places. At this time the wealthy were expected to provide food and drink for common folk. The ritualized disorder provided a kind of annual safety valve against smoldering class resentments and grievances.

By the early seventeenth century, when the rapid growth of cities, technological advance, and new cross-cultural connections were transforming the old social order, the safety valve stopped working. The king of England, James I, was concerned that such developments as sprawling urbanization and the disturbing outspokenness of women were eroding traditional values. He commissioned his chief propagandist, the playwright and poet Ben Jonson, to create a performance called *Christmas, His Masque*, to be presented around Christmas Day, 1616. This play would mark the first literary appearance of the prototype of Santa Claus, called Father Christmas. Jonson described him as "attir'd in round Hose, long Stockings, a close Doublet, a high crownd Hat with a Broach, a long thin beard, a Truncheon, little Ruffes, white Shoes, his Scarffes, and Garters tyed crosse, and his Drum beaten before him." Accompanied by his ten children (Mis-rule, Carroll, Minc'd-Pie, Gamboll, Post and Paire, New-Yeares-Gift, Mumming, Wassail, Offering, and Babie-Cocke), he appealed for a return to "a right Christmas, as of old it was."

Christmas, His Masque was intended to encourage people to resist the enticements and corruptions of modernity and return to traditional values in the hope of restoring the more stable social order of earlier times. At the same time, it sought to check the growing influence of religious hard-liners such as the Puritans, who opposed the celebration of Christmas. In this it failed — within a generation the monarchy would be overthrown, to be replaced by the religious extremists.

The Puritans, who rejected ceremony in favor of direct communion with God, were opposed to all of the old seasonal celebrations. They also objected to the license and disorder of the winter festivals. Among the practices they took exception to during the Christmas season festivities was cross-dressing, a vestige of ancient winter saturnalias. Role reversals were a common feature of the winter celebrations: the fool would be king for the day, peasants would temporarily command the wealthy, men and women would exchange roles. According to a minister writing in the early 1700s, Christmas mumming often involved "a changing of Clothes between Men and Women; who when dressed in each other's habits, go from one Neighbor's house to another . . . and make merry with them in disguise." The merry making involved the objectionable habit of caroling, which, the minister said, occurred "in the midst of Rioting, Chambering [fornication], and Wantonness."

The Puritans brought their opposition to Christmas to the new world. Suppression of Christmas began in the first year of the Plymouth Rock colony, when its governor came across some revelers who had taken Christmas Day off and forced them to return to work. The observance of Christmas was declared a criminal offense by the Massachusetts General Court in 1659.

My own great-great-great-great-great-great-grandmother, a woman named Dorothy Jones, was convicted in the town of Wilmington, near Philadelphia, in 1672 of "propagating ye Throne of wickedness." According to court records, she was charged with "masking" in men's clothes the day after Christmas, "walking and dancing in the house of John Simes at 9 or 10 o'clock at night.'" Simes, who hosted the party, was charged with keeping a disorderly house, "a nursery of Debotch ye inhabitants and youth of this city . . . to ye greef of and disturbance of peaceful minds."

As the old winter festivities became repressed, they turned more bitter and vehement. Christmas carolers, or wassailers, asserted their right to seasonal largesse with the threat of violence. A Scottish wassailing song contains such lines as

> We've come here to claim our right . . .
> And if you don't open up your door,
> We'll lay it flat upon the floor . . .
> God bless the mistress and her man,
> Dish and table, pot and pan:
> Here's to the one with yellow hair,
> She's hiding underneath the stair:
> Be you maids or be you none,
> Although our time may not be long,
> You'll all be kissed ere we go home.

Young men from the fringes of society formed bands who went from house to house demanding gifts of food and drink. One wassailing song asserted the petitioners' right to sample the lord's best goods and not just ordinary stock:

> Come, butler, draw us a bowl of the best
> Then we hope your soul in heaven shall rest
> But if you draw us a bowl of the small
> Then down will come butler, bowl, and all

If the petitioners were not let in, they would sometimes enter homes by force. On Christmas night of 1679 one landholder near

Salem refused to grant the demands of such a gang of young men. His case is known through the court record it has left; it is retold in Stephen Nissenbaum's excellent *The Battle for Christmas*. After his refusal, he testified, "they threw stones, bones, and other things . . . They continued to throw stones for an hour and a half with little intermission. They also broke down about a pole and a half of fence, being stone wall, and a cellar, without the house, distant about four or five rods, was broken open through the door, and five or six pecks of apples were stolen."

The colonists succeeded, with difficulty, in suppressing Christmas for a time, but immigrants to North America from other parts of Europe (such as Germany, the Netherlands, and Scandinavia) continued to bring their various seasonal traditions with them. With a more diverse populace, by the beginning of the nineteenth century Christmas was on the way to revival. It emerged from its years of suppression in a new form. Since each group observed the holiday in its own way, it no longer took the form of a rowdy public festival, gradually becoming transformed into a quieter domestic observance.

Gift-giving had not been a feature of traditional Christmas celebrations, which had emphasized feasting and drinking. But over the course of the nineteenth century, with the growth of industrialization, as manufacturers looked to develop new markets, the holiday became commercialized. Though some employers, like Dickens's Ebenezer Scrooge, still saw it as a kind of scam, when he was forced to "pay a day's wages for no work," others made a different calculation — they saw the momentarily idle workers as a potential market for their products. By the end of the century, it became customary in the U.S. to purchase and exchange manufactured goods at Christmastime.

In the end it was probably a bad deal for the workers. What was once a worker-oriented festival had been subsumed into an economic system that in recent years has resulted in staggering levels of economic inequality. "My little girl don't understand why Daddy can't afford no Christmas here," Merle Haggard once sang. Today, as SantaCon meets and mingles with the Occupy movement, people are again demanding a better share of the wealth during the holiday season. It might be wise to take their protests seriously. There are centuries of tradition behind them.

Sadakichi and America

A CASE OF TAKEN IDENTITY

❦❦❦

After all, not to create only, or found only,
But to bring, perhaps from afar, what is already founded,
To give it our own identity, average, limitless, free;
To fill the gross, the torpid bulk with vital religious fire;
Not to repel or destroy, so much as accept, fuse, rehabilitate;
To obey, as well as command — to follow, more than to lead;
These also are the lessons of our New World . . .

> — Opening of "Song of the Exposition" by Walt
> Whitman, presented by the author in proof sheet to
> Sadakichi Hartmann on their first meeting

Nobody called him Carl, the name he shared with his father, Carl Herman Oskar Hartmann. To Walt Whitman he was "that Japanee." To W. C. Fields he was "Catch-a-Crotchie," "Itchy-Scratchy," or "Hootchie-Coochie." To the critic James Gibbons Huneker he was "a fusion of Jap and German, the ghastly experiment of an Occidental on the person of an Oriental," and years later John Barrymore would call him "a living freak presumably sired by Mephistopheles out of Madame Butterfly." A 1916 magazine profile (calling him "our weirdest poet") insisted he was "much more Japanese than German." During World War II, because of his Japanese and German heritage, he was accused of being a spy, and he barely escaped internment. More recently, in 1978, scholars Harry W. Lawton and George Knox, in their introduction to his selected photography criticism, *The Valiant Knights of Daguerre*, presented him as "Sadakichi Hartmann (1867–1944), the Japanese-German writer and critic." And so Hartmann is usually introduced, as if his ethnicity were the most important thing about him. But despite his ancestry Carl Sadakichi Hartmann was not Japanese

◀ Sadakichi Hartmann (detail), 1903, by Edward J. Steichen. Photograph: direct carbon print. *Metropolitan Museum of Art, Alfred Stieglitz Collection, 1933, 33.43.52.*

or German — he was American. He lived most of his life in the United States. He wrote what stood as the standard textbook on American art for decades. H. L. Mencken, of all people, got it right: "Hartmann is an exotic — half German and half Japanese by birth," he noted, "but thoroughly American under it all."

Hartmann was born in 1867 in Dejima, Nagasaki, of a Japanese mother and a German father shortly after the opening of Japan during the post–Edo early Meiji period. But his mother died when he was still a toddler, and he left Japan in his father's tow not long afterward, never to return. Still, he retained an interest in Japanese art and culture throughout his life. He is said to have introduced haiku to America. Two years after publishing *A History of American Art* he followed up with *Japanese Art.* He became expert enough on the subject to be consulted by collectors of Japanese art. Recently I encountered Hartmann in an essay by Julia Meech in *The Printer's Eye: Ukiyo-e from the Grabhorn Collection* (a book I produced for the Asian Art Museum in San Francisco). Meech writes:

> Between 1937 and 1941, when [Judson D.] Metzgar was acting as agent for Tod Ford and his brother Freeman, he sold the Grabhorns at least thirty-five prints, including a stunning Utamaro large-head portrait of a courtesan on an apricot mica ground. The asking price for the entire Ford group was $25,000, based on an appraisal by the art critic Sadakichi Hartmann (1867–1944).

Hartmann's "Japaneseness" was a fundamental aspect of his identity, not only because of his interest in Japanese culture but also because everyone kept reminding him of it. Japanese people had visited America, and even settled in the port of Acapulco before the closing of Japan at the beginning of the Edo period (as I described in *1616: The World in Motion*). But after the closing of Japan that connection was shut down, with the result that most Americans had never seen a Japanese person (apart from a few rare shipwrecked individuals) until 1860, when two ships carrying Japanese diplomats landed in San Francisco. It was Japan's first official diplomatic delegation to a Western nation in nearly two and a half centuries. And it was only a couple of decades after that first contact that Sadakichi came to an America that had never seen anything like him.

Unlike those initial ambassadors, and most of the Japanese immigrants who would follow, he arrived in America across the Atlantic. After the death of his mother he had been raised by his father's family in Hamburg. There he attended private schools and received a solid European education (by nine he had read the works of Goethe and Schiller). As a result, Hartmann's cultural foundation was strongly European. He was particularly interested in the theater. But around the time his father remarried, when Hartmann was thirteen, he was sent off to a naval academy. Later in life he would make several Atlantic crossings, but it is hard to imagine him a naval officer. He wasted little time in running away to Paris. Afterward he faced an enraged father who gave him $3 and packed him off to relatives in Philadelphia. Hartmann would describe them as a "plebian, philistine grand uncle and aunt." According to Hartmann's unpublished autobiography (in the archives of the UC Riverside library), he parted his father with a mere handshake. They had little to do with each other thereafter. "Events like these," he observed, "are not apt to foster filial piety."

Maybe Hartmann's estrangement from his father contributed to his adopting his Japanese name rather than using the Western name they shared. But Sadakichi was not the only name he used. He also maintained several others. Among the pseudonyms under which he published were Caliban, Hogarth, Juvenal, Chrysanthemum, Innocent De La Salle, and even A. Chameleon. (Of Sidney Allan I will speak in a bit.) Gertrude Stein said, "Sadakichi is singular, never plural," yet in many ways he was plural. "My father was a genuine freethinker; the rest of my family were mildly Lutheran. My stepmother was a Catholic. One of my aunts a French Jewess. My mother presumably was a Buddhist," he pointed out. "These influences shaped my early view point."

Arriving in Hoboken in 1882 at the age of fourteen, Hartmann found no relatives or their agents there to meet him, and he made his own way to Philadelphia. There he worked for a time in a printmaking shop and at other jobs, though at no time in his life did he excel at steady employment. He frequented libraries and bought many books. One of the booksellers suggested he visit Walt Whitman, who was just across the Delaware River in Camden. In November 1884, Hartmann paid a call. He was seventeen; the good gray poet was sixty-five. Lacking a father in his life, the teenager imprinted strongly on the old man. The two met often. "The depth of the relationship between the young Hartmann and the old Whitman," says scholar Jane Calhoun Weaver, "was apparently astonishingly deep." Hartmann's relationship with Whitman, she says, "adds credibility to the notion that Hartmann's zealous Americanism sprang from the purest source imaginable in the late nineteenth century, the crooning poetry of Walt Whitman's native songs."

Hartmann wrote of that first visit: "There was nothing overwhelming to me in Whitman's face, but I liked it at once for its healthy manliness. It seemed to me a spiritually deepened image of contemporary Americans: an ideal laborer, as the Americans are really a nation of laborers." Hartmann said that Whitman was the most important person in his life, next to his mother (whom he barely knew). "I am bound to thee forever, thy works were to me, except Love and Nature, the grandest lessons of my life," he wrote in an early poem. He made careful note of the poet's pronouncements and casual remarks, which he would publish a few years later in the *New York Herald*. The publication irritated the poet and most of his circle, since some of the comments were impolitic and not meant for public consumption. Whitman called the comments Hartmann reported "the projected camel of his imagination." Friends of the poet accused Hartmann of fabricating the quotes. He insisted that he had not, and he would go on to write about his recollections of Whitman on several more occasions.

He got in trouble too for his attempt to start a Walt Whitman Society in Boston, where he had relocated in 1887.

> I dreamt of having a huge sign in gold lettering across my bay window announcing "THE WALT WHITMAN SOCIETY." Of course I would also rent the lower floor. We would have a

reading room, a Whitmanea department, lectures, classes and many other wonderful things. And I, of course, would be the curator of this self-created establishment.

Unfortunately, he appointed officers to his society without informing either them or others. When he convened the first meeting, it did not go well, and the society fizzled. Hartmann was too young, too impecunious, and too advanced and European in his literary tastes for Boston society. His attempt to introduce Bostonians to the works of Ibsen, for example, also ended in failure.

Despite these sorts of annoyances, Whitman seems to have retained an affection for Hartmann. "I have more hopes of him, more faith in him than any of the boys," he told his confidant Horace Traubel. He bequeathed his personal copy of the 1876 edition of *Leaves of Grass* to Hartmann. "They all seem to regard him as a humbug — or if not that, a sensationalist anyhow, or an adventurer. I can't see it that way. I expect good things of him — extra good things." George Knox and Harry W. Lawton, who were responsible for reawakening interest in Hartmann a few decades after his death, identified the impact Whitman had on Hartmann:

First Ibsen Performance in Boston, ca. 1915, by Lillian Bonham. Postcard; pen and ink. *Collection of Dorothea Gilliland.*

> Whitman was probably the most important single influence on the literary career of Sadakichi Hartmann. It was not so much that Whitman affected Hartmann's style of writing as

that he influenced the literary pose which Hartmann adopted toward the world. As an impressionable youth in Philadelphia, Hartmann closely observed Whitman's stance and attempted to emulate some aspects of it, refining those qualities which he borrowed until he developed his own posture as a literary figure. What remained, however, was Hartmann's reliance on Whitman's techniques of self-promotion, a belief in democracy despite his tendency toward seeing art as primarily for the elite, the use of press-agentry methods pioneered by Whitman, and an assertive Bohemianism traceable to Whitman.

But just as Hartmann had multiple identities, so he had multiple mentors. After selling his library, he returned to Europe in 1885. At that time he still thought of Europe as home. It was the first of four trips he would make to the continent over the next eight years. There he attended theater performances, visited art galleries, and called on literary figures, including Stéphane Mallarmé, whom he would meet in 1893, and with whom he would keep up a correspondence; he could lay claim to being the first to introduce Symbolist poetry to the U.S. He ended up in Munich, where he attached himself to its leading literary figure, Paul Heyse, who would be awarded the Nobel Prize in 1910. (Hartmann kept in contact with Heyse during the intervening years. After Heyse received the Nobel, Hartmann, in an echo of his experience with Whitman, would cause a strain in his relationship with his former mentor by publishing remarks attributed to him.) Despite winning the Nobel — one of the judges said that "Germany has not had a greater literary genius since Goethe" — Heyse is little remembered today, though some of his stories, poems, lieder, and translations from Italian are occasionally praised. Classically trained, he was the leader of a rearguard action against naturalism and other new directions in the arts. In most ways his writing could not be less like Whitman's. When Hartmann sought to introduce Heyse to the works of Whitman, Heyse remarked that he preferred flowers to leaves of grass. Hartmann was torn between mentors, and between continents. In the end, he chose America, where, as the turn of the century approached,

Parents and mentors: *Top left:* Carl Hartmann, nd. *Bottom left:* Sada Hartmann, 1867. *Top center*: Paul Heyse, nd. *Bottom center:* Paul Heyse, from a tribute published in the *Munich City Chronicle* on the occasion of his eightieth birthday. *Top right:* Walt Whitman, 1854, frontispiece to *Leaves of Grass.* Steel engraving by Samuel Hollyer from a lost daguerreotype by Gabriel Harrison. *Morgan Library and Museum.* Bottom right: Walt Whitman, 1870. Photograph. Known as the "Quaker photo."

he developed a literary and bohemian persona modeled largely on Whitman. In 1894 he became an American citizen.

Hartmann built a precarious career as a freelance writer. His literary efforts brought him a meager income. He spent Christmas 1893 in jail for his "erotic play" *Christ* — called by the *New York Sun* "the most daring of all decadent productions" — which was judged obscene in Boston. (The New England Society for the Suppression of Vice made a show of publicly burning copies of the play.) His most ambitious theatrical efforts often met with crushing rejection. In 1902 he would attempt "A Trip to Japan in Sixteen Minutes," a performance piece presented at New York Theatre on Broadway, that was described as a "melody in odors." Hartmann was well versed in the synesthetic affectations of decadent French poetry; unfortunately, he was ignorant of the chemical and technological issues in the manufacture of aromas. He attempted to fill the theater with various scents with the aid of giant electric fans. Although the performance was planned to run sixteen minutes, it only lasted four. By that point "the audience stamped, cheered derisively," a reporter wrote, "and began to pour out of the theater." And later, in San Francisco, Hartmann revived the notion of staging Ibsen. He decided to present *Ghosts*, and he hatched a plan to light a real fire outside the play's venue, a mansion on Russian Hill, to coincide with a fire in the second act. Predictably, the fire got out of control, Hartmann was again arrested, and he was prohibited from further performances in the city.

He had better success as an art critic, the role with which he would mainly support himself for three decades. In fact, Jane Calhoun Weaver asserts that "few writers were as important to the art of the United States at the end of the nineteenth century and beginning of the twentieth century as Sadakichi Hartmann. . . . A reading of the 1890–1915 era in American art is virtually impossible without recourse to Hartmann's writings. From the beginning Hartmann demonstrated a remarkable ability to identify the artists and ideas that would become the primary focus of twentieth-century American art." As a boy in Hamburg, Hartmann had received an excellent education in European art. He was blessed with a discerning eye. A contemporaneous painter, E. E. Simmons, made a fair appraisal: "Hartmann may be capricious and malicious, and rather careless at times, but he is, after all, the only critic we have who knows a good picture when he sees it and who is not afraid of expressing his opinion." He helped to introduce artists such as Paul Gauguin, August Rodin, Maurice Denis, Henri Matisse, and Félicien Rops to U.S. audiences. "As an art critic, he was the most astute of his time in America," in the judgment of Kenneth Rexroth, "and spotted the right people, from Winslow Homer and Ryder to Marin, Maurer, and Weber, long before anybody else." Among other American artists he was one of the first to champion were Robert Henri, George Luks, Thomas Eakins, and Marsden Hartley.

Besides his knowledge and eye for art, Hartmann had another advantage that is uncommon in the art world: he could write well. He was hired as a roving reporter for Samuel McClure's first American newspaper syndicate, under whose auspices he traveled to Paris in the winter of 1892–1893, where he met such artists as Whistler, Monet, and Maurice Maeterlinck (who would win a Nobel Prize in 1911, the year after Hartmann's Munich mentor, Paul Heyse). On returning to Boston he launched a magazine called *The Art Critic*. He traveled up and down the Eastern Seaboard selling subscriptions, and among the approximately 750 subscriptions appear the names of many leading artists and critics. The magazine's editorial perspective was strongly influenced by the European Symbolist movement. Unfortunately, it lasted only three issues, folding after the fiasco of his presentation of *Christ* in Boston. In 1902 he cobbled together many of his writings (his forte was the short essay) into *A History of American Art*, which would remain a standard textbook on the subject through the early decades of the twentieth century. (His *The Whistler Book* is actually his best book-length work on art.) Despite his familiarity with avant-garde currents in European art and literature, in his *History*, as elsewhere, Hartmann championed an assertively American art. In doing so, he quoted a version of these lines from *Leaves of Grass*:

> Others may praise what they like;
> But I, from the banks of the running Missouri, praise
>   nothing in art or aught else,
> Til it has breathed well the atmosphere of this river —
>   also the western prairie scent,
> And fully exudes it again.

Calling Whitman "a voice in the wilderness," Hartmann complained that "the artists have taken no heed of it. Only men like Winslow Homer and Thomas Eakins have endorsed it to a certain extent with their work in the art of painting, and at the same time have strong, frank, and decided ways of expressing something American."

Soon Hartmann himself would explore the American heartland and, eventually, relocate west. The indirect cause was his association with Alfred Stieglitz. When the two men met in 1898, Hartmann was the better known and established, but Stieglitz quickly asserted himself. Sharing interests in art and photography and a connection to Germany, the two men established a rapport. Stieglitz considered Hartmann's writings on art of the utmost importance, and he cited Hartmann as his most important influence in the years between 1898 and 1907. In June of 1898, Hartmann published "An Art Critic's Estimate of Alfred Stieglitz" in *The Photographic Times*. In October his first essay in *Camera Notes*, the photographic journal of the Camera Club of New York, which was then edited by Stieglitz, appeared. It was titled "A Few Reflections on Amateur and Artistic Photography." Hartmann soon became a leading advocate for the recognition of photography as a fine art. In 1904, when Stieglitz resigned as editor to organize his landmark "Photo-Secession" and launched *Camera Work*, the most historically important publication devoted to art photography, he made Hartmann one of the mainstays of the magazine. No one wrote more or better articles for *Camera Work* than Hartmann, but he bristled at Stieglitz's imperious control of the Photo Secessionist movement. In 1904, he wrote a letter informing Stieglitz that he had "simply got tired of your dictatorship." The breach continued until 1908, when Hartmann, typically short of funds, wrote asking Stieglitz to "lend a helping hand for old time's sake." He resumed writing for the magazine through 1912.

The break with Stieglitz may have precipitated some kind of emotional response in Hartmann, or he may simply have been looking for a new source of income. In any case, he began to publish at that time under the name Sidney Allan. The last name was probably an homage to Edgar Allan Poe, an American poet much beloved by the French intellectual set that Hartmann hoped to connect with avant-garde America. But Sidney Allan, unlike Sadakichi Hartmann, was not really in the artistic vanguard. Nor was he merely a pseudonym. Hartmann fashioned a complete new persona for Allan. He bedecked himself with a monocle, derby hat, and three-piece suit. Sidney Allan's publications on photography far outnumber Hartmann's. While Sadakichi Hartmann wrote penetrating articles about vanguard art, Sidney Allan wrote practical guidance for aspiring photographers. While Hartmann wrote for the coastal urban cognoscenti, Allan was much beloved by the heartland. In his Allan persona Hartmann toured the country giving lectures. Allan's standard lecture was on the topic "Good Taste and Common Sense." He made quite an impression. "The photographers worship the ground over which Allan walks," enthused a reporter from the *Des Moines Register and Leader* in the paper's October 5, 1906, edition about Allan's appearance at the Iowa State Photographic Convention. "He is harsh and brutal at times in his criticism, but he hits the nail on the head every time."

Sidney Allan, 1898. Photo by by Zaida Ben-Yusuf.

While Allan was captivating the heartland, Hartmann was conquering radical New York. In 1915 most of the magazine *Greenwich Village* was devoted to (or written by) Hartmann. The magazine annointed him "the King of Bohemia." His pranks and outrages were legendary (and amount to something of a distraction in trying to understand the man and his accomplishments). "During my lifetime there have been hundreds of claimants to the throne of bohemia," said Kenneth Rexroth, "but no one who

Sadakichi Hartmann, 1907. *Photo by B. J. Falk.*

could compare with Sadakichi." It almost seemed that Sidney Allan's conservatism pushed Sadakichi Hartmann to new extremes.

In 1912, in one of his last essays for *Camera Work*, Hartmann championed the infant motion picture medium not as an entertainment for the masses but as an art form. He had written about motion pictures before, as early as 1898. He correctly predicted the coming of color, sound, and home movies. Now, in "The Esthetic Significance of the Motion Picture," taking advantage of his experiences as Sidney Allan, he wrote that "people in the larger cities can hardly imagine what this entertainment means to town and village populations. It is cheap and within the reach of all. And it is in many communities the one regular amusement that is offered. A town of six thousand inhabitants will easily support three to four houses with continuous performances of three reels each." His championing of motion pictures as an art form echoes his earlier battles on behalf of photography. "Readers may ask whether I take these pictures seriously and whether I see any trace of art in them," he wrote. "Yes," he answered, "honestly, I do." Hartmann was less interested in the medium's narrative potential than in its visual effects: "It is generally not the story which interests me but the expression of mere incidents, a rider galloping along a mountain path, a handsome woman with hair and skirts fluttering in the wind, the rushing water of a stream, the struggle of two desperate men in some twilight atmosphere."

In 1916 he decided to move west. He was seeking relief from a serious case of asthma and removing himself from a failed marriage, as well as a less than satisfactory working relationship with Stieglitz. He ended up in the San Francisco Bay Area, where he connected with the bohemian scene that centered on George Sterling and Jack London. In 1923 he moved to Los Angeles, where he became Hollywood correspondent for the English magazine *The Curtain*. He continued to lecture and write but produced mostly light journalistic work (an exception was an insightful essay on Sergei Eisenstein). He appeared in 1924 in *The Thief of Bagdad*, starring Douglas Fairbanks, in which Hartmann was cast as the Court Magician. But his alcoholism and independent spirit made him unreliable and undesirable as a character actor.

Still a flamboyant figure despite poor health, he hooked up with the Hollywood rat pack of the day, a circle that included Douglas Fairbanks, John Barrymore, the painter John Decker, W. C. Fields, and others. They admired him as a comical and pathetic Pierrot whose stories of his association with figures such as Whitman, Mallarmé, and Stieglitz were not to be credited. This image was popularized by Gene Fowler in his *Minutes of the Last Meeting*, which describes the group's antics while purporting to be a profile of Hartmann. Fowler captures the wild and crazy figure Hartmann cut at the time, but he shows scant interest in his subject's actual accomplishments.

Hartmann spent the last years of his life in a shack he built on the Morongo Indian Reservation in Banning, California, on property belonging to his daughter Wistaria Hartmann Linton, who was married to a Cahuilla cattle rancher. Some people probably figured him for an Indian. You can't get more American than that. He relied on small donations from people like Ezra Pound, who had not forgotten him. He died in 1944 while visiting another daughter in Florida.

Identity is a kind of negotiation an individual makes with society. Hartmann refashioned his identity multiple times. At times to different audiences he presented more than one identity simultaneously. Who was Sadakichi Hartmann? In the end he had found perhaps his most enduring identity in one of the last roles he played — the Court Magician. That was an exotic role; Hartmann managed to be both exotic and fiercely American. He signaled the advent of an increasingly multicultural America.

If you search for "Sadakichi Hartmann dancing" on YouTube you will find a short film clip that gives a sense of his expressive presence. After that you can also watch on the same site Fairbanks's *Thief of Bagdad*. "Be sure to see it," Kenneth Rexroth advised. "It's Hollywood at its best, and Sadakichi plays himself. He doesn't look as though he'd even used any makeup, and the Hollywoodized Oriental robes are the clothes he always should have been able to wear. They robe his vision of himself, for that's what he was: court magician to two generations of American intellectuals."

▶ Sadakichi Hartmann as the Court Magician in *The Thief of Bagdad*, 1924.

SOURCES

These would be good to begin with. I omit Hartmann's own voluminous work, except as collected and edited by others.

Fowler, Gene. *Minutes of the Last Meeting.* Mattituck, NY: Rivercity, 1954.

Hartmann, Sadakichi. *Sadakichi Hartmann, Critical Modernist: Collected Art Writings.* Jane Calhoun Weaver, ed. Berkeley: University of California Press, 1991.

———. *The Valiant Knights of Daguerre: Selected Critical Essays on Photography and Profiles of Photographic Pioneers.* Harry W. Lawton and George A. Knox, eds. Berkeley: University of California Press, 1978.

———. *White Chrysanthemums: Literary Fragments and Pronouncements.* George A. Knox, ed. New York: Herder and Herder, 1971.

Knox, George. *The Whitman-Hartmann Controversy: Including Conversations with Walt Whitman and Other Essays.* Bern: Herbert Lang, 1976.

Knox, George, and Harry W. Lawton. *The Life and Times of Sadakichi Hartmann, 1867–1944: An Exhibition Presented and Cosponsored by the University Library and the Riverside Press-Enterprise Co., at the University of California, Riverside, May 1 to May 31, 1970.* Riverside, CA: Rubidoux, 1970.

Legro, Michelle. "A Trip to Japan in Sixteen Minutes." *The Believer.* www.believermag.com/issues/201305/read=article_legro.

Index of Persons and Works

River of Ink: Literature, History, Art was published in December 2014 by Counterpoint Press, Berkeley, which graciously allowed me to design and typeset the book in Garamond Premier Pro, make the section opening globes, execute the photo/graphics work, and prepare the index. The book was printed in China on 128 gsm Sun Matte paper, with smyth sewn binding, by RR Donnelley.

I owe thanks to many people, beginning with the original publishers of these essays. Carol Christensen, who read them on first publication, was always encouraging. Ellen Christensen read the manuscript and saved me from many embarrassing mistakes, as did copy editor Sara Walker and proofreader Daniel King. If only editors got the acclaim they deserve!

Speaking of editors, Jack Shoemaker, editorial director at Counterpoint, has been steadily congenial throughout our recent collaborations, and he helped spark my interest in Sadakichi Hartmann. (I plan to pursue that interest in a future book.) Emma Cofod, production manager at Counterpoint, put up stoically with my nonstandard working methodologies, while Sharon Wu is doing her best to publicize a difficult title. Beth Metrick and Sabrina Plomitallo managed the printing with their usual assurance and aplomb. Dear reader, consider rewarding these good folks by inflicting these essays on a friend.